D0572706

POETS
FOR YOUNG ADULTS

POETS

FOR YOUNG ADULTS
Their Lives and Works

Mary Loving Blanchard
and Cara Falcetti

GREENWOOD PRESS
Westport, Connecticut • London

Library of Congress Cataloging-in-Publication Data

Blanchard, Mary Loving, 1952–
    Poets for young adults : their lives and works / Mary Loving Blanchard
    and Cara Falcetti.
        p.   cm.
    Includes bibliographical references and index.
    ISBN 0–313–32884–6 (alk. paper)
    1. American poetry—Bio-bibliography—Dictionaries—Juvenile literature. 2. Poets,
    American—Biography—Dictionaries—Juvenile literature. I. Falcetti, Cara. II. Title.
    PS305.B57 2007
    811'.009—dc22
    [B] 2006029475

British Library Cataloguing in Publication Data is available.

Library of Congress Catalog Card Number: 2006029475
ISBN: 0–313–32884–6

First published in 2007

Greenwood Press, 88 Post Road West, Westport, CT 06881
An imprint of Greenwood Publishing Group, Inc.
www.greenwood.com

Printed in the United States of America

The paper used in this book complies with the
Permanent Paper Standard issued by the National
Information Standards Organization (Z39.48–1984).

10   9   8   7   6   5   4   3   2   1

This book is dedicated to the memory of

Cortney Jerome Rivers (1984–2005),

a young poet whose light burned brightly.

Contents

List of Entries

List of Entries

Preface

In *Cultural Capital: The Problem of Literary Canon Formation*, literary critic John Guillory observes that the problem of canonization is a problem of the syllabus and of the curriculum, which are the primary institutional forms by which great works are preserved and by which the school's function—the dissemination of knowledge—might be realized. In contrast to the classroom, in which a select few of all available literary works are presented to students, Guillory credits libraries, given their function to preserve everything, with providing opportunities for students' increased access to knowledge. Often excluded from such acts of preservation and dissemination are the texts of women writers and writers of color.

Poets for Young Adults brings together in a single collection poets who represent 163 years of participation in the American literary tradition. Of the seventy-five poets included in this collection, forty-one, or a bit more than one-half, are women. Of that number, approximately seventeen, or a bit more than one-third, are women of color. Of the remaining thirty-four entries, all of which are concerned with the work of male poets, approximately nine, or about one-fourth, provide biographical and bibliographical data, including primary as well as secondary source information, on men of color. The inclusion of these writers reflects the authors' conscious efforts to highlight the texts of poets who may escape attention in the present-day classroom.

Poets for Young Adults also showcases writers whose poetic voices announce the arrival of a generation of artists who are creating new forms or combining several genres to produce imaginative verse. To that end, readers will discover in these pages entries on poets Tupac Amaru

Shakur, John Lennon, Lydia Omolola Okutoro, Ntozake Shange, and Ray Anthony Young Bear. This reference guide for young scholars acknowledges as well the contributions of writers whose poetic voices recorded important moments in our country's history. In that regard, we have compiled entries on poets ranging from those who wrote during the colonial era to those writing about contemporary issues. Poets whose verse imagines a human experience free from subjugation or gives voice to cries of protest and to instances of witness are represented here in entries on Ishmael Reed, Carolyn Forché, Robert Trammell, Carl Sandburg, James Weldon Johnson, Jean Toomer, Mercy Otis Warren, Phillis Wheatley, and Jane Colman Turell.

Poets for Young Adults includes within its pages entries on poets who immigrated to colonial America as well as poets who immigrated to contemporary America. Selections on Annis Boudinot Stockton and on more recent immigrants such as Julia Alvarez and Jessica Hagedorn reveal surprising similarities in the imaginative verse produced by writers separated by a distance of more than one hundred years. The collection includes entries on poets who were lawyers or librarians. Some of the writers included here obtained advanced degrees in various fields, and many of them are or were teachers. Other poets received less in the way of traditional preparation. Each poet included in this collection participated in creating a Western literary tradition that is still alive, thriving, and dynamic.

Despite its emphasis, *Poets for Young Adults* is much more than a celebration of lesser-known poets. The text also includes biographical and bibliographical information on mainstream writers, acknowledged masters in the American and British literary traditions, including William Blake, Anne Bradstreet, Countee Cullen, Ralph Waldo Emerson, E. E. Cummings, Emily Dickinson, Gwendolyn Brooks, Robert Frost, John Keats, and Edgar Allan Poe. There are entries on poets who keep the old traditions alive even as they demonstrate inventiveness and daring. Young readers will discover in this collection descriptions of poets who employ traditional verse and meter along with articles on poets who explode and reinvent traditional forms. To that end, we include entries on poets Elizabeth Bishop, Gloria Anzaldúa, Maya Angelou, Hilda Doolittle, Yusef Komunyakaa, and Jack Kerouac.

In recognition of the contemporary student's ready access to data in an age of advancing technology, many entries include the poet's home page or an Internet address for a site such as Poem Hunter, a delightful search engine that encourages young scholars to pursue additional research on a favorite poem or poet.

Young readers will find much to like in this collection. Although the poets included here come from a variety of backgrounds and produce imaginative verse that is diverse in its exploration of themes and its use of languages, imagery, sound, and voice, these poets were chosen for this collection precisely because those differences permit them to speak with a single voice from a myriad of cultures and identities. The poets included here have produced wildly wonderful, often silly, sometimes somber verse. Each voice is a single element in that complex mosaic known as the Western literary canon.

Acknowledgments

Thanks to Debra Adams, who inherited the project. Both *Poets for Young Adults: Their Lives and Works* and its authors have been the beneficiaries of her guidance, support, and encouragement. Thanks as well to the copyeditor, Dave Mason, at Publication Services, who worked with us to finalize this project.

A special thanks to the folks at the New York Public Library's Teen Central, Books of Wonder, the J. Erik Jonsson Branch of the Dallas Public Library's Young Adult Center, Young Audiences of North Texas, Black Images Book Bazaar in Dallas, and the Miller Branch Library in Jersey City for their efforts to help readers rediscover the pleasure of poetry.

Thanks to the parents, the faculty, and the students of St. Francis of Assisi School in Queens County, New York, as well as to the parents, faculty, and students at University Charter High School in Jersey City, New Jersey, and at W. E. Greiner Arts Academy in Dallas, Texas, for their energy, their commitment, and their love of poetry.

Cara Falcetti sends an extra special thanks to friends Brian Selznick, Muriel Feldshuh, and Gerry Catoggio; to family members Kevin, Larry, Cathy, Felicia, and John for their good humor; to her children, Laura and Andrew, for their patience; and to her mom for putting books in her hands in the first place.

Mary Loving Blanchard thanks New Jersey City University (Jersey City) for awarding her a research grant, which reduced her teaching load and allowed her to devote time to the completion of this project.

Both authors wish to acknowledge the unsung poets whose imaginative verse fills our ordinary lives with extraordinary delight.

Arnold Adoff
(1935–)

Arnold Adoff's contributions to the body of children's and young adult literature go beyond the books he has written and the collections he has anthologized. He is considered one of the primary forces in creating a base of multicultural works for young readers—a mission he started when he discovered few high-quality books available that depicted people from various racial and cultural backgrounds. Adoff has concentrated on selecting, promoting, and writing the stories of people not adequately represented in literature, while avoiding the promotion of materials that reinforce stereotypes or attempt to oversimplify complex issues. Adoff has an intuitive understanding about a work's inherent narrative value and its ability to tell a good story as it reflects inclusiveness and respect for different cultural and racial backgrounds.

Arnold Adoff was born in New York City on July 16, 1935, to pharmacist Aaron Jacob Adoff and Rebecca Stein Adoff. Arnold's father was a Jewish immigrant from a town along the border between Poland and Russia. The Adoffs settled in a working-class neighborhood in the South Bronx, and Arnold grew up in a home rich in books and conversation. The political climate in his home was decidedly liberal, and the women in his family were particularly vocal about social issues.

Adoff entered a Zionist school around the age of ten to begin studying his faith. By age eleven, he was an ardent reader who often carried stacks of books home from the public libraries. The themes found in the young scholar's writing broadened to reflect his evolving interests in psychology, religion, culture, language, and music. His imaginative verse during this period reflected a strong influence from the rhythms and structure of jazz, a true American innovation in music, verse, and movement.

Adoff entered the Columbia University School of Pharmacy in 1955, but the following year he left the school to matriculate in history and literature at the City College of the City University of New York, where he received a degree in history and government. Adoff became an activist in the civil rights and civil liberties activities and rallies at school, and he wrote for the college newspaper. At this time Adoff developed friendships with the writers James Joyce and Gertrude Stein as well as with the musician Charles Mingus, whose career he would later manage.

In 1958, Mingus introduced Adoff to writer Virginia Hamilton. The two married in 1960, and they moved to Europe to work on writing projects, but they later moved back to the United States to take a more active part in the civil rights movement. Adoff began teaching and counseling in Harlem and on Manhattan's Upper West Side and took courses at the New School for Social Research, including one taught by Filipino American poet José Garcia Villa, who became an important force in Adoff's life. Adoff later joined projects affiliated with other schools, including New York University and Connecticut College.

In his teaching positions, Adoff found that his black students wanted poems, stories, artwork, and plays that related to their lives and experiences. Adoff assembled his own collection of materials and included many of them in his first anthology, *I Am the Darker Brother: An Anthology of Modern Poems by Negro Americans*, published in 1968. He published several more anthologies within a few years: *City in All Directions* (1969), *Black Out Loud* (1970), *It Is the Poem Singing into Your Eyes* (1971), and *The Poetry of Black America: Anthology of the 20th Century* (1973). The works were prodigious in size, especially *It Is the Poem Singing into Your Eyes*, for which Adoff selected 600 poems from the thousands submitted by young poets. Even the title came from a young writer. *Poetry of Black America* remains one of the largest anthologies of black poetry.

In 1971, Adoff published his first book of original poetry, *MA nDA LA*. In 1973, he wrote about a subject both topical and personal, that of an interracial family. Adoff and his African American wife Virginia Hamilton were raising their own biracial children, and he wrote a book that reflected his home life, *black is brown is tan*. He continued this theme in *All the Colors of the Race*, based on a girl's questions and her loving reflections on her own mixed-race family. Other juvenile works included a child's journey as retold in *Where Wild Willie* (1978), and one of Adoff's own favorites, *OUTside/Inside Poems* (1981), a cycle of poems that chronicles a little boy's day and that invites young people to express themselves in writing that is emotional and that describes their personal experiences as members of a family and as members of a community.

Adoff has written for middle-grade readers. *Sports Pages* is a collection of pieces about young people in sports. *Flamboyan* (1988) is a prose picture book about a little girl who dreams of escaping her environs as she watches birds in flight. In *Chocolate Dreams* (1989) Adoff blends wit, wordplay, and altered rhyme to produce poetry that appeals to the senses, and his collection of poetry, *Slow Dance Heart Break Blues* (1995), combines lyricism with the intense emotions felt by teenagers.

Adoff and his wife moved to Yellow Springs, Ohio, after many years in New York City. Both of their children have careers in the arts. Son Jaime Levi worked for many years as a musician, and he has since published several books, including an acclaimed first collection of poetry, *The Song Shoots Out of My Mouth*. Daughter Leigh Hamilton is an opera singer. Virginia Hamilton died in 2002.

Adoff continues to write and to work at promoting and adding to a body of literature for young people that is fully inclusive and that reflects the mosaic of human experience without diminishing the dignity of racial and cultural differences or engaging in simplistic or stereotypical writing. He has received an impressive, eclectic assortment of awards, including the National Council of Teachers of English Award for Excellence in Children's Poetry in 1988, and the Virginia Hamilton Award, which was established to honor his late wife. Adoff has described the job of the poet as that of changing attitudes. It is a tribute to Adoff's work that its appeal among preteens and teens is not specific to any one racial group; his words appeal to what they have in common, while recognizing and validating their differences. Adoff has been an advocate for equity, and an energetic voice for the changes he so wanted to effect.

Website

"Arnold Adoff." http://www.arnoldadoff.com

Juvenile Poetry

MA nDA LA. Pictures for Emily Arnold McCully. New York: Harper & Row, 1971.

All the Colors of the Race: Poems. Illustrated by John Steptoe. New York: Lothrop, Lee & Shepard, 1982.

Birds: Poems. Illustrated by Troy Howell. New York: Lippincott, 1982.

The Cabbages Are Chasing the Rabbits. Illustrated by Janet Stevens. San Diego: Harcourt Brace Jovanovich, 1985.

Sports Pages. New York: Lippincott, 1986.

Greens: Poems. Illustrated by Betsy Lewin. New York: Lothrop, Lee & Shepard, 1988.

Chocolate Dreams: Poems. Illustrated by Turi MacCombie. New York: Lothrop, Lee & Shepard, 1989.

In for Winter, Out for Spring. Illustrations by Jerry Pinkney. San Diego: Harcourt Brace Jovanovich, 1991.

Slow Dance Heart Break Blues. Artwork by William Cotton. New York: Lothrop, Lee & Shepard, 1995.

Street Music: City Poems. Illustrated by Karen Barbour. New York: HarperCollins, 1995.

Love Letters. Illustrated by Lisa Desimini. New York: Blue Sky Press, 1997.

Touch the Poems. Illustrated by Lisa Desimini. New York: Blue Sky Press, 2000.

The Basket Counts. Illustrated by Michael Weaver. New York: Simon & Schuster Books for Young Readers, 2000.

Fiction

Flamboyan: Story. Pictures by Karen Barbour. San Diego: Harcourt Brace Jovanovich, 1988.

Hard to Be Six. Illustrated by Cheryl Hanna. New York: Lothrop, Lee & Shepard, 1991.

The Return of Rex and Ethel. Illustrated by Catherine Deeter. San Diego: Harcourt, 2000.

Daring Dog and Captain Cat. Illustrated by Joe Cepeda. New York: Simon & Schuster Books for Young Readers, 2001.

Nonfiction

Black on Black: Commentaries by Negro Americans. New York: Macmillan, 1968.

Edited Collections

I Am the Darker Brother. Drawings by Benny Andrews. New York: Macmillan, 1968.

City in All Directions: An Anthology of Modern Poems. Drawings by Donald Carrick. New York: Macmillan, 1969.

Black Out Loud: An Anthology of Modern Poems by Black Americans. Drawings by Alvin Hollingsworth. New York: Macmillan, 1970.

It Is the Poem Singing into Your Eyes: Anthology of New Young Poets. New York: Harper & Row, 1970.

The Poetry of Black America: Anthology of the 20th Century. New York: Harper & Row, 1973.

My Black Me: A Beginning Book of Black Poetry. New York: Dutton, 1974.

Celebrations: A New Anthology of Black American Poetry. Chicago: Follett, 1977.

References and Suggested Reading

Rand, Donna, and Toni Trent Parker. *Black Books Galore! A Guide to Great African American Children's Books about Girls.* New York: Jossey-Bass, 2000.

Rand, Donna, and Toni Trent Parker. *Black Books Galore! A Guide to Great African American Children's Books about Boys.* New York: John Wiley & Sons, 2001.

Julia Alvarez
(1950-)

Although she was born in New York City, shortly after her birth Alvarez returned with her parents and her sister to the Dominican Republic, where their father was a doctor in charge of a small hospital. In the Dominican Republic, Alvarez lived in a compound with her parents, her siblings, a maid, and an assortment of family members from her mother's side. In 1960, when she was approximately ten years old, her family returned to New York following her father's involvement in an unsuccessful attempt to overthrow the Trujillo dictatorship. Her family's hurried relocation resulted in culture shock for the young Alvarez, who, like many immigrants to the United States, carried with her a storybook image of life in the big city.

However, that storybook image was marred by the harsh realities of her life as an immigrant. Alvarez was uprooted from the intimate familiarity of a culture and language she had known since immediately after birth, and moved to a city that was foreign to her. She was forced to learn a new language; what is more, the family structure to which she had been accustomed was radically changed. The youngster sought comfort from the shock of the major changes within her family and in her own life. She found that comfort in reading and writing. Alvarez reports that books became her new home, once she discovered that books permitted her to carry home around in her head. Books gave the writer a place to go, a place to recover from the frantic pace of her young life and her subsequent feelings of displacement and alienation.

By age seventeen, Alvarez had attended several boarding schools and had completed high school; along the way, she became an avid reader and writer. In 1971, Alvarez received her Bachelor of Arts degree, summa cum laude, from Middlebury College in Vermont. She received her Master of

Fine Arts in 1975 from Syracuse University. Reflecting on her early years as a poet and teacher, Alvarez reports that after her graduation she became a wanderer who would eventually claim fifteen different addresses over the next thirteen years. From 1975 to 1977 she served with the Kentucky Arts Commission as one of three poets in that state's poetry-in-the-schools programs. In 1978 she was involved with a bilingual program in Delaware and with a senior citizen program in North Carolina, both pilot projects funded by the National Endowment for the Arts.

Alvarez compares her frequent changes of address during those years to the travels of another poet, Walt Whitman. She confides that for her, the freedom to travel translated into poetic freedom, explaining that she belonged to no one place but was free to go anywhere. Her recent travels have found her in the birthplace of her parents. In the late nineties, Alvarez returned to the Dominican Republic with her husband, Bill Eichner, to reclaim a small coffee farm. Her latest work, *A Cafecito Story,* although a work of fiction, is described as a poetic, modern fable about humans working in concert with the earth, to nurture and sustain it rather than polluting or misusing it.

In addition to her work during her years as a self-described migrant poet, Alvarez received grants from the National Endowment for the Arts and from the Ingram Merrill Foundation. She served as Robert Frost Fellow in Poetry at the 1986 Bread Loaf Writers Conference and was professor of Creative Writing and English at Andover Academy in Massachusetts, the University of Vermont, and the University of Illinois. She has won several awards, including the 1986 General Electric Foundation Award for Young Writers and the 1991 PEN Oakland/Josephine Miles Award for excellence in multicultural literature.

Comfortable in several genres because each one provides her with "a different form, rhythm, voice" from which to explore language, Alvarez has written poetry, children's books, stories, novels, and essays. Her stories and poems are semi-autobiographical, for they, in significant ways, relate the story of an immigrant's assimilation into American culture. However, although her 1995 collection of poetry, *El Otro Lado: The Other Side,* relates the immigrant's narrative of struggling to maintain self-identity, of being acutely aware of class consciousness, and of childhood memories of the *old country*, Alvarez's memories, unlike those of many immigrants from Latin American countries, include a live-in maid. Still, despite criticism that her work depicts a reality far different from that of the majority of Latin immigrants to the United States, Alvarez's work highlights experiences of the Latina by bringing a bilingual and bicultural voice to the stories of girls and young women to reflect both her own and her young readers' transformation into "an American girl, coming home at last."

Despite her initial discomfort in her birth country, Alvarez became a productive and innovative writer of prose and poetry for young people. Much of her work is bilingual (Spanish and English), and it can be accessed by young Latinas who may have recently immigrated to the United States and who are learning a second language. In fact, Alvarez's work can be enjoyed by children throughout the world. For example, in addition to Spanish, her texts have been translated into Dutch as well as Italian.

Websites

Official Alvarez website: http://www.juliaalvarez.com
"Café Alta Gracia." http://www.cafealtagracia.com

Poetry

The Other Side/El Otro Lado. New York: Plume 1996.
Homecoming: New and Collected Poems. New York: Plume, 1996.
Seven Trees. North Andover, MA: Kat Ran Press, 1998.
The Woman I Kept to Myself. Chapel Hill, NC: Algonquin, 2004.

Nonfiction

Something to Declare. Chapel Hill, NC: Algonquin, 1998.

Fiction

In the Time of the Butterflies. Chapel Hill, NC: Algonquin, 1994.
Yo! Chapel Hill, NC: Algonquin, 1997.
In the Name of Salome. Chapel Hill, NC: Algonquin, 2000.
Saving the World. Chapel Hill, NC: Algonquin, 2006.

Juvenile Fiction

A Gift of Gracias: The Legend of Altagracia. New York: Knopf Books, 2005.

References and Suggested Reading

Behar, Ruth. "Revolutions of the Heart." *The Women's Review of Books* (May 1995): pp. 6–7.
Clinton, Catherine, and Stephen Alcorn. *A Poem of Her Own: Voices of American Women Yesterday and Today.* New York: Harry N. Abrams, 2003.
DuBois, Ellen Carol. *Unequal Sisters: A Multicultural Reader in United States Women's History.* New York: Routledge, 1994.
Johnson, Kelli Lyon. *Julia Alvarez: Writing a New Place on the Map.* Albuquerque: University of New Mexico Press, 2005.

Jones, Vanessa A. "Writing Her Book of High Grace: Novelist/Poet Julia Alvarez Has Forged a Career Doing the Unexpected." *Boston Globe* (June 28, 2000).

Miller, Susan. "Family Spats, Urgent Prayer: Fiction: Celebrating the Strength of Latinas." *Newsweek* (October 17, 1994): p. 77.

Saillant-Torres, Silvio, and Ramona Hernandez. *The Dominican Americans.* Westport, CT: Greenwood Press, 1998.

"Singing Makes Everything Else Possible: An Interview with Julia Alvarez." *River Styx* 53 (Fall 1998).

Sirias, Silvio. *Julia Alvarez: A Critical Companion.* Westport, CT: Greenwood Press, 2001.

Maya Angelou
(1928–)

Angelou's distinct voice has been heard in poetry and prose, in autobiography, and in performance. She is an actress, a biographer, a singer, an activist, an educator, and a poet, and she is fluent in six languages. Angelou was nominated for a Pulitzer Prize in 1971 for her poetry collection *Just Give Me a Cool Drink of Water 'Fore I Diiie*, and in 1992 she was named inaugural poet for President Bill Clinton. Dr. Maya Angelou has received more than twenty honorary degrees from various universities, and she is recognized as being among the more influential writers in contemporary American letters.

Maya Angelou. Courtesy of Photofest.

She was born Marguerite Johnson in St. Louis, Missouri, to Bailey and Vivien Johnson. Her father worked as a dietitian in the Navy; her mother later owned a San Francisco boardinghouse. She adored her brother, Bailey, who began calling her *Maya* because he could not pronounce Marguerite. Following her parents' divorce, Marguerite and Bailey spent much of their early childhood in Stamps, Arkansas, raised by their grandmother, Momma. Momma was a source of strength and stability for the children, and a role model who ran her own store and property, and extended loans to other blacks and to whites in the community.

When Maya and Bailey returned to their mother's home, eight-year-old Marguerite was raped by her mother's friend. Her uncles extracted their own revenge, killing the rapist following his brief prison stay. Terrified that her part in identifying the attacker led to his death, the girl retreated into silence. For five years she refused to speak, and her mother sent Marguerite back to grandmother Momma in Arkansas. Angelou recovered there, largely because of the encouragement and understanding of her grandmother and a family friend, Mrs. Bertha Flowers. Maya and Bailey eventually rejoined their mother in California, where Maya attended high school as well as dance and drama classes. At seventeen, Angelou held a position as San Francisco's first black streetcar conductor. That same year, she graduated high school and gave birth to a son, initially named Clyde Bailey Johnson; he subsequently renamed himself Guy.

Throughout the early 1950s, Angelou went through a series of transitory jobs; she also traveled to New York frequently, and she continued to pursue a career in the arts. Angelou was married briefly to sailor Anastasias (Tosh) Angelos. Angelou's stage career took off with a twenty-two-country tour of *Porgy and Bess.* Her son's reactions to Angelou's absence were both emotional and physical, and he developed a stress-related skin condition. This convinced Angelou that she should leave the touring company. She continued to work as an actress and singer, moving to Brooklyn to work with the Harlem Writers Guild. Angelou raised money for Dr. Martin Luther King Jr.'s Southern Christian Leadership Conference and became a regional coordinator for the organization.

In 1960, Angelou married South African freedom fighter Vasumzi Make. The following year, she left New York with her son and husband for Egypt, where she worked for a weekly newspaper. Make and Angelou separated and subsequently divorced. Angelou and her son left Cairo for Ghana following Guy's graduation from high school. Angelou became a professor at the University of Ghana, and while teaching there she helped to stage a rally in support of Dr. King's march on Washington. In 1965, Angelou joined the faculty of the University of California at Los Angeles. She wrote for educational television, then published her first book in 1970. The memoir *I Know Why the Caged Bird Sings* was an immediate critical success. Five subsequent autobiographical works, *Gather Together in My Name* (1974), *Singin' and Swingin' and Gettin' Merry Like Christmas* (1976), *The Heart of a Woman* (1981), *All God's Children Need Traveling Shoes* (1986), and *A Song Flung Up to Heaven* (2002) chronicle her life as a young mother, performer, and emerging activist.

Angelou's career as a poet has not been limited to print; she is also a gifted speaker with an austere yet warm stage presence. Angelou commands audiences with readings of her own works as well as those of other artists. Her body of work features themes ranging from the deeply personal to public calls for social change. Her poetry is rhythmic and made for recitation. Her work relies equally on imagery and on the many voices that speak from the pages of her work.

Angelou has written several volumes of poetry and she has received numerous honors and recognition, including the National Association for the Advancement of Colored People's (NAACP) Spingarn Medal. She has also received appointments from presidents Ford, Carter, and Clinton. The Maya Angelou Child Protection Team and Family Center was established in London in her honor.

Angelou embraces all aspects of the human condition. Her poetry speaks of resiliency and hope as it celebrates diversity and cautions against intolerance or complacency. Her work reflects her determination to keep language alive and to place the concerns of women, children, the homeless, and the disenfranchised at the center of conversations about rights and responsibility. Angelou is a respected and frequently read contemporary writer who currently lives in Winston-Salem, North Carolina.

Websites

Maya Angelou's official website: http://www.mayaangelou.com
"Academy of American Poets." http://www.poets.org

Poetry

Just Give Me a Cool Drink of Water 'Fore I Diiie. New York: Random House, 1971.
Oh Pray My Wings Are Gonna Fit Me Well. New York: Random House, 1975.
And Still I Rise. New York: Random House, 1978.
Shaker, Why Don't You Sing? New York: Random House, 1978.
Poems. New York: Random House, 1986.
I Shall Not Be Moved. New York: Bantam Books, 1991.
On the Pulse of Morning. New York: Random House, 1993.
The Complete Collected Poems of Maya Angelou. New York: Random House, 1994.
Phenomenal Women. New York: Random House, 1994.
A Brave and Startling Truth. New York: Random House, 1995.
Even the Stars Look Lonesome. New York: Random House, 1997.
Oh, Pray My Wings Are Gonna Fit Me Well. New York: Random House, 1998.
Amazing Peace: A Christmas Poem. New York: Random House, 2005.

Juvenile Fiction

My Painted House, My Friendly Chicken, and Me. New York: Alfred A. Knopf, 2003.
Kofi and His Magic. New York: Alfred A. Knopf, 2003.

Nonfiction

I Know Why the Caged Bird Sings. New York: Bantam Books, 1969.
Gather Together in My Name. New York: Random House, 1974.
Singin' and Swingin' and Gettin' Merry Like Christmas. New York: Random House, 1976.
The Heart of a Woman. New York: Random House, 1981.
All God's Children Need Traveling Shoes. New York: Random House, 1997.
A Song Flung Up to Heaven. New York: Random House, 2002.
Even the Stars Look Lonesome. New York: Random House, 2002.

Recordings

Our Sheroes and Heroes. Los Angeles: Pacifica Tape Library, 1983.
Life Doesn't Frighten Me. New York: Stewart, Tabori, Chang, 1993.
On the Pulse of Morning. New York: Random House Audio, 1993.
And Still I Rise. New York: Random House Audio, 1996.
Black Pearls: The Poetry of Maya Angelou. Los Angeles: GWP Records, 1998.
Making Magic in the World. Ukiah, CA: New Dimensions Foundation, 1998.
The Maya Angelou Poetry Collection. New York: Random House, 1999.

References and Suggested Reading

Graham, Joyce L. "Maya Angelou." *Writers for Young Adults.* Ed. Ted Hipple. New York: Charles Scribner's Sons, 1997.
Pettis, Joyce. *African American Poets: Lives, Works, and Sources.* Westport, CT: Greenwood Press, 2002.

Gloria Evangelina Anzaldúa (1942–2004)

The themes of family, friendship, loss, recovery, and growth found in Anzaldúa's imaginative verse reflect as much the poet's strong roots in the culture of the towns along the Texas–Mexico border as they do the poet's efforts to identify and explore a politics of identity. Her efforts are as much personal as global, for in attempting to localize the point from which her strengths arise, Anzaldúa gives voice to young lesbians of color in the United States.

The self-described "Chicana dyke feminist" is the daughter of migrant workers, and she entered the fields with her family when she was eleven years old. Anzaldúa suffered from bouts of illness as a young girl; she often took to her bed for several days after harvesting crops in the towns along the Texas–Mexico border and in Arkansas. It was at these times that she found comfort in books. Anzaldúa was an avid reader who loved language. Books soothed the many aches in her young life and encouraged her to imagine anew her life's circumstances.

After graduating with a bachelor of arts in English and secondary education, she returned to Hargill, Texas, as a teacher to the children of migrant families. While teaching in Hargill, Anzaldúa enrolled in graduate school and earned a master of arts in English and education from the University of Texas. After receiving her graduate degree, she taught in a bilingual pre-school program. In addition, she has taught courses in feminism, Chicano studies, and creative writing at the University of Texas at Austin, at Vermont College of Norwich University, and at San Francisco State University.

In her poetry, as well as in her prose, Anzaldúa blends Spanish and English to create language variants. These variants are, in fact, new languages that the poet uses to speak specifically to the different members of her audience. Her intimacy with Spanish and English allows speakers of either language to know, immediately, the meaning of the new words she has created, words whose meaning must be understood connotatively.

Anzaldúa infuses language with emotion and circumstance; the result is often seemingly simplistic verse that echoes in readers' thoughts long after they have completed reading her poetry. Although her texts have been criticized as being filled with anger and rage, Anzaldúa's poetry is a call for young people to join in the struggle to identify self, rather than a call to arms. Her poetry is not about anger as much as it is about reclamation, and is not about pain as much as it is about pride. These are the gifts she offers young readers.

Anzaldúa's writing reflects both her spirituality and her attention to the tiny things that often escape notice. Her use of language to create imagery evokes the torturous heat that burns the skin of the youngster who picks crops with her family in the poem, "Sus Plummas el Viento." And because Anzaldúa has drawn a verbal picture in the poem, "Immaculate, Inviolate: Como Ella," the reader is able to count along with the narrator as she describes the wrinkles on her grandmother's face.

Although much of Anzaldúa's work appears in anthologies, she has also written several books for children, including poetry and fiction. Much of her work for young people examines the clash of cultures, not to offer solutions, but simply to draw attention to the existence of such conflicts and to engage people from different cultures in discourse about possible solutions. For example, her poem, "The Horse," examines disparate cultural responses to the maiming of an animal to suggest that such responses provide opportunities to examine relationships between cultures and among races.

In other imaginative work for young people, she creates a persona, Prietita, who relates autobiographical experiences that Anzaldúa then connects to the experiences of young girls the world over. Indeed, this Chicana poet has won several awards that reflect the scope and breadth of her reach. Anzaldúa received the Lambda Lesbian Small Book Press Award, a National Endowment for the Arts (NEA) Award, the Before Columbus Foundation American Book Award, and the Sappho Award of Distinction.

This American poet suffered throughout her life from compromised health. She was completing her dissertation at the University of California, Santa Cruz, when she died. Friends of Anzaldúa created a Web altar for the poet, and, in July 2005 The Benson Latin American Collection acquired an archive of her work. The archive contains manuscripts of the poet's major published works along with unpublished manuscripts, notebooks, correspondence, and lectures as well as audio and video interviews.

Websites

"Web Altar for Gloria." http://gloria.chicanas.com
"Nettie Lee Benson Latin American Collection, University of Texas Libraries, The University of Texas at Austin." http://www.lib.utexas.edu/

Nonfiction

Making Face, Making Soul/Haciendo Caras: Creative and Critical Perspectives by Women of Color. St. Paul, MN: Consortium Books, 1990.
Borderlands/La Frontera: The New Mestiza. St. Paul, MN: Consortium Books, 1999.
This Bridge Called My Back: Writings by Radical Women of Color. Berkeley, CA: Third Woman Press, 2001.

Juvenile Fiction

Friends from the Other Side/Amigos Del Otro Lado. Illustrator: Consuelo Mendez. Bt Bound, 1999.
Prietita and the Ghost Woman/Prietita y La Llorona. Illustrator: Maya Christina Gonzalez. Minneapolis, MN: Pub Group West, 2001.

References and Suggested Reading

Alarcon, Norma. "Anzaldúa's Frontera: Inscribing Gynetics." *Chicana Feminisms: A Critical Reader*. Ed. Gabriela F. Arredondo, Aida Hurado, Norma Klahn, Olba Nijera-Ramirez, and Patricia Zavella. Durham, NC: Duke University Press, 2003.
Cassell's Encyclopedia of Queer Myth, Symbol and Spirit: Gay, Lesbian, Bisexual and Transgender Lore. Herndon, VA: Cassell, 1997.
Heyck, Denis. *Barrios and Borderlands*. New York: Routledge, 1994.
Ikas, Karin Rosa. *Chicana Ways: Conversations with Ten Chicana Writers*. Reno, NV: University of Nevada Press, 2002.
Kaup, Monika. "Constituting Hybridity as Hybrid: Métis Canadian and Mexican American Formations." *Mixing Race, Mixing Culture: Inter-American Literary Dialogues*. Ed. Monika Kaup and Debra J. Rosenthal. Austin: University of Texas Press, 2002.
Keating, AnaLouise, ed. *Entre Mundos/Among Worlds*. New York: Routledge, 2005.
———, ed. *Gloria E. Anzaldúa: Interviews/Entrevistas*. New York: Routledge, 2000.
———. *Women Reading Women Writing: Self-Invention in Paula Gunn Allen, Gloria Anzaldúa and Audre Lorde*. Philadelphia: Temple University Press, 1996.
Rodenberger, Laura Payne Butler, and Jacqueline Kolosov. *Writing on the Wind: Anthology of West Texas Women Writers*. Lubbock: Texas Tech University Press, 2005.

Ruiz, Vicki. *Latinas in the United States: A Historical Encyclopedia.* Bloomington: Indiana University Press, 2006.

Steele, Cassie. *We Heal From Memory: Sexton, Lorde, Anzaldúa and the Poetry of Witness.* New York: Palgrave, 2000.

Torres, Lourdes, and Inmaculada Pertusa, eds. *Tortilleras: Hispanic and U.S. Latina Lesbian Expression.* Philadelphia: Temple University Press, 2003.

Elizabeth Bishop
(1911–1979)

Elizabeth Bishop published her first poem at age twenty-four. Her early work received critical attention; however, she did not achieve widespread recognition until late in her career. A perfectionist who strove for elegance of expression in her poetry, which addresses themes ranging from spiritual rebirth to the nature of art, Bishop is now one of the most highly regarded poets in American literature. Her poetry is recognized for its clarity and precision, for its sense of immediacy and of place, and for its imagery, which creates layers of meanings.

The only child of William and Gertrude May Boomer Bishop, Elizabeth Bishop's earliest days were marked by loss. Her father died of kidney disease when Elizabeth was but a year old. Soon thereafter her mother, overwhelmed by her circumstances and consumed by grief, attempted suicide. Bishop's maternal grandparents became caretakers of both her and her mother. When Elizabeth was five years old, her grandparents committed their daughter, the young girl's mother, to the Nova Scotia Hospital, where she remained until her death in 1934. Elizabeth was twenty-two years old when her mother died. For the better part of her life, Elizabeth was separated by death and disease from the two most important people in her world.

Despite an adolescent marked by loss and estrangement, Bishop developed an intellectual and creative curiosity that was fostered by her maternal aunt, who owned a large number of books, including anthologies of poetry, and who introduced the young girl to the classics. Bishop was an enthusiastic albeit sporadic reader who was drawn to fairy tales. Influenced by the imaginative verse she discovered in her aunt's collections, she wrote her first poem at the age of eight. Home-schooled by her aunt, Bishop made a delayed entry into the public school arena, at age fourteen. She went on to enroll at the North Shore Country Day School in Swampscott, where she wrote for a literary magazine, contributing a ballad, essays, and a short story.

Bishop became a boarding student at the Walnut Hill School for Girls in 1927, when she was approximately sixteen years old. There she wrote for the school's literary magazine, *The Blue Pencil.* During her teen years, she became more keenly aware of, and sensitive to, her complicated family situation; with her mother's hospitalization and only the extended family to take her in, Bishop was often forced to spend holidays and vacations at the nearly vacant boarding school.

In 1930 Bishop entered Vassar College, where she majored in English literature and attended classes with other writers, including Mary McCarthy, Eleanor Clark, and Muriel Rukeyser. During this period she published a number of pieces in the *Vassar Review.* While a senior at Vassar, Bishop forged a close friendship with fellow poet Marianne Moore, and she was a member of a group of students that created a literary magazine, *Con Spirito,* to compete with the more staid Vassar publication.

Upon graduating from Vassar, Bishop became determined to earn a living as a writer. She moved to New York City, and she began to travel extensively. Her experiences in countries throughout Europe became an invaluable source of inspiration for her writing, much of which reflected her yearning for a sense of place. After sharing a friend's home in Florida, Bishop settled in Key West, where she purchased a home.

Although her work continued to appear in various publications—including *The Paris Review* and a 1936 entry in *Trial Balances,* an anthology of works by new writers—it would be ten years before Bishop published a collection of her own work. Her first full-length collection, *North and South,* was published in 1946 to immediate critical acclaim. The collection won the prestigious Houghton Mifflin Prize fellowship. In her first collection, readers discover many of Bishop's most frequently anthologized poems, including "The Monument," "Roosters," "The Imaginary Iceberg," and "The Fish."

"The Fish" is, perhaps, Bishop's best-known poem. The simply written narrative, similar to other pieces in the collection, tells a layered story, one that follows a girl in search of the beautiful. Much of Bishop's poetry reads as autobiographical, as the poet's attempt to order her life in verse. However, Bishop's poetry is equally concerned with the craft of poetry. Bishop examines the craft of making, of creating something new. The protagonist in "The Fish" releases the creature back into the sea in recognition of her power to create both death and life. Her words, the simple descriptive narrative, are the creature's link to life—not the rainbow she views in his skin; the rainbow is, after all, her own reflection. Although the subject of the poem is not human, Bishop explores human emotions in this work, as she examines relationships marked by estrangement, witness, clarity, and sheer determination. In "The Monument," Bishop encourages readers to consider the value of art. She wants readers to question not only what qualities are inherent to art, what its aesthetics are, but also who makes the decisions about those inherent qualities.

After winning a Guggenheim Fellowship for *North and South,* Bishop served as poetry consultant at the Library of Congress. She won the Amy Lowell Travel Fellowship in 1951 and traveled to South America in November of that year. Bishop returned to New York City only to settle some affairs before relocating to Brazil, where she would take up residence for fifteen years. Bishop's time in Brazil was productive; she worked with Enrique E. Mindlin on a book about Brazilian architecture and composed seventeen poems for the release of an expanded edition of *North and South*, now subtitled *A Cold Spring* (1955). The volume included some of her best-reviewed pieces, notably "At the Fishhouses," a highly descriptive allegory set on the Nova Scotia coastline. Bishop was awarded the Pulitzer Prize for this book.

Bishop worked on translations and did work in nonfiction over the next years; she also continued her travels, including a trip down the Amazon River. Her 1965 collection, *Questions of Travel,* may partially explain the poet's self-exile in Brazil. In this collection the poet recalls moments of intense sadness as well as moments of intense joy; she re-creates those moments in the two sections of her collection titled "Brazil" and "Elsewhere." Bishop's exacting ability with language and her keen skills of observation combine in *Questions of Travel* to produce a simple yet elegant retelling of history and culture.

Bishop taught at the University of Washington in Seattle in 1966 and again in 1973. In between her teaching stints in Seattle, Bishop released *Complete Poems,* for which she won the 1969 Book Award for poetry. Although she suffered from health difficulties, Bishop continued to travel, giving readings and making public appearances. She taught at Harvard, taking a four-year position as lecturer and later taught a semester at New York University.

In 1976, Bishop released *Geography III,* yet another collection attesting to her fascination not only with travel but also with history and culture, and with the implications of supposedly benign travel for both the adventurers and those left behind. The 1976 collection featured works such as the monologue "Crusoe in England," in which an aging Crusoe ruminates his return to civilization, and "The End of March," in which a beachcomber—presumably Bishop—strolls along the sea on a harsh day, contemplating and then rejecting retirement as sanctioned idleness.

Bishop died on October 6, 1979, in Massachusetts. She left behind a body of work that secures her place as a maker of American literary traditions. In her work, young readers observe the steady hand of a craftsman whose persnickety attention to word choice, imagery, and detail result in imaginative verse that is as telling as it is secretive, as provocative as it is evocative.

Websites

"Academy of American Poets." http://www.poets.org
"Poets Online." http://www.poets.org

Poetry

Selected Poems. London: Chatto &Windus, 1967.
The Ballad of the Burglar of Babylon. New York: Farrar, Straus & Giroux, 1968.

Nonfiction

Brazil. Collaboration with the editors of *Life* magazine. New York: Time/Life World Library, 1962.
Becoming a Poet: Elizabeth Bishop with Marianne Moore and Robert Lowell. By David Kalstone. Edited with a preface by Robert Hemenway. New York: Farrar, Straus & Giroux, 1989.

References and Suggested Reading

Bloom, Harold, ed. *Elizabeth Bishop: Bloom's Major Poets Series.* Broomall, PA: Chelsea House, 2002.
The Collected Prose. New York: Farrar, Straus & Giroux, 1984.
Fountain, Gary, and Peter Brazeau. *Elizabeth Bishop: An Oral Biography.* Amherst: University of Massachusetts Press, 1994.
Giroux, Robert, ed. *One Art: Elizabeth Bishop.* New York: Farrar, Straus & Giroux, 1994.
Miller, Brett C. *Elizabeth Bishop: Life and the Memory of It.* Berkeley: University of California Press, 1993.

William Blake
(1757–1827)

Although he was given no formal education as a young child, William Blake seemed marked for distinction from an early age. And while he never made his living exclusively as a writer, he produced a highly influential body of work in poetry for adult and young adult audiences. He also created what are recognized as the first picture books and he wrote literary criticism specific to the children's book field. His works were largely unrecognized until four decades after his death, but they have endured and still provoke lively speculation as to their intended audience and purpose.

William Blake was born on November 28, 1757, in the Soho district of London, to hosier James Blake and Catherine Hermitage Blake. The two had wed in 1752; it was a second marriage for the previously widowed Catherine. The couple had seven children, two of whom died in infancy. William was the third-born son.

Blake had a happy childhood, in part due to the freedom allowed him by his parents. He wandered through nearby fields and the streets of London, and he learned to read and write from his mother. By four, the young Blake claimed to have visions, announcing that he saw the face of God at a window; a few years later, he claimed to have seen a vision of a tree of angels. Throughout his life, he would assert that he was visited by poets, prophets, and mystics. And while his parents nurtured and supported the young poet, often purchasing art supplies for him, on at least one occasion his report of having seen visions earned him a whipping from them.

His parents determined that William was not suited to training in the family's business, and they sent him for instruction in drawing, painting, and engraving. At ten, he became a student at a drawing school in the Strand, under the tutelage of Henry Pars. He studied with Pars for approximately five years. The young Blake became an apprentice to an engraver;

however, he had difficult relationships with the other students, and after two years he was dismissed from tutelage. By age twenty-one, Blake was studying at the Royal Academy and he became an active member of a community of artists during this period. He also became acquainted with a publisher who later guided him as he prepared his children's work for publication.

On August 18, 1782, William Blake married Catherine Boucher, the daughter of his landlord. Catherine was illiterate, but Blake trained his wife to work as an assistant printer and color artist. The Blakes found themselves part of local gatherings of artists in Soho.

William Blake continued to produce works such as illuminated prints, text, and relief done on a single plate. Blake used this style in *Songs of Innocence*, a work containing twenty-three lyrics. Some of the poems were published in an expanded edition, *Songs of Innocence and of Experience*. A child muse introduces the book, asking the speaker to sing the songs "in a book that all may read," reflecting, perhaps, Blake's efforts to speak to a larger and more diverse audience. Blake's allusions and use of conventional literary forms make his work an intriguing read for both the young and not so young. As he became increasingly aware of movements in children's literature meant to eschew the traditional, oral forms of narrative for the less traditional unrhymed verse, he began to employ the rhymes, rhythms, and themes of folklore and Mother Goose in his work.

The Blakes relocated to Lambeth, a more rural area, in 1790. Some of Blake's works from this period have not been definitively dated, but he began to write of his views on the complexity of the soul and refused to consider the worlds of children and adults as mutually exclusive. He saw the darker sides of childhood and the price of innocence. This was reflected in some of his poetry, in his almost cryptic titles, and in the surprising complexities of works that seemed primarily aimed at the juvenile market. His book *For Children: The Gates of Paradise*, was later reworked as *For the Sexes: The Gates of Paradise.* Lyrics and illustrations in the work focused on the mundane and the materialistic, self-awareness and morality, skewing the lines between juvenile and adult readership.

Blake continued to support himself through sales of his engravings and his artwork, noted primarily for his illustrations of earlier poets' works. Blake's less than social disposition and his eccentricities alienated many around him, friends and patrons alike. He died at the home of an in-law on August 12, 1827.

Websites

"The Literature Network." http://www.online-literature.com
"William Blake Archive." http://www.blakearchive.org/blake/

Poetry

The Complete Poetry and Prose of William Blake. Berkeley: University of California Press, 1965.
Songs of Innocence and of Experience. Princeton, NJ: Princeton University Press, 1991 (reprint).

Nonfiction

Letters from William Blake to Thomas Butts, 1800-1803. London: Oxford University Press, 1926.

References and Suggested Reading

Ackroyd, Peter. *William Blake: A Biography.* New York: Alfred A. Knopf, 1996.
Davis, Michael. *William Blake: A New Kind of Man.* Berkeley: University of California Press, 1977.
King, James. *William Blake: His Life.* New York: St. Martin's Press, 1991.
Lister, Raymond. *William Blake: An Introduction to the Man and to His Work.* New York: Frederick Ungar, 1969.
Wilson, Mona. *The Life of William Blake.* London: Oxford University Press, 1971.

Arna Wendell Bontemps
(1902-1973)

This twentieth-century American poet was a chronicler of African American cultural heritage. He recorded and preserved the cultural origins and artifacts of an emerging African American self, both in his imaginative verse and in his work as a librarian. Bontemps's work is marked by decorum and by a restrained, elegant composition. Although he often composed in free verse, his poetry is noted for its adherence to traditional forms. Most of Bontemps's poems were published in the United States during the 1920s; however, a pamphlet of his verse, *Personals,* was published in London.

Bontemps was born in Alexandria, Louisiana, on October 13, 1902, the first child of a Roman Catholic bricklayer and a Methodist schoolteacher. However; Bontemps grew up in California under the watchful eye of members of the Seventh Day Adventist Church, where he attended primary school. After completing college, he moved from California to New York, where he accepted a teaching position in Harlem. His arrival was propitious: it was the height of the Harlem Renaissance, and Bontemps was quickly ushered into that society of black intellectuals, artists, and writers given the designation of "New Negro."

Unlike Countee Cullen and Jean Toomer, poets who rejected racial identity as an adjective to describe their poetry, Bontemps appeared to have been a model of what Alain Locke had in mind when he, along with other black intellectuals of the period, coined the term "New Negro" to describe a generation of African Americans no longer bound by the travesty of slavery and its implications, and sufficiently race conscious without being radical.

A skilled and meticulous writer of imaginative verse, Bontemps stumbled into writing children's verse when he collaborated with Langston

Hughes on a travel book of verse for children. The success and wide appeal of the work compelled him to add the role of children's writer to his roles as a writer of poetry, fiction, and folklore. In addition to several collaborations with Hughes, Bontemps also taught at various colleges and became involved in the local chapter of the National Association for the Advancement of Colored People (NAACP). Bontemps also produced another book of juvenile verse, *You Can't Pet a Possum,* and after a visit to Fisk University in Nashville, Tennessee, he turned his attention to a project that would occupy him for the next several years: recovering the neglected histories of former slaves.

In 1938, Bontemps was appointed as editorial supervisor to the Federal Writers' Project of Illinois and he dedicated his efforts to the collection and archival preservation of narratives from former enslaved men, women, and children. He also edited his first compilation of poetry, *Golden Slippers: An Anthology of Negro Poetry for Young Readers,* published a humorous American tall tale for children, and was awarded grants to pursue a graduate degree.

Bontemps completed a master of arts degree in library science at the University of Chicago and subsequently was appointed as librarian at Fisk University. His early interest in the narratives written by slaves that were held in repository at Fisk had come full circle. With this appointment, Bontemps had an opportunity to ensure future additions to and preservation of those holdings. In fact, an assortment of histories and biographies, largely written with young people in mind, distinguished Bontemps's tenure at Fisk. In addition, during this period, Bontemps, in collaboration with Hughes, produced two noteworthy collections: *The Book of Negro Folklore* and *The Poetry of the Negro,* comprehensive collections of poems and folklore by and about black Americans. After Hughes's death in 1967, Bontemps produced *Hold Fast to Dreams,* a collection of poems by black and white writers clearly centered on acknowledging the significance of Hughes's contributions to poetry and to writers.

Bontemps's collections of poetry include *Personals,* from which the poem "Nocturne at Bethesda" is taken. This work clearly shows that Bontemps's decision to accept his role as a model of the New Negro was not undertaken without his knowledge of the importance of a people's attempts to define themselves, not in relationship to their hardships, but in relationship to their accomplishments and dreams. The speaker in "Nocturne at Bethesda" has indeed survived; his spirit has been bludgeoned, but his head is lifted high in a show of strength and determination. *Personals* serves as a repository that marks the growth of African American literature during the 1920s. In much of his work, Bontemps links the evolution of an African American self to the cycle of the seasons to suggest a natural, and inevitable, evolution. His poetry often simply states the obvious in verse that is intricately woven. For example, in "A black man talks of reaping," Bontemps observed that it is illogical for a man not to benefit from his own labor and offers a biting indictment against the ills of slavery that had filtered into then present laws and that resulted in disparate wages and standards of living for many African American and poor white workers.

On the whole, Bontemps's poetry speaks to the persistent will of African Americans to endure beyond the failed promises of Reconstruction. His poetry describes a race of dignified people, earnest workers whose commitment to kith and kin deserve both acknowledgment and valorization. This multitalented writer's most distinguished work was *The Story of the Negro,* a race history of Africans and African Americans since Egyptian civilization that won him the Jane Addams Children's Book Award in 1956.

Retirement from Fisk in 1966 brought with it recognition for Bontemps in the form of two honorary degrees and distinguished professorships at the University of Illinois and at Yale, where he was Curator of the James Weldon Johnson Collection at the Beinecke Library. Bontemps also returned to Fisk as a writer in residence. The vast body of extant correspondence between Bontemps and Hughes is housed in the Johnson Collection at Yale.

Website

"Internet School Library Media Center, Arna Bontemps's Page." http://falcon.jmu.edu/~ramseyil/bontemps.htm

Poetry

Fast Sooner Hound. By Arna Bontemps and Jack Conroy. Illustrated by Virginia Lee Burton. Boston: Houghton Mifflin, 1942.

Five Black Lives: The Autobiographies of Venture Smith, James Mars, William Grimes, the Rev. G. W. Offley, [and] James L. Smith. Introduction by Arna Bontemps. First edition. Middletown, CT: Wesleyan University Press, 1971.

Recordings

Anthology of Negro Poetry for Young People. Edited and read by Arna Bontemps. Folkways Records FC 7114, 1958.

Arna Wendell Bontemps Reading His Poems with Comment at Radio Station WPLN, Nashville Public Library, May 22, 1963. Library of Congress Archive of Recorded Poetry and Literature.

References and Suggested Reading

Andrews, William L., Francis Smith Foster, and Trudier Harris, eds. *The Oxford Companion to African American Literature.* New York: Oxford University Press, 1997.

Bader, Joan. "History Changes Color: A Story in Three Parts. (Remembering African American Educators Carter Woodson and Arna Bontemps on the Occasion of Black History Month)." *Horn Book Magazine* (January 11, 1997).

Jones, Kirkland C. *Renaissance Man from Louisiana; A Biography of Arna Wendell Bontemps.* Westport, CT: Greenwood Press, 1992.

Nichols, Charles H., ed. *Arna Bontemps, Langston Hughes: Letters, 1925–1967.* New York. Paragon House, 1990.

Parini, Jay, ed. *The Columbia History of American Poetry.* New York: Columbia University Press, 1993.

Anne Bradstreet
(ca. 1612–1672)

Although Anne Bradstreet's poetry has earned her a fixed place in the American canon purely by means of its own literary merits, Bradstreet is also the subject of extensive study on a sociological level. Considered by many critics to be the first authentic American poet, Bradstreet provided an atypical reflection of the lifestyle and sensibilities of seventeenth-century women. Her works force readers to consider two options: the view of Bradstreet as a renegade, or the view that Puritan society was not as rigid and uncompromising as postulated by the majority of studies on the era.

Bradstreet was born Anne Dudley in either 1612 or 1613 in Northamptonshire, England, one of six children of Dorothy Yorke and Thomas Dudley, a former solder under Queen Elizabeth and a clerk to a nobleman at the time of the girl's birth. The Bradstreets moved in 1619 when her father began service as a steward to the Earl of Lincolnshire. Bradstreet was educated at home, primarily by her father. Her contact with the outside world was filtered through her father's tutelage; indeed, she met her future husband, Simon Bradstreet, in 1621 when the Cambridge graduate was hired to work with her father. The young master Bradstreet lived on the same property as the Dudley family for several years; between 1621 and 1628, Anne Dudley and Simon Bradstreet spent four years apart. The two married in 1628, after they were reunited and following Anne's bout with smallpox.

In 1630 the young couple sailed to the New World on the *Arabella*, arriving at Salem in the Massachusetts colony. They quickly fled the harsh environment, first for Massachusetts and then, in 1631, to Cambridge. By 1635 they had settled in Ipswich. It was during this time that Anne Bradstreet began to write lengthy, formal poetry as well as shorter descriptions of her life as a young wife and mother in the Americas, later addressing many of her reflections to her eight children. Simon Bradstreet became a judge, a royal councilor, a legislator, and a two-term governor. After a decade in Ipswich, the Bradstreets relocated to North Andover, Massachusetts, where they lived until Anne's death.

The only work published during Bradstreet's lifetime was *The Tenth Muse,* a collection that her brother-in-law, the Reverend John Woodbridge, published in England in 1647 without Bradstreet's consent. In the introductory letter to readers, Woodbridge repeatedly apologizes to Bradstreet for taking it upon himself to submit the manuscript for publishers' consideration, asserting that Bradstreet never intended to make the poems public. Some poems in the collection were addressed to the poet's father; others contained breaks in style or segued into musings. Bradstreet did not attempt to publish her works because she was cautious about entering the public arena as the author of work that might be viewed as outside the purview of women. Although Bradstreet wrote extensively, her writing remained a part of the private, rather than the public sphere during her lifetime.

Several Poems was released in 1678, six years after her death, and *The Works of Anne Bradstreet in Prose and Verse* about two hundred years later, in 1867. After Bradstreet's death, her works were initially handled by a group of literary friends, including editor John Rogers and publisher John Foster. The last volume, *Works*, was edited by John Harvard Ellis. Her forays into prose, including the aphoristic "Meditations," have been mostly dismissed as critical disappointments.

Bradstreet's voice is distinctive, and in "The Prologue" she offers her own assessment of how society views the woman poet. She describes herself as "obnoxious to each carping tongue," referring to those naysayers who dared proclaim that women's endeavors were better limited to the sewing needle than to the pen. The duality of her writing career—the vast body of work she created juxtaposed against her own resistance to having her poetry made public—remains the subject of conjecture. Bradstreet resisted being characterized as unfit to create imaginative verse because of her gender; however, she made few, if any, attempts to seek opportunities to publish her verse. Had her brother-in-law not traveled with the manuscript of what became *The Tenth Muse*, her works might have remained within the family.

In poetry written for her family, Bradstreet employs an intimate but sophisticated voice to chronicle her spiritual growth and to reflect on her various roles, from daughter, to mother, and finally to grandparent. Her early poems also provide an intimate view of Bishop's perception of family milestones, notably births and deaths. She uses imagery to project an appreciation of nature and to address her own religious convictions. Her work reflects her efforts to reconcile in verse the Puritan resistance to pleasure. Bradstreet's genuine appreciation of the corporeal world—her warmth and humanity—permit Bradstreet's words to transcend the social confines of the culture within which she wrote.

Website

Anne Bradstreet's website: http://ww.annebradstreet.com

Poetry

The Tenth Muse Lately Sprung Up in America, by a Gentlewoman in Those Parts. London: Stephen Bowell, 1650.

Revised: Several Poems Compiled with Great Variety of Wit and Learning, Full of Delight, by a Gentlewoman in New England. Boston: John Foster, 1678.

The Complete Works of Anne Bradstreet. Ed. Joseph R. McElrath, Jr., and Allan P. Robb. Boston: Twayne, 1981.

References and Suggested Reading

Elliott, Emory, ed. "Anne Bradstreet." *Dictionary of Literary Biography, Volume 24: American Colonial Writers: 1606–1734.* Princeton, NJ: Princeton University Press, Gale Group, 1984, pp. 29–34.

Lancashire, Ian, ed. "Selected Poetry of Anne Bradstreet." *Representative Poetry Online.* Toronto: University of Toronto Press, 2003.

McElrath, Joseph R., and Allan P. Robb, eds. *The Complete Works of Anne Bradstreet.* Boston: Twayne, 1981.

Wilson, Douglas. *Beyond Stateliest Marble: The Passionate Femininity of Anne Bradstreet.* Nashville, TN: Cumberland House, 2001.

Martha Wadsworth Brewster (1725–1757)

Brewster was one of a handful of American women poets who produced imaginative verse in the two centuries that mark the beginning of an American poetic literary tradition. Brewster's immediate predecessors and poetic models included Anne Bradstreet (1612–1672) and Jane Colman Turell (1708–1735). But while Bradstreet's and Turell's work reflects the early focus of colonial American women writers-primarily on religion and family life—Brewster's work reflects a shift from those themes to focus on the evils of war and its cumulative effect on a nation and its citizens.

Brewster's principal work, *Poems on Diverse Subjects,* contains poems, prose, and letters. Perhaps because she exactingly examined topics that were considered outside both the experience and the ability of eighteenth-century women, a doubting public pressed Brewster to authenticate her ability to compose verse by paraphrasing, on demand, a psalm. In this regard, the reception of Brewster's poetry can be compared to the reception that greeted the work of another eighteenth-century poet, Phillis Wheatley (1753?–1784). Indeed, the restrictions placed on women's ability to compose imaginative verse transcended both race and class: the male gender, because of property and job rights, possessed the power of the pen, and works by women were greeted with doubts that were not easily assuaged.

Brewster shares another similarity to Wheatley, for like that poet, Brewster's work also appeared on broadside, an early type of publication that resembled the modern-day flyer. And like flyers, broadsides were also posted in public places, and were read by the members of a community as they went about their daily errands. In addition, Brewster commemorated historical events in her poetry; in 1745, she set to meter a piece describing the capture of Cape Breton from the French by the British.

Brewster produced imaginative verse much different from that of her contemporaries. Much of her work focuses on military invasion and conquest, and locates a woman's voice alongside those of the male founders of our country. Brewster's work occupies a place not only in an American literary tradition but also in a history of ideas relative to manifest destiny and its implications. Her texts are a link from the works of early Puritan women writers to those of colonial women writers who voiced their opinions on matters of political and national consequence, including slavery, war, and the rights of women. No single volume of Brewster's work is now extant; however, she is mentioned frequently in historical records describing the early formation of American life and culture.

Website

"Men and Women of the Revolutionary War."
    http://members.aol.com/mayflo1620/revolutionary_war.html

References and Suggested Reading

American Poetry, 1609-1870: A Guide to Microfilm Collection. Research Publications, 1982.

Burt, Daniel S. *The Chronology of American Literature.* Boston: Houghton Mifflin, 2004.

Elliott, Emory, ed. *The Cambridge Introduction to Early American Literature.* Cambridge, UK: Cambridge University Press, 2002.

Hopkins, Lee Bennett, and Stephen Alcorn. *My America: A Poetry Atlas of the United States.* New York: Simon & Schuster Children's Publishing., 2000.

Morgan, Robert J. "The Loyalists of Cape Breton." *Cape Breton Historical Essays.* Ed. Don McGillivray and Brian Tennyson. 2nd ed. Sydney, NS: College of Cape Breton Press, 1981.

Sigourney, Lydia Howard. *The Girl's Reading-Book: In Prose and Poetry, for Schools.* New York: J. Orville Taylor, 1838.

Trent, W. P., J. Erskine, S. P. Sherman, and C. Van Doren, eds. *The Cambridge History of English and American Literature in Eighteen Volumes. Volume 15: Colonial and Revolutionary Literature: Early National Literature, Part I.* New York: Putnam, 1907–21.

Gwendolyn Elizabeth Brooks (1917-2000)

Gwendolyn Elizabeth Brooks. Courtesy of Photofest.

She called Chicago home, but Gwendolyn Elizabeth Brooks was born in Topeka, Kansas, the first child of David and Keziah Brooks. Her family moved to Chicago shortly after her birth; it was there that her two siblings were born. In 1939, when she was twenty two years of age, she married Henry Blakely. The couple had two children: a son, Henry, Junior, and a daughter, Nora.

Although Brooks traveled extensively and spent time in major universities of the United States, she considered herself a Chicagoan. And since her death in the first year of this century, Brooks has remained associated with the people, the culture, and the sounds and life of Chicago's South Side. Nevertheless, Brooks produced poetry that embodies all of Chicago. Readers need look no further than her 1967 commemorative ode "Chicago Picasso" and the 1967 poem "The Wall of Respect" to find evidence of that embodiment. "Chicago Picasso" was read at an unveiling ceremony attended by social and business dignitaries, and "The Wall of Respect" commemorated a mural erected in the heart of Chicago's black community. Brooks's lifelong service to her adopted city is reflected in the positions she held as a resident of Chicago; she was publicity director for the Chicago branch of the National Association for the Advancement of Colored People (NAACP) during the 1930s, and she succeeded the poet Carl Sandburg as poet laureate of Illinois in 1968.

Brooks worked diligently to make poetry accessible to the public. Described as one of America's most visible poets during her lifetime, she was active in introducing poetry to inner-city children through poetry-in-the-schools programming. In these formats, Brooks emphasized to young writers that while creating poetry required time and work, such creation was not closed to them, but was within their reach and understanding.

Brooks's poetry is infused with an intimacy that comes from her own lived experiences even as it recites the tales of everyday American people. Her poetry is both tribal and universal; the voices that characterize her verse may be drawn from the inner city, but universal themes of parents' aspirations for their children and the importance of community are not so easily categorized by class background. Brooks was a poet of the people, all of the people. She saw in black people the faces of various nations, and her poetry is an attempt to bridge the differences between groups by highlighting their human similarities.

Brooks's interests both in poetry and in social protest began early and informed much of her life. Brooks's mother discovered the seven-year-old girl's penchant for writing and encouraged her daughter by exposing her to literature and libraries. Because Brooks was a shy young girl who made few friends in school, she spent endless hours in her room, where she created a world of her own by reading and writing stories and poems. As a young poet, she met James Weldon Johnson and Langston Hughes and was inspired to become more involved in the growing Black Arts movement. Brooks eventually became one of the more visible poets of that movement. Critics note that as her voice became angrier and angrier in its protest against social ills, that voice never resorted to diatribe; Brooks's commitment to principles of form and structure are evinced in her poetry, which never screams in its demand for answers. The poet issues complaints from the vantage point of a rational observer. In this regard, her poetry embodies qualities observed in work by the metaphysical poet John Donne as well as in work by the Harlem Renaissance poets Langston Hughes and Countee Cullen.

And although her poetic voice has been described as objective, Brooks is invested in the event she describes far beyond the engagement required of a simple observer. Her poems are poignant in their simplicity and in the use of minimalism. A well-known Brooks poem, "We Real Cool," is a simply stated, painfully poignant narrative that predicts the future of teenager boys who have decided to skip school and spend the day playing pool. To be sure, Brooks possessed a clear, unmuted, and persuasive voice that was not a carbon copy of any poet in recent or past history.

During her lifetime, Brooks both experimented with and reinvented form in her work. Her use of structure ranged from a juxtaposition of lyric, narrative, and dramatic poetic forms to free verse, which has been described as "brilliantly jagged." Her poetry depicted the turbulence and sense of isolation felt by many inner-city youth during the 1960s yet was often framed in the traditional forms of the ballad and the sonnet. Still, her poetry is an affirmation of her own young life, for much of her work is a celebration of the genius and potential of young people who inhabit Chicago's South Side.

Her poetry also praises recent and past historical figures, from the social reformer Jane Addams to Winnie Mandela, the wife of the former president of South Africa. Other poetry praises Alabama's civil rights workers; Brooks has incorporated their speech into her poetry, thereby giving readers a history lesson on an important period in our country's development. In 1945, Brooks was selected as one of *Mademoiselle Magazine's* "Ten Young Women of the Year"; she won her first Guggenheim Fellowship that same year and became a fellow of the American Academy of Arts and Letters. In 1950, Brooks's poem "Annie Allen" won the first Pulitzer Prize to be awarded to an African American woman.

Websites

"Interview with Gwendolyn Brooks": http://www.jmu/edu/furiousflower/interview.html

"A Tribute by Rita Dove": http://www.math.buffalo.edu/~sww/brooks/brooks-biobib.html

Poetry

In the Mecca: Poems. New York.: Harper & Row, 1968.
Riot. Detroit: Broadside Press, 1969.
Family Pictures. Detroit: Broadside Press, 1970.
The World of Gwendolyn Brooks. New York: Harper & Row, 1971.

Juvenile Fiction

Jump Bad: A New Chicago Anthology. Detroit: Broadside Press, 1971.
A Broadside Treasury, 1965-1970. Detroit: Broadside Press, 1971.
Aloneness. Illustrated by Leroy Foster. Detroit: Broadside Press, 1971.
The Tiger Who Wore White Gloves: Or, What You Are Your Are. Chicago: Third World Press, 1974.

Nonfiction

Report from Part One. Prefaces by Don L. Lee and George Kent. Detroit: Broadside Press, 1972.

A Capsule Course in Black Poetry Writing. Detroit: Broadside Press, 1975.

References and Suggested Reading

Dickle, Margaret, and Thomas Travisana, eds. *Gendered Modernisms: American Women Poets and Their Readers.* Philadelphia: University of Pennsylvania Press, 1996.

Hughes, Gertrude R. "Making It Really New: Hilda Doolittle, Gwendolyn Brooks, and the Feminist Potential of Modern Poetry." *American Quarterly* 42.3 (September 1990): pp. 375–401.

Kent, George E. *A Life of Gwendolyn Brooks.* Lexington: University Press of Kentucky, 1990.

Loff, Jon N. "Gwendolyn Brooks: A Bibliography." *College Language Association Journal* 17 (1973): pp. 21–32.

Madhubuti, Haki R., ed. *Say That the River Turns: The Impact of Gwendolyn Brooks.* Chicago: Third World Press, 1987.

Melhem, D. H. *Gwendolyn Brooks: Poetry and the Heroic Voice.* Lexington: University Press of Kentucky, 1987.

Miller, Baxter R., ed. *Black American Poets between Worlds, 1940–1960.* Knoxville: University of Tennessee Press, 1986.

Mootry, Maria K., and Gary Smith, eds. *A Life Distilled: Gwendolyn Brooks, Her Poetry and Fiction.* Urbana: University of Illinois Press, 1987

Shaw, Harry B. *Gwendolyn Brooks.* Boston: Twayne, 1980.

Tate, Claudia, and Tillie Olsen. *Black Women Writers at Work.* New York: Continuum, 1983.

Lewis Carroll
(1832–1898)

Lewis Carroll. Courtesy of Photofest.

He came to the field of children's literature in a slightly roundabout way; he was a clergyman, a mathematician, and a highly regarded photographer before discovering his talent for writing imaginative verse. His early interests are reflected in his poetry, which is readily accessible to teens and young adults. The poet uses imagery, unusual language, and tone to captivate readers' imaginations. It was a lifelong interest in children and a penchant for blending logic with the absurd that established Lewis Carroll as an original voice in Western literary traditions.

A lifetime resident of Oxford University, Carroll was named Charles Lutwidge Dodgson at his birth on January 27, 1832. During his lifetime, he published under his given name, under a pseudonym, and anonymously.

Carroll bought his first camera in 1856. Primarily self-taught, he nonetheless became a highly acclaimed photographer of children, including many celebrities' youngsters. His rapport with children put his subjects at ease, and his photographs are considered typical of the early art of portraiture. During his work as a photographer, Carroll became acquainted with Alice Liddell, the daughter of Henry Liddell, headmaster of Westminster School. Carroll spent a great deal of time with the family, and a story he told to the Liddell children on a boating trip became the basis for *Alice's Adventures in Wonderland.* In addition to the Liddells, Carroll maintained life-long relationships with friends made in his youth. One such friend was Ellen Tracy, whom Carroll first met after her performance in a drama.

Throughout the early 1860s, Carroll published pamphlets and treatises on mathematics and philosophy. In 1862, he focused on storytelling and poetry, and, in a pivotal episode in the author's life, began the story of the fictional Alice while boating with the Liddells. By March of 1863, he had a manuscript tentatively titled *Alice's Adventures Under the Ground.* The work was complex, using satiric rhymes and word play. In 1864, John Tenniel was commissioned to illustrate the manuscript. Under the revised title *Alice's Adventures in Wonderland*, Carroll was able to distribute the book to friends by July of 1865. Critics reviewed the commercial release with great enthusiasm.

Carroll never married or had children of his own; however, his verse has continued to captivate and entertain young readers for more than one hundred years. In 1897, Carroll was diagnosed with a bronchial infection, and he died shortly thereafter, on January 14, 1898.

Carroll will be remembered for his fiction—in particular for the *Alice* books, which were early literary models—as well as for his poetry, which continues to garner attention within academic and literary circles. Educators often use his classic poem "Jabberwocky" and "You Are Old, Father William" to encourage students' engagement with his work. In these, as in his other works, Carroll plays with words and sounds, and masterfully combines the logical and illogical to encourage young readers to view reading as silly fun rather than as a scary chore. Carroll makes reading fun for his scores of young readers, as well as for their parents and teachers.

Website

"Lewis Carroll Society." http://www.lewiscarrollsociety.org.uk/

Poetry

Phantasmagoria and Other Poems. London: Macmillan, 1869.
The Hunting of the Snark, An Agony in Eight Fits. London: Macmillan, 1876; Boston: James R. Osgood, 1876.
Three Sunsets and Other Poems. London: Macmillan, 1898.

Fiction

Alice's Adventures in Wonderland. London: Macmillan, 1865; New York: Appleton, 1866.
Through the Looking-Glass, and What Alice Found There. London: Macmillan, 1872; Boston: Lee, Sheppard & Dillingham, 1872.
Sylvie and Bruno. London and New York: Macmillan, 1889.
Sylvie and Bruno Concluded. London and New York: Macmillan, 1893.

Juvenile Fiction

Christmas Greetings from a Fairy to a Child. London: Macmillan, 1884.
The Nursery Alice. London: Macmillan, 1889.

References and Suggested Reading

Clark, Anne. *Lewis Carroll, A Biography.* London: J. M. Dent & Sons, 1979.
Leach, Karoline. *In the Shadow of the Dream Child.* London: Peter Owen, 1999.
Lovett, Charlie. *Lewis Carroll's England: An Illustrated Guide for the Literary Tourist.* London: Lewis Carroll Society, 1998.
Stoffel, Stephanie Lovett. *Lewis Carroll and Alice.* London: Thames & Hudson., 1997.
Woolf, Jenny. *Lewis Carroll in His Own Accounting.* London: Jabberwock Press, 2005.

Ana Castillo
(1953-)

This American poet is also a novelist, a writer of short stories, and an essayist. Castillo is of Mexican ancestry; however, she is also a baby-boomer who was born in Chicago and who grew up during the turbulent 1960s and 1970s, when social protests against war and against the United States' domestic policies on education, civil rights, and women's issues were recurring events. Castillo is prominent among the American poets who use their poetry as a forum for their activism, and she often laces her work with irony and humor. She writes narrative poetry that recounts stories and events in history that are in danger of being lost or forgotten. While Castillo is concerned with recapturing the voices of Chicanas, her attention to highlighting the voices and experiences of young women renders her work particularly suitable for young readers who are in the process of discovering their own life goals.

Castillo is one of the leading writers to give voice to a Chicana experience, and her work has been critically acclaimed and widely anthologized in the United States and abroad. She is a daring and inventive writer of imaginative verse, who, by virtue of the quality of her work, has earned a place in an American poetic literary tradition. She has been compared favorably with other American writers whose use of irony allows them to speak candidly on themes that are at once public and private. For example, her imaginative verse often speaks to issues ranging from the role of the Catholic Church to the roles assigned to women. Castillo relies on the many nuances of language to create meaning in her work. And although her themes are global in that readers from diverse cultural, racial, and economic backgrounds can discover their personal stories reflected in Castillo's verse, the poet has been an equally influential voice for Mexican American readers and writers.

Following her graduation from high school, Castillo attended Chicago City College for two years before entering Northeastern Illinois University, where she received a bachelor of arts in secondary education and served as a writer in residence for the Illinois Arts Council. In addition, Castillo was a community activist during her undergraduate years. She organized Latino artists into a group called *The Association of Latino Brotherhood of Artists* in an attempt to form alliances between men and women, between Latinos and non-Latinos, and among Latinos in the United States. Her imaginative verse, which often critiques sexism, racism, and classism, also uses examples drawn, in many instances, from her personal experiences. An early publication, *The Invitation*, contained poetry written in response to sexism in groups such as the one she herself had organized. In addition to her involvement with community groups, Castillo has taught English as a Second Language, Mexican and Mexican American history, women's studies, creative writing, and Chicano literature at the University of New Mexico, Mill College of Oakland, Santa Rose Junior College, and Mount Holyoke College.

Castillo earned a master of arts in Latin American and Caribbean Studies from the University of Chicago in 1979. During the 1980s, she was a dissertation fellow in the Chicano Studies Department at the University of California, Santa Barbara. While enrolled in the graduate program, she continued working on her poetry. The collection, *I Ask the Impossible,* was published during this period. The poet elected to complete her doctoral work outside of the United States; she received a PhD in American Studies from the University of Bremen, Germany in 1991, and in 1995, she won a fellowship from the National Endowment for the Arts.

Writing protest poetry gave Castillo a direction both as a poet and as a political being in that it helped her to define herself in opposition to mainstream feminism and to a culture of machismo that required her silence. Her body of work evinces her attempts to reconcile her sense of self as a Chicana feminist. Castillo has been compared to another Chicana writer, Gloria Anzaldúa. Both writers explore what it means to be caught between or on the edge of borders, whether those borders are between languages, cultures, races, or genders. Castillo's work, like Anzaldúa's, attempts to challenge essentialist categories of race, gender, and sexuality, even as it speaks to the specificity of a Chicana experience in the United States.

Like many Chicana and Latina writers of the 1980s, Castillo began publishing with an independent press. Arte Público published her collection of poetry *Women Are Not Roses* in 1984, and West End Press published another poetry volume, *My Father Was a Toltec*, in 1988. Perhaps because of her position at the margins, Castillo has long supported the independent bookseller. In fact, she has written a collection of short stories in which a character owns a bookstore that specializes in books on spirituality. A reader cannot help but notice that even in her fiction, Castillo's themes remain consistent to similar themes explored in her poetry. Her attempts to unravel and then reconstruct the many identities of Chicana selfhood introduce themes of spirituality, sexuality, gender, race, and class, all lenses through which she examines notions of identity. And although Castillo's work is now available through booksellers such as W. W. Norton and Barnes and Noble and has appeared in the popular magazine *Vanity Fair*, her work has not always been well received by mainstream audiences.

Castillo has been a guest speaker at the Sorbonne University in Paris and a lecturer in Germany. She was honored by the Women's Foundation of San Francisco, and she has been twice awarded a National Endowment for the Arts fellowship. The University of California at Santa Barbara houses seven linear feet of Castillo's papers, divided into five series, including the poet's personal and biographical information from 1974 to 1990 as well as the poet's published and unpublished writings from 1973 to 1990.

Website

Ana Castillo's official website: http://www.anacastillo.com

Poetry

My Father Was a Toltec, Poems 1973–1988. New York: Norton., 1996.
My Daughter, My Son, The Eagle, The Dove. New York: Dutton Books, 2000.
I Ask the Impossible. New York: Anchor, 2001.
Watercolor Women. Willimantic, CT: Curbstone Press, 2005.

Fiction

The Mixquiahuala Letters. New York: Anchor, 1992.
Loverboys: Stories. New York: Norton, 1996.
Carmen la Coja. New York: Vintage, 2000.
Peel My Love Like an Onion. New York: Anchor, 2000.

References and Suggested Reading

Alarcon, Norma. "The Sardonic Powers of the Erotic in the Work of Ana Castillo." In *Breaking Boundaries: Latina Writing and Critical Readings.* Amherst: University of Massachusetts Press, 1989.
Bower, Anne L. *Epistolary Responses: The Letter in Twentieth-Century American Fiction and Criticism.* Bloomington: University of Indiana Press, 1996.

Castillo, Debra A. "Borderliners: Federico Campbell and Ana Castillo." In *Reconfigured Spheres: Feminist Explorations of Literary Space*. Ed. Margaret R. Higonnet and Joan Templeton. Amherst: University of Massachusetts Press, 1994.

Castillo-Speed, Lillian. *Latina: Women's Voices from the Borderlands*. New York: Touchstone, 1995.

Fernandez, Roberta, ed. *In Other Words: Literature by Latinas of the United States*. Foreword by Jean Franco. Houston, TX.: Arte Publico Press, 1994.

Her Heritage: A Biographical Encyclopedia of Famous American Women. CD-ROM. New York: Pilgrim New Media, 1996.

Trujillo, Carla, ed. *Chicana Lesbians: The Girls Our Mothers Warned Us About*. Berkeley, CA: Third Woman Press, 1991.

Lucille Clifton
(1936–)

Lucille Clifton. Courtesy of Photofest.

Thelma Lucille Sayles Clifton was born on June 27, 1936, into a family of storytellers. Her father, Samuel Louis Sayles, Sr., worked at a steel mill and was also an oral storyteller. Her mother, Thelma Moore Sayles, was a folk poet. The young poet lived with her family in the steel-mill town of Depew, New York; later the family relocated to Buffalo, New York, where the young poet attended high school.

On graduating from high school at the age of sixteen, Clifton accepted a full scholarship to Howard University. She left Howard after two years. Clifton has observed that she was not a diligent student in her early college years; however, she eventually completed her education at Fredonia State Teachers College in New York, earning a bachelor's degree in 1958. During the same year, she married philosophy professor Fred James Clifton, with whom she had six children. This poet—who traces her ancestry to the West African Dahomey tribe that boasted a well-trained army of women in service to the king through the nineteenth century—has worked as a claims clerk in the New York State Division of Employment and as literature assistant in the Office of Education in Washington, D.C.

Clifton's first book, *Good Times: Poems* (1969) featured poems about ordinary days in an urban community, told in various tones that represent voices of the members of the community. Many of the poems in this collection subtly address the charged issues of the decade, and the last sequence of poems, told in the voices of two boys, addresses the riots and unrest of the Civil Rights movement and depicts the day-to-day struggle of life in the shadow of sweeping social reforms. The book was well-received, garnering positive critical attention, including a position as one of the *New York Times* Top Ten Best Books of the year.

In 1970 Clifton wrote *Some of the Days of Everett Anderson,* the first in what would become a series of children's books. Shortly after the publication of *Everett Anderson,* Clifton accepted a position as poet-in-residence at Coppin State College in Baltimore. Her experiences there helped her to hone her already strong writing, and she emerged from the residency as a full-time working writer. During this period, Langston Hughes accepted several of her poems for inclusion in his *Poetry of the Negro, 1746–1970* (1970).

While at Coppin, Clifton wrote *Good News About the Earth* (1972) and *An Ordinary Woman* (1974). Clifton avoided the angry tones of protest in her poetry; instead she coolly examined the tumultuous social, historical, and political scenes by juxtaposing them against personal events and encouraging each reader to come to his or her own decisions about policies that affected those already disenfranchised.

Clifton's poetry reflects her effort to link generations as she recites stories that evoke and honor the past while mirroring the present. Her references to her own rich family history are interspersed with universal stories of the human experience and of the endurance of the human spirit. Clifton infuses the voices of young people with critical powers of observation, resulting in a poetic language that is simultaneously complex and accessible.

Clifton has written more than twenty books for children. Some of these are in verse, others in prose, although even the prose is often rhythmic. Her work in the picture book field features African American characters whose experiences, triumphs, and mishaps reflect those that young readers find familiar regardless of race. For example, the Everett Anderson books feature collections of poems arranged thematically around the events in the title character's life. Clifton's poems depict events and activities in the boy's life, including the months he spends awaiting the birth of a sibling, and the shock and sorrow he feels when his father dies.

During the 1980s, Clifton held positions as visiting writer at Columbia University's School of Arts and at George Washington University. She taught at the University of California at Santa Cruz and at St. Mary's College in Maryland. In 1987, *Next: New Poems* was released; it was a work rich in historical images, weaving together the stories of slaves, war stories, and stories of personal loss. *Quilting: Poems 1987–1990* compiles works that pay homage to forefathers, recognize the strength of women in the act of creation, and mourn a child in Soweto.

In *The Terrible Stories* (1993), Clifton reflects on her role as survivor and chronicles her battles with cancer, kidney failure and transplant, and mastectomy surgery. This is not to the exclusion of more sweeping themes; Clifton includes poems about African ancestors and their modern descendents. *Blessing the Boats: New and Selected Poems 1988–2000*, arranges poems carefully by theme and period. Together they form a glimpse at Clifton's body of work throughout those years, in an eclectic mix of hope and caution. Clifton addresses concrete issues of violence, illness, transformation, and personal enlightenment. The collection won the 2001 National Book Award.

Throughout her career, Clifton has embraced her heritage as a descendent of the Dahomey women of West Africa and her role as a voice for women and children. She has demonstrated her determination to celebrate and to mourn the vastness of human experience in an effort to compel young readers to give voice to their own causes.

Website

"Academy of American Poets." http://www.poets.org/

Poetry

Good Times: Poems. New York: Random House, 1969.
Good News About the Earth: New Poems. New York: Random House, 1972.
An Ordinary Woman. New York: Random House, 1974.
Two-Headed Woman. Amherst: University of Massachusetts Press, 1980.
Good Woman: Poems and a Memoir, 1969–1980. Rochester, NY: BOA Editions, 1987.
Next: New Poems. Rochester, NY: BOA Editions, 1987.
Quilting: Poems 1987–1990. Brockport, NY: BOA Editions, 1991.
The Book of Light. Port Townsend, WA: Copper Canyon Press, 1993.
The Terrible Stories. Rochester, NY: BOA Editions, 1996.
Blessing the Boats: New and Selected Poems 1988–2000. Rochester, NY: BOA Editions, 2000.
Mercy: Poems. Brockport, NY: BOA Editions, 2004.

Juvenile Fiction and Poetry

The Black ABCs (alphabet poems). Illustrations by Don Miller. New York: Dutton, 1970.
The Times They Used to Be. Illustrations by Susan Jeschke. New York: Holt, 1974.

My Brother Fine with Me. Illustrations by Moneta Barnett. New York: Holt, 1975.
Three Wishes. Illustrations by Stephanie Douglas. New York: Viking, 1976.
Amifika. Illustrations by Thomas DiGrazia. New York: Dutton, 1977.
The Lucky Stone. Illustrations by Dale Payson. New York: Delacorte, 1979.
My Friend Jacob. Illustrations by Thomas DiGrazia. New York: Dutton, 1980.
Sonora Beautiful. Illustrations by Michael Garland. New York: Dutton, 1981.
Dear Creator: A Week of Poems for Young People and Their Teachers. Illustrations by Gail Gordon Carter. Garden City, NY: Doubleday, 1997.

"Everett Anderson" Series for Children

Some of the Days of Everett Anderson. Illustrations by Evaline Ness. New York: Holt, 1970.
Everett Anderson's Christmas Coming. Illustrations by Evaline Ness. New York: Holt, 1971.
Everett Anderson's Year. Illustrations by Ann Grifalconi. New York: Holt, 1974.
Everett Anderson's Friend. Illustrations by Ann Grifalconi. New York: Holt, 1976.
Everett Anderson's 1 2 3. Illustrations by Ann Grifalconi. New York: Holt, 1977.
Everett Anderson's Goodbye. Illustrations by Ann Grifalconi. New York: Holt, 1983.
One of the Problems of Everett Anderson. Illustrations by Ann Grifalconi. New York: Holt, 2001.

References and Recommended Reading

Pettis, Joyce. *African American Poets: Lives, Works, and Sources.* Westport, CT: Greenwood Press, 2002.

Judith Ortiz Cofer
(1952–)

Because the United States annexed Puerto Rico in 1898 and granted American citizenship to people who were Puerto Rican by birth in 1917, it is not entirely correct to say that Judith Ortiz Cofer immigrated with her family to New York City when she was a youngster. Cofer's father was in the United States Navy, and although this American poet was born in Hormingueros, Puerto Rico, she spent her early years moving between Puerto Rico and Paterson, New Jersey, where her father was stationed. Whenever her father earned extended leave from his naval duties, she and her family returned to Puerto Rico, where they spent time at her la casa de abuela (grandmother's house) and where the young girl was a ready audience for the many stories that were told about her family's history. Those early years spent listening to her grandmother recite family stories fueled Cofer's passion for writing.

Like many Latin Americans who have immigrated to the United States, Cofer's family was among the group of people who have relocated since the end of World War II. After the war, employment opportunities drew large numbers of Puerto Ricans to New York and to other American industrial centers. Today, approximately one-half of the people of Puerto Rican ancestry who live in the United States reside in New York City. The themes in Cofer's poetry and prose reflect her efforts to examine the effects of colonization on her homeland and the subsequent spreading out of its populace. Her poetry also contains themes that center on the absence of authority or male figures, and on women who wait, sometimes patiently, for them to return. No doubt her imaginative verse, particularly in this instance, has been influenced by her own young life as the daughter of a father who was required to spend time away from his family. Cofer also writes verse that recounts a history of immigration into the United States by people from Latin American countries, characterizing such immigration both as an avenue of mobility and as a tool of division.

Cofer, who is bilingual, often combines the use of Spanish and English in her imaginative verse. She reflects her inheritance from both her motherlands in her language; her voice is a confluence of two nations. And while she celebrates both languages in her poetry, speaking to the ordinary and extraordinary life experiences of a young woman, she often confronts issues regarding the dominance of the English language in her poetry and prose as well. Her work is a cultural hybrid that reflects and examines rituals, customs, traditions, and beliefs inherent to her dual identity.

Cofer is the author of several collections of poetry and prose, including *A Love Story Beginning in Spanish: Poems*, *Terms of Survival: Poems*, and *The Latin Deli: Prose and Poetry*. She has also written a young adult novel, *Call Me Maria*, and a collection of essays, *Woman in Front of the Sun: On Becoming a Writer.* Her work has appeared in *The Georgia Review*, *Kenyon Review*, *Southern Review*, and other journals (as well as *Glamour*), and she has been anthologized in numerous textbooks including *The Norton Book of Women's Lives*, *The Norton Introduction to Literature*, and *The Norton Introduction to Poetry*.

Cofer has received numerous awards and honors for her writing. *The Latin Deli* was selected for the 2005 Georgia Top 25 Reading List, a project of the Georgia Center for the Book. In 2005, her young adult novel *Call Me Maria* received Honorable Mention for the Americas Award, sponsored by the National Consortium of Latin American Studies Programs. Her work has been included on the New York Public Library's "Books for the Teen Age 2004 List." In addition, Cofer has received several fellowships and grants, including awards from the University of Georgia Research Foundation, the University of Georgia Center for the Humanities and Arts, the Rockefeller Foundation, and the National Endowment for the Arts. Cofer is currently the Regents' and Franklin Professor of English and Creative Writing at the University of Georgia.

Website

University of George Faculty Page: http://www.english.uga.edu/~jcofer/home.html

Poetry

Peregrina. Golden, CO: Riverstone Press, 1986.
Terms of Survival. Houston, TX: Arte Publico Press, 1987.
The Latin Deli. Athens: University of Georgia Press, 1993.

The Year of Our Revolution: New and Selected Stories and Poems. Houston, TX: Arte Publico Press, 1998.

Young Adult Fiction

The Meaning of Consuelo. New York: Farrar, Straus & Giroux, 2003.
Call Me Maria. New York: Scholastic, 2004.
Riding Low on the Streets of Gold: Latino Literature for Young Adults. Houston, TX: Piñata Books, 2004.

Nonfiction

Silent Dancing: A Partial Remembrance of a Puerto Rican Childhood. Houston, TX: Arte Publico Press, 1990.
An Island Like You: Stories of the Barrio. New York: Orchard Books, 1995.
Sleeping with One Eye Open: Women Writers and the Art of Survival. Athens: University of Georgia Press, 1999.
Woman in Front of the Sun: On Becoming a Writer. Athens: University of Georgia Press, 2000.

References and Suggested Reading

Payant, Katherine B., and Toby Rose, eds. *The Immigrant Experience in North American Literature: Carving Out a Niche.* Westport, CT: Greenwood Press, 1999.
Rivera, Carmen Haydee. *Latino and Latina Writers.* Vol. 2, Scribner's Writers Series. New York: Charles Scribner's Sons, 2004.

Billy Collins
(1941–)

By the time Billy Collins was selected the nation's poet laureate in 2001, he had produced a number of volumes of poetry that enjoyed both critical success and an impressive level of popularity among readers from a wide range of ages. In his position as laureate, it was the young adult audience he most actively sought to reach, mobilizing a movement to reinvigorate poetry in classrooms across America through a project he called Poetry 180, named not only for the number of days in a typical school year but also for the number of degrees in a complete about-face turn. Collins compiled poems that would appeal to young adults, and he suggested that schools allow one poem to be read each day, possibly over the public address system. He set up a website and published two books, *Poetry 180* in 2003 and *180 More* in 2005. The books contain poems described by Collins as "short, clear, and clean." He served two terms as poet laureate, concluding his second term in 2003.

Billy Collins was born in New York City on March 22, 1941, the only child of William Collins, an electrician who later became successful as an insurance broker, and Katherine Collins, a nurse. The family lived in Queens, New York, throughout Collins's early childhood; he attended public-school kindergarten, but from first grade through college he attended Catholic schools. When Collins was in middle school, the family moved from Queens to suburban Westchester County, outside New York City.

Collins took an early interest in writing. He created his first poem at the age of twelve, and in high school he joined the staff of the school's literary magazine.

After receiving his bachelor of arts degree from the College of the Holy Cross in 1963, Collins moved to the West Coast. While working on his doctorate at the University of California in Riverside, and inspired by the Beat poetry movement and the counterculture in California, he wrote poems for publications such as *Rolling Stone* magazine. Collins earned his Ph.D. in Romantic poetry in 1971 and moved back east to take a position as a professor of English at the City University of New York's Lehman College in the Bronx.

Collins continued to write poetry while teaching, and in 1977 he published his first collection, *Poker Face*. The poems, including "On the Speed of Snakes," "Too Close for Comfort," and a set of poems bearing the names of Looney Tunes characters "Porky," "Bugs," "Daffy," and "Elmer," exhibit some of the everyday images that would continue to find expression in Collins's poetry.

More recently, in 2004 Collins received the Mark Twain Award for his use of humor in his work, and in 2005 he published *The Trouble with Poetry and Other Poems*. The collection contains pieces that offer lyrical views of his world as well as a defense of the poet's poetic style.

Collins continues to be a fan of jazz music. He incorporates its syncopated rhythms into his everyday existence. His poem "Man Listening to Disc" is written in first person and recounts the poet's experience listening to music through his headphones as he walks along a street in New York City. He and his wife live in Somers (Worchester County), New York.

Websites

"Academy of American Poets." http://www.poets.org/poet.php/prmPID/278
"Po' Jazz: Artist Biographies." http://www.writerscenter.org/pojazzbios01.html

Poetry

The Art of Drowning. Pittsburgh: University of Pittsburgh Press, 1995.
Picnic, Lightning. Pittsburgh: University of Pittsburgh P, 1998.
Questions about Angels. New York: Morrow, 1991; Pittsburgh: University of Pittsburgh Press, 1999.
Taking Off Emily Dickinson's Clothes. London: Picador, 2000.
Sailing Alone Around the Room: New and Selected Poems. New York: Random House, 2001.
Nine Horse: Poems. New York: Random House, 2002.
The Trouble with Poetry and Other Poems. New York: Random House, 2005.

As Editor

Poetry 180. New York: Random House, 2003.
180 More. New York: Random House, 2005.

References and Suggested Reading

Alleva, Richard. "A Major Minor Poet." *Commonweal 129.1* (January 11, 2002).

Barnett, Catherine. "The Laureate and the Loudspeaker." *Arts Education Policy Review 104.1* (September–October 2002): pp. 35–37.

"Billy Collins." In *Authors and Artists for Young Adults,* Vol. 64. Farmington Hill, MI: Thomson Gale, 2005; reproduced in *Biography Resource Center*, Farmington Hill, MI: Thomson Gale, 2006.

Cavalieri, Grace, and Billy Collins. "Grace Cavalieri Interviews Poet Laureate Billy Collins." *Pembroke Magazine 35* (2003): pp. 252–69.

Citino, David, ed. *The Eye of the Poet: Six Views of the Art and Craft of Poetry.* New York: Oxford University Press, 2001.

Countee Porter Cullen
(1903(?)-1946)

New York City, Baltimore, Maryland, and Louisville, Kentucky, have been given as birthplaces of this enigmatic American poet, translator, playwright, and children's writer. Although Cullen never publicly corrected the misconceptions regarding his place and year of birth, he did give his birthplace as Louisville when he applied for admission to college in New York. Biographers of this extremely private poet have observed that other than those matters of public record, there is not much that can be documented about Cullen's early years. And although questions about Cullen's sexuality have garnered a great deal of attention, he left critics to their speculations rather than attempting to clarify or expand upon their perceptions of him or of his work. Young readers will appreciate Cullen's wit and use of irony to combat hate and racism. For example, one of his more popular works, "Yet Do I Marvel," while easily read as the poet's frustration with the burdens associated with being a black poet, is no less a humorous yet scathing commentary regarding the attention paid to a writer's race.

The poet's early years reflect the tragedy of race and class. Born to a young mother, he was raised by his maternal grandmother, and from all accounts, he did not know his birth father. Upon his grandmother's death, he was unofficially adopted by Carolyn Belle Mitchell Cullen and her husband, Frederick Cullen, a pioneer black activist minister who established a church in a storefront upon his arrival in New York City in 1902. Cullen was approximately fifteen years old at the time of his adoption in 1918, and six years later, by 1924, he had helped his adoptive father to move the storefront church to the site of a former white church in Harlem and to increase the congregation's membership to more than 2,500.

The young Cullen was raised in the conservative environment and precepts of the Methodist Church, and his adoptive father was a particularly strong influence. Cullen and his adoptive father were very close; they often traveled together, and it appears that the latter considered the young poet as his heir. The elder Cullen fully invested his adoptive son in the family's resources as well as in its responsibilities.

Cullen achieved considerable literary fame during the era known as the Harlem Renaissance. This literary moment signaled the emergence of a black school of writers, artists, and intellectuals identified as the "New Negro." According to thinkers such as W. E. B. Du Bois and Alain Locke, this group represented a talented tenth of black Americans who represented the best the race had to offer. It is not clear that all writers welcomed the designation. Cullen, like Jean Toomer, resisted being described as a black poet; he sought to be recognized as an American poet. Still, despite being a shy, private young man, Cullen personified the coming of a new black artist, a first-generation, academically trained literary figure who composed imaginative verse that appealed not only to black audiences but to mainstream audiences as well. In his work, Cullen employed romantic lyrics, sonnets, and quatrains to record a black experience that had been perceived as lacking in refinement and grace. His work is a twentieth-century representative of a tradition of American poetry produced by writers who self-consciously learned the craft of poetry.

Much of Cullen's poetry reflects his attempts to examine or otherwise reconcile the values of his conservative upbringing and his own artistic and personal desires, which often seemed in opposition to those values.

An outstanding student, Cullen attended New York's DeWitt Clinton High School, where he edited the school's newspaper, assisted in editing the literary magazine, and began to achieve notice for his poetry. He became a member of the Arista honor society, and in his senior year he received the Magpie Cup from his peers in recognition of his scholarly and literary achievements. He also served as vice president of his senior class and as treasurer of his school's poetry club. Cullen won an oratorical contest sponsored by the film actor Douglas Fairbanks, and his poetry continued to appear regularly in school publications as well as in wider venues. The young poet won his first contest in high school when his poem "I Have a Rendezvous with Life" placed first in a citywide competition.

Upon completion of high school, Cullen received a scholarship to New York University, and during his years as an undergraduate student he produced the poems that would become three poetry collections: *Color*, published in 1925; *Copper Sun*, and *The Ballad of the Brown Girl*, both published in 1927. Cullen was elected to the Phi Beta Kappa fraternity in his junior year, and he earned a bachelor of arts degree from New York University before enrolling in the graduate program at Harvard University. In 1926,

Cullen received a master of arts from Harvard; in the same year, he won the *Crisis* magazine award in poetry. His poems were also published in *Bookman*, *The American Mercury*, *Harper's Magazine*, *Century*, and *Nations*.

At one point prior to his graduation from Harvard, Cullen was one of the more popular black American literary figures in the United States. His contributions to children's literature include *The Lost Zoo* and *Christopher Cat*. The collections are not intended just for children's amusement; they are also models for writers of children's verse. Cullen wrote both texts during a period when children's writing was not generally being produced by black writers. He won major literary prizes and awards during the period, including first prize in the Witter Bynner Poetry contest, *Poetry* magazine's John Reed Memorial Prize, and second prize in *Opportunity* magazine's first poetry contest. He was also awarded a Guggenheim Fellowship. However, *The Black Christ and Other Poems*, published in 1929, was not critically well received, and from the 1930s until his death, Cullen seemed to have relegated writing to a secondary place in his life. Still, he produced some of his more complex sonnets during his later years. However, for many years after his death and until recently, his work stood as a footnote to other writers of the Harlem Renaissance. In the final years before his death, Cullen taught French at Frederick Douglass Junior High, where James Baldwin was a student in his class.

Much of Cullen's poetry is anthologized, and single volumes of his work are no longer in print; however, the Amistad Research Center, located at Tulane University, houses Cullen's personal papers dated from 1921 to 1969, comprising more than 4,000 manuscripts and photographs in thirty-nine volumes. In addition, the James Weldon Johnson collection in the Beinecke Library at Yale University houses more than nine hundred letters and manuscripts written by, to, and about the poet.

Websites

"Perspectives in American Literature (PAL)." http://www.csustan.edu/english/reuben/home.htm

"Modern American Poetry: An Online Journal and Multimedia Companion to *Anthology of Modern American Poetry*." http://www.english.uiuc.edu/maps/index.htm

Poetry

The Black Christ and Other Poems. New York: Harper & Bros., 1929.

My Soul's High Song: The Collected Writings of Countee Cullen. New York: Harper & Bros., 1947.

References and Suggested Reading

Bontemps, Arna. *The Harlem Renaissance Remembered*. New York: Dodd, Mead, 1972.
———, ed. *The Harlem Renaissance Remembered*. New York: Dodd, Mead, 1972.
Daniel, Walter C. "Countee Cullen as Literary Critic." *College Language Association Journal XIV* (March 1972): pp. 281–90.
Davis, Arthur. *From the Dark Tower: African-American Writers 1900–1960*. Washington, DC: Howard University Press, 1974.
Davis, Arthur P. "The Alien-and-Exile Theme in Countee Cullen's Racial Poems." *Phylon 14* (1953): pp. 390–400.
Dorsey, David F. "Countee Cullen's Use of Greek Mythology." *College Language Association Journal 13* (1970): pp. 68–77.
Early, Gerald, ed. *My Soul's High Song: The Collected Writings of Countee Cullen, Voice of the Harlem Renaissance*. New York: Doubleday, 1991.
Kirby, David. "Countee Cullen's Heritage: A Black Waste Land." *South Atlantic Bulletin 4* (1971): pp. 14–20.
The Oxford Companion to African American Literature. New York: Oxford University Press, 1997.
Perry, Margaret. *A Bio-Bibliography of Countee P. Cullen, 1903–1946*. Westport, CT: Greenwood Press, 1966.
Rodgers, Marie E. *The Harlem Renaissance: An Annotated Reference Guide*. Englewood, CO: Libraries Unlimited, 1998.
Wagner, Jean. *Black Poets of the United States*. Urbana: University of Illinois Press, 1973 (Part II).
Webster, Harvey Curtis. "A Difficult Career." *Poetry 70* (1947): pp. 224–25.

Edward Estlin Cummings
(1894-1962)

According to family diaries, this American writer began exploring his artistic inclination at an early age. As a small child, Cummings wrote poetry and produced pencil drawings as gifts for his mother, his grandmother, his aunt, his younger sister, and his versatile, energetic, and highly articulate father. In particular, his love of language was nurtured by his mother, who made up word games to encourage his blossoming creativity. His love of language and his penchant for producing art developed as the young writer grew up. Intensely creative, he continued to demonstrate his aptitude for language throughout his primary and secondary education. He enrolled in Harvard, and in 1915 he graduated magna cum laude with a bachelor of arts degree in the classics. A year later, in 1916, he was awarded his masters' degree from Harvard's Graduate School of Arts and Sciences. He met another writer, John Dos Passos, who was also a student at Harvard during his time there. Later, in 1917, he, Dos Passos, and others published the collection *Eight Harvard Poets*.

In addition to writing poetry, Cummings was also a fine graphic artist, playwright, and novelist who is well known for his typographic innovations. In 1923, Cummings published a collection of verse, *Tulips and Chimneys*, in which he contrasted war and its outcome against the world in what he considered its natural state, unsullied by violence. The poet expressed dissatisfaction with industrial innovations, because he viewed mass production as a threat to individuality.

By 1925, he had published *XLI Poems* and had won the prestigious Dial Award. His stylistic choices resulted in poetry that captivated both the reader's ear and the reader's eye. Consistently inconsistent, Cummings was also interested in contemporary slang as an unorthodox form of language. His poetry often expresses a rebellious, confrontational attitude toward religion, politics, authority, and conformity; however, it also celebrates the simple joys of life and the beauty of the natural world. In some of his work, the words become pictorial signifiers that suggest, for example, in his poem, "mOOn Over tOwns mOOn", the movement of the full moon.

Cummings had a long relationship with *Vanity Fair;* he contributed not only poetry but also drawings in charcoal, ink, oil, and pastel to that popular magazine. He received his first Guggenheim Fellowship in 1933 for the purpose of writing a book of poems. However, by 1935 he had finished the manuscript and was unable to find a publisher. He titled his book *No Thanks* and published it with the help of his mother. He dedicated the book to the fourteen publishing houses that had turned him down. The first exhibition of his drawings occurred in New York in 1931; some twenty years after he self-published *No Thanks*, Cummings won a second Guggenheim Fellowship for his drawings. A prolific artist who never confined himself to a single genre or form, Cummings produced a play and exhibited his paintings and drawings. However, his work in these areas has not attracted the critical and popular acclaim he has received for his poetry.

Although Cummings experimented with form, punctuation, spelling, and syntax in his writing and attracted attention for his eccentric punctuation, the commonly held belief that he legally changed his name to lowercase letters is false. In *E. E. Cummings Revisited*, published in 1994, Richard S. Kennedy states that Cummings's name should be capitalized; the E. E. Cummings Society has been working to correct the notion that Cummings had an all lower-case version of his name legalized.

Later in his career, the poet was criticized for not allowing his poetry to grow beyond the idiosyncratic structures and uses of language that became his trademark. Despite such criticism; however, the simplicity of his language, his playful manner, and his attention to everyday, commonplace subjects have garnered and sustained great popularity, especially among young readers. At the time of his death in 1962, Cummings was second only to Robert Frost as the most widely read contemporary poet in the United States. From 1952 until 1953, Cummings was a professor at his alma mater, Harvard, and in 1957, he received both a special citation from the National Book Award Committee and the Bollinger Prize in Poetry for his collection of verse, *Poems 1923–1954*. Currently, the E. E. Cummings Society publishes a journal, *Spring*, that includes reproductions of Cummings's artwork as well as critical essays on the poet.

Website

"Academy of American Poets." http://www.poets.org

Poetry

101 Select Poems. New York: Grove/Atlantic, 1954.

95 Poems. New York: Harcourt Brace Jovanovich, 1958.

E. E. Cummings: Complete Poems 1904–1962. Ed. George Firmage. New York: Liveright, 1991

Complete Poems, 1904–1962, rev. ed. New York: Liveright, 1994.

References and Suggested Reading

Beacham, Walter. *Research Guide to Biography and Criticism, Literature.* Washington, DC: Research Publishing, 1985.

Friedman, Norman. *E. E. Cummings, the Art of His Poetry.* Baltimore: Johns Hopkins University Press, 1960.

———, ed. *E. E. Cummings: A Collection of Critical Essays.* Englewood Cliffs, NJ: Prentice Hall, 1972.

Harmon, William. *The Top 500 Poems.* New York: Columbia University Press, 1992.

Kennedy, Richard S. *E. E. Cummings Revisited.* New York: Twayne, 1994.

Winters McBride, Katherine, ed. *A Concordance to the Complete Poems of E. E. Cummings* (Cornell Concordances). Ithaca, NY: Cornell University Press, 1989.

Emily Elizabeth
Dickinson (1830–1886)

Born in Amherst, Massachusetts, the oldest of three children, Dickinson is remembered as a reclusive, sensitive young woman. Many instances of her withdrawal from public life have been recorded by biographers and critics. An early example of her affinity for solitude is found in the incapacitating homesickness that compelled her to return home after one year away at college. In the years that followed her departure from Mount Holyoke, Dickinson seldom received visitors or ventured far from the confines of her home and garden. By 1860, the young woman lived in almost absolute seclusion from the outside world and from its distractions. Family journals suggest that Dickinson was an independent thinker, a healthy, happy, and precocious young girl surrounded by a close circle of friends. Rather than being a recluse, it appears that Dickinson may simply have possessed a preference for solitude over society, for she maintained close family ties and friendships with chosen intimates throughout her life.

Although Dickinson published little during her lifetime, critics are still discovering her poems, particularly in letters to friends and in her journal entries. In fact, after Dickinson's death, her younger sister, Lavinia, discovered more than 1,000 poems in Emily's bureau. During Dickinson's voluntary withdrawal from public life, she not only read widely but also cultivated and maintained correspondence with several people. For despite suppositions that the young woman was either extremely shy or antisocial or both, Dickinson's extant work evinces her real need for human connections as well as her interest in the world beyond her garden. Dickinson was once referred to by a family friend as "the Queen Recluse"; however, her life was not nearly as sheltered as biographers have implied. One of the people with whom Dickinson maintained correspondence was Thomas Wentworth Higginson, who was the first to publish Dickinson's work after her death.

A productive writer, Dickinson produced approximately 1,700 or more poems during her life; however, only six were published during her lifetime, and those were published without her active pursuit of such publication. Although Dickinson routinely enclosed poems in letters to friends, the first volume of her work was not published until 1890, four years after her death.

Dickinson's style was heavily informed by the metaphysical poets of seventeenth-century England and, naturally, by her own poetic sensibility. Although she read the work of Robert and Elizabeth Barrett Browning as well as that of John Keats, her parents dissuaded her from reading Walt Whitman, who was considered unconventional and thus, dangerous to the developing mind of the young Victorian woman. Ironically, despite her parents' efforts to protect their daughter from Whitman's bad influence, today Walt Whitman and Emily Dickinson are regarded as progenitors of a uniquely American poetic voice. Indeed, Dickinson's accomplishments in imaginative verse have been recognized since the publication of her first volume of poems; interest in her work has grown steadily since that first publication. Readers recognize Dickinson as a poet of immense depth and stylistic complexity. Her experimentation with form is read as a defiance of literary and social authority by feminist critics, who also celebrate her work as representing an original voice in Western literary traditions.

Dickinson's poetry is noteworthy for its marriage of the scientific and natural worlds. Few poets have incorporated scientific concepts and language into their work as seamlessly as has Dickinson, who possessed a comprehensive and exact scientific vocabulary—a benefit of her time at Amherst Academy, where she learned the value of close, dedicated study. Extensive developments in science and technology that took place during her childhood influenced Dickinson's poetry. During the first ten years of Dickinson's life, the young poet witnessed firsts in American and European politics, in mass transportation, and in science, including the discovery of chloroform, the invention of photography, and the invention of the telegraph.

Dickinson's precise use of the language of science found fertile ground in her poetry, for she has written more than one hundred poems in which she explores the sciences from physics to psychology. Her poems argue that the manifestation of science—technology—is harmful to the natural world. Dickinson viewed science as neutral; her poetry suggests that man, rather than technology, became the machine in the garden of public life.

Dickinson's scientifically themed poems have been read as explications of her desire to demystify the heavens. Much of her work seems an effort at demystification, that is certain. However, Dickinson is equally concerned with demystifying the physical world, for her poetry examines the mysteries of mortality and immortality, in part to explore where the two separate and in part to fuse the severed parts into one. Dickinson's poetry reflects her concern with both the physical and the spiritual planes. And for the past few decades, it has been Dickinson herself that readers and critics have sought to demystify; still, she remains a literary Mona Lisa, enigmatic, unknowable, and adored.

Website

"The Literature Network." http://www.online-literature.com

References and Suggested Reading

Anderson, Charles. *Emily Dickinson's Poetry: Stairway of Surprise*. Westport, CT: Greenwood, Press 1982.

Benfey, Christopher. *Emily Dickinson and the Problem of Other*s. Amherst: University of Massachusetts Press, 1984.

Buckingham, Willis J. *Emily Dickinson: An Annotated Bibliography*. Bloomington: Indiana University Press, 1970. (Covers 1850–1968.)

Cameron, Sharon. *Choosing Not Choosing: Dickinson's Fascicles*. Chicago: University of Chicago Press, 1992.

Capps, Jack L. *Emily Dickinson's Reading: 1836–1886*. Cambridge, MA: Harvard University Press, 1966.

Cody, John. *After Great Pain: The Inner Life of Emily Dickinson*. Cambridge, MA: Belknap-Harvard University Press, 1971.

The Emily Dickinson Journal. Baltimore: Johns Hopkins University Press, 2005.

Erkkila, Betsy. *The Wicked Sisters: Women Poets, Literary History, and Discord*. New York: Oxford University Press, 1992.

Farr, Judith. *The Passion of Emily Dickinson*. Cambridge, MA: Harvard University Press, 1998.

Grabher, Gudrun. *The Emily Dickinson Handbook*. Amherst: University of Massachusetts Press, 1999.

Juhasz, Suzanne, ed. *Feminist Critics Read Emily Dickinson*. Bloomington: Indiana University Press, 1983.

Juhasz, Suzanne, Cristanne Miller, and Martha Nell Smith. *Comic Power in Emily Dickinson*. Austin: University of Texas Press, 1993.

Sewall, Richard B. *The Life of Emily Dickinson*. 2 vols. New York: Farrar, 1974.

Smith, Martha Nell. *Rowing in Eden: Rereading Emily Dickinson*. Austin: University of Texas Press, 1992.

St. Armand, Barton Levi. *Emily Dickinson and Her Culture*. New York: Cambridge University Press, 1984.

Hilda Doolittle (H.D.)
(1886–1961)

Hilda Doolittle was born on September 10, 1886, in Bethlehem, Pennsylvania, to Charles Leander Doolittle, a professor and amateur astronomer, and Helen Wolle Doolittle. Hilda grew up in the community of Upper Darby, Pennsylvania, surrounded by a confluence of artistic and scientific influences; her mother was a pianist, her father an academic.

An eager student, Hilda was among the top-ranked girls in her class at Friends' Central School when she enrolled in 1902. Enrolling in the school's Classical Studies section, she was educated in classical languages and in ancient history. Following her graduation from Friends' Central, Doolittle went to Bryn Mawr College, where she met Marianne Moore. Doolittle left the school in 1906 because of poor health; she was struggling academically as well.

Doolittle cultivated a friendship with Ezra Pound, whom she met when she was fifteen and he sixteen. The two shared literary interests as well as companionship, and Pound introduced her to a fellow student at the University of Pennsylvania, William Carlos Williams. Pound and Doolittle were briefly engaged twice, but Hilda's father interceded and put an end to the young couple's plans. They were further separated by Pound's 1908 expulsion from nearby Wabash College; he left to study in Europe.

After withdrawing from Bryn Mawr, Doolittle spent several years staying close to her family home. She was writing, at first focusing on prose sketches, publishing Sunday school stories or astronomy articles directed at younger readers in local newspapers and small journals. Following a brief period of time living and writing in New York City in 1910, Doolittle embarked on a trip to Europe.

Ezra Pound, who had assigned Hilda the nickname "H.D.," introduced her to much of London's literary community. H.D., Pound, Richard

Aldington, and F. S. Flint formed their own writers' community, discussing movements in poetry and sharing their own verses. Each had a specialized literary background, in terms of education: Flint knew a great deal about French poetry, H.D. and Aldington were versed in the Greek and Latin classics, and Pound was concerned with esthetics. They determined to forge their own collective style, embracing clear, tangible images, with tight, concise use of language and verse. These writers altered conventional meter and worked in a style contrary to symbolism—images were direct rather than oblique. Some of Hilda's poems were included in *Poetry* magazine in 1913, submitted and titled under Pound's direction. Her work was included in the first anthology of Imagist poetry, *Des Imagistes* (1914).

Doolittle married Richard Aldington in October of 1913. As England plunged into World War I, Doolittle suffered the birth of a stillborn daughter. Doctors advised Doolittle against attempting another pregnancy while doctors were in such short supply because so many were needed for the war effort. The couple began to drift apart, and Aldington strayed from the marriage. He was badly injured in the war. Doolittle separated from him, though she would not pursue finalizing the divorce until 1938.

In 1916, Doolittle began serving as editor for the journal *The Egoist* and worked on translations. Her first collection, *Sea Garden*, was published the same year. The twenty-seven poems comprising the first collection were written in free verse, with frequent allusions to Greek culture and to mythology. One poem, "Eurydice," is more personal; in it, H.D. uses references to Orpheus and Eurydice to express a personal crisis, that of a woman whose husband's infidelity causes her despair.

H.D.'s second book was published in 1921. Though it was considered still in the Imagist style, there was more emotion—and more passion—expressed through the voices of women. The Imagist movement, as such had not lasted long as a collaborative or cooperative, but H.D.'s poems were again praised for their precision. *Heliodora and Other Poems* (1924) along with the first two volumes of H.D.'s previously published work were released as *Collected Poems* in 1925. Many of the narrators that populate the landscape of the work are mythological creatures; H.D. uses them as a dramatic device to represent universal experiences.

The 1940s was a productive period for Doolittle. In 1941, she published a collection entitled *Red Roses for Bronze*. She wrote a tribute to Sigmund Freud, with whom she'd had sessions for many years, and a poetry collection, *What Do I Love?*

World War I influenced H.D.'s works; she wrote the novels *Walls Do Not Fall*, *Tribute to the Angels*, and *The Flowering of the Rod*, referred to as her war trilogy. These books chronicle the war in both concrete and visionary terms, reflecting specific stages of the war. The role of the artist, the struggle to cling to the humane while surrounded by acts of inhumanity, and the very real consequences of intolerance are explored. The fires following bombings are compared to the devastation of Pompeii; death is all around, and Doolittle offers an unflinching series of visuals, beginning with the narrator surveying the wreckage of a blitz.

Doolittle's part in pioneering a new form of poetry and her consistent use of the techniques of Imagism throughout her career put her at the forefront of studies of that literary movement. Her poetry is among that more often included in texts for secondary students, as are studies on her uses of the mythic. H.D. died on September 27, 1961, following a heart attack and complications from a stroke.

Websites

Hilda Doolittle's home page: http://www.cichone.com/jlc/hd/hd.html
"Academy of American Poets." http://www.poets.org

Poetry

Sea Garden. London: Constable, 1916; Boston: Houghton Mifflin, 1916.
The Tribute and the Circe: Two Poems. Cleveland: Clerk's Private Press, 1917.
Hymen. London: Egoist Press, 1921; New York: Henry Holt, 1921.
Heliodora and Other Poems. Boston: Houghton Mifflin, 1924.
Hippolytus Temporizes. Boston: Houghton Mifflin, 1927.
Red Roses for the Bronze. London: Chatto & Windus, 1931; Boston: Houghton Mifflin, 1931.
The Walls Do Not Fall. London and New York: Oxford University Press, 1944.
What Do I Love? London: Brendin, 1944.
Tribute to the Angels. London and New York: Oxford University Press, 1945.
The Flowering of the Rod. London and New York: Oxford University Press, 1946.
By Avon River. New York: Macmillan, 1949.
Helen in Egypt. New York: Grove Press, 1961.
Hermetic Definition. New York: New Directions, 1972.
Trilogy. New York: New Directions, 1973.

Fiction

Palimpsest. Boston: Houghton Mifflin, 1926.
Hedylus. Boston: Houghton Mifflin, 1928.
Kora and Ka. Dijon: Darantiere, 1934.
The Usual Star. Dijon: Darantiere, 1934.
Bid Me to Live (a Madrigal). New York: Grove Press, 1960.
HERmione. New York: New Directions, 1981.

Within the Walls. Iowa City: Windhover, 1990.
Asphodel. Durham, NC: Duke University Press, 1990.

Translations

Choruses from Iphigenia in Aulis. London: Egoist Press, 1916.
Choruses from the Iphigenia in Aulis and the Hippolytus of Euripides. London: Egoist Press, 1919.
Euripides' Ion. London: Chatto & Windus, 1937.

Nonfiction

Borderline: A Pool Film with Paul Robeson. London: Mercury, 1930.
Writing on the Wall. New York: Pantheon, 1956.
End to Torment: A Memoire of Ezra Pound. New York: New Directions, 1979.
The Gift. New York: New Directions, 1982.
Notes on Thought and Vision and the Wise Sappho. San Francisco: City Lights, 1982.

Editions

Collected Poems of H.D. New York: Boni & Liveright, 1925.
Selected Poems of H.D. New York: Grove Press, 1957.
Collected Poems, 1912–1944. Ed. Louis L. Martz. New York: New Directions, 1983.
Selected Poems. Ed. Louis L. Martz. New York: New Directions, 1988.

References and Recommended Reading

Boughn, Michael. *H.D. A Bibliography 1905–1990.* Charlottesville: University of Virginia Press. 1993.
Morris, Adalaide. *Modern American Writers.* Consulting Ed. Elaine Showalter. New York: Charles Scribner's Sons, 1991.
Robinson, Janice. *H.D.: The Life and Work of an American Poet.* Boston: Houghton Mifflin, 1982.

Rita Dove
(1952–)

Rita Dove. Courtesy of Photofest.

This American poet was born in Akron, Ohio. Her father was one of the first African American research chemists in the United States. Dove's early years read like a fairy tale; however, the comfort of those times was no doubt tempered by the discomfort of being in the public eye. Her poetry reflects a return not to the black middle-class status of her childhood, but to the working-class origins of her grandparents. Dove's poetry celebrates the ordinary lives of ordinary people; it lays bare the fabric of those lives in an effort to capture and to restore the history of a people with whom she is intimately familiar.

Dove is a scholar-poet who has long received public acclaim. In 1970, at the tender age of eighteen, she became a Presidential Scholar, and three years later she graduated summa cum laude from Miami University. She won a Fulbright Scholarship and spent two semesters in Germany immediately following her graduation. Upon returning from Germany, Dove joined the University of Iowa Writers' Workshop. There she met another Fulbright scholar, the German writer Fred Viebahn, whom she married in 1976. Dove earned a Master of Fine Arts degree from Iowa in

1977 and published her first collection of poetry, *Ten Poems*, shortly after graduation.

Critics describe Dove's verse as concise, evocative recitations of history seen from an African American perspective. The poems are so much more: Dove recites an American identity; she explores the history as well as the myth of a people who are not hyphenated citizens but rather the progenitors of an American ethos. Many of her poems recontextualize slavery; she evokes the frightful institution's presence in unexpectedly gentle verse. She displaces slavery, moves its past-tense atrocities to a present tense to reveal its immediate and its long-term dangers. And she does so in the voices of those individuals maligned in its service. Her efforts render a different view of enslaved Africans: they become American citizens; their cries are those of a people demanding the privileges of such citizenship. However, Dove's poetry is not dedicated exclusively to pointing out different perspectives on past historical events, for in other poems, she writes similarly about mother–daughter relationships, travel, and the craft of poetry.

Still, in interviews Dove has confided that her poetic imagination is often spurred by historical events. She discusses her habit of being drawn into history at the same time that she has learned to distance herself from the experiences she relates. Dove acknowledges that she has a way of looking back at historical events with an eye that allows her to view what lies underneath those events. She searches not for what has always been seen or what is expected about a particular event, but for the things that can't be related in the sober voice of history. The language of poetry allows her to bring history alive. She acknowledges that when she is writing, she is very conscious of the sounds in the words, and that when she writes about historical figures that the world recognizes, it is important to her that the characteristics of the particular person that are familiar to her readers are depicted in that poem. She balances historical accuracy with imagination to create poems that are at once restricted to a particular time yet true of all time.

Dove has won many awards, including the Pulitzer Prize for "Thomas and Beulah," which was published in 1986. The poem is the story of her grandparents' life in verse and contains themes of perseverance, freedom, and dignity. The theme of a hard-won freedom is present in much of her poetry. She composed the poem "Lady Freedom Among Us" to be read at a ceremony both commemorating the two-hundredth anniversary of the United States Capitol and celebrating the restoration of the Freedom Statute on the Capitol's dome. The poem was published by Janus Press of Vermont in a limited edition that became the four-millionth acquisition of the University of Virginia Libraries. A multimedia version of the verse play *The Darker Face of the Earth* was made accessible globally by the University of Virginia; it was one of the earliest such publications by a major American writer to be made available in this way.

From 1993 to 1995, Dove was poet laureate of the United States, the first African American to hold the post. Other honors she has garnered include the Academy of American Poets' Lavan Younger Poets Award, a Mellon Foundation grant, and National Association for the Advancement of Colored People (NAACP) award for her work restoring dignity to the memories of enslaved African Americans. In 2004 she was named poet laureate of the Commonwealth of Virginia. Dove's verse play *The Darker Face of the Earth* won critical acclaim at its world premiere at the Oregon Shakespeare Festival in Ashland, Oregon, in the summer of 1996. In 1999, the verse play opened at the Royal National Theatre in London and was published in Great Britain by Oberon Press. In addition to poetry and the verse play, Dove has written short stories and a novel.

Her books of poetry include *American Smooth*, published in 2004, and *On the Bus with Rosa Parks*, published in 1999. The collection of poetry on the American icon Rosa Parks was named a New York Times Notable Book of the Year and was a finalist for the National Book Critics Circle Award. Other poetry collections include *Mother Love*, published in 1995; *Selected Poems*, published in 1993; and *Grace Notes*, also published in 1993.

Websites

Rita Dove's home page: http://www.people.virginia.edu/~rfd4b/
"Women of Color, Women of Words." http://www.scils.rutgers.edu/~cybers/
  dove2.html

Poetry

Thomas & Beulah. Pittsburgh: Carnegie Mellon University Press, 1986.
Grace Notes. New York: Norton, 1991.
Selected Poems. New York: Vintage, 1993.
Mother Love. New York: Norton, 1996.
On the Bus with Rosa Parks. New York: Norton, 2000.
American Smooth. New York: Norton, 2004.

Fiction

Through the Ivory Gate. New York: Vintage, 1993.

Drama

Darker Face of the Earth. Ashland, OR: Storyline Press, 2000.

References and Suggested Reading

Righelato, Pat. *Understanding Rita Dove.* Columbia: University of South Carolina Press, 2006.

Steffen, Therese. *Crossing Color: Transcultural Space and Place in Rita Dove's Poetry, Fiction and Drama.* New York: Oxford University Press, 2001.

———. "The Darker Face of the Earth: A Conversation with Rita Dove." *Transition: An International Review 7.2.74* (1998): pp. 104–23.

Bob Dylan
(1941–)

Bob Dylan. Courtesy of Photofest.

Few things appeal to teen and young adults readers as much as the voice of a rebel. Bob Dylan has forged a career on challenging his readers and his listeners by incorporating into music poetic elements that have helped define his times. Fiercely candid in his writing yet guardedly private in his personal life, Bob Dylan remains both icon and enigma. Still, at times he has defined himself, proclaiming "I'm a poet, and I know it."

Robert Allen Zimmerman was born in Duluth, Minnesota, on May 24, 1941, to a working-class Jewish couple, Abraham and Beatrice Zimmerman. Even as a toddler, Bob showed an early interest in singing. In 1946, shortly after the family welcomed a second son, Abraham suffered an attack of polio, which left him disabled and out of work. The Zimmermans relocated to Hibbing, Minnesota, where Abraham joined a family business.

Dylan, then known as Bobby Zimmerman, attended public school and was trained in the Jewish faith. His religion—and subsequent conversion to an evangelical branch of Christianity in adulthood—has often influenced his writing. Dylan was a quiet teenager in school, and at home he composed tunes at his piano. Dylan listened to radio stations that featured the work of country artists such as the legendary Hank Williams and Johnny

Ray. Dylan became a fan of the storytelling elements and the emotive nature of Williams's songs. He admired Johnny Ray's soulful voice, especially in Ray's songs about unrequited love. Dylan embraced the styles he saw in the 1955 film *Rebel Without a Cause*, suddenly shunning his conservative school clothes in favor of jeans, motorcycle jacket, and boots, as worn by the James Dean character with whom he sympathized.

In 1955, as rock and roll music made its dramatic breakthrough on radio stations across the country, Dylan was drawn to rhythm and blues artists like Little Richard. He and some friends formed an a cappella group called the Jokers, singing pop songs in harmony at local events. They cut a record in 1956 for which they were paid only a few dollars. After the Jokers disbanded, Dylan and three friends put together a rock band; they called themselves the Golden Chords. Their 1958 appearance at a high school talent competition apparently succeeded more in surprising the audience with the group's loud, raw music than in impressing the judges; they lost to a pantomime artist. They played at other small, local venues, once making an appearance on a Duluth television show, but Dylan split from the group when he became discontented with playing simple rock and roll songs. He also decided to change his name to Dylan, though he has never made the reason for that choice clear; he claimed it was not as a tribute either to poet Dylan Thomas, to Matt Dillon, hero of a popular 1950s television Western series, or to a well-known Hibbing family.

Dylan had no career ambitions other than to be a musician, and a job at a café would be the only one he ever held outside of the music industry. His parents, who had tolerated their son's rebellious teen stages (even buying him his motorcycle and allowing him his music as a hobby), begged him to earn a degree and stop writing poetry. They were able to persuade Dylan to enroll at the University of Minnesota at Minneapolis–St. Paul.

Dylan joined a fraternity, but began cutting classes. He spent time in nearby Dinkytown, a suburb of St. Paul, a neighborhood with clubs that welcomed beatniks—young people who shunned conservative ideas in favor of more liberal political causes and who formed their own subculture. They were more interested in folk music—which often addressed their ideologies—than in rock music. Dylan was drawn to the story-telling elements and the themes of folk music. The songs were often rallying cries for social justice and activism. He became a fan of singers Odetta Holmes and Woody Guthrie, especially appreciating that they wrote most of their own songs. Dylan left school to try for more exposure in clubs in Denver and then headed to New York.

New York City had a vibrant music scene, and Dylan began playing in coffeehouses and small clubs. John Hammond, a major record producer, spotted Dylan, and in the summer of his first year of the city, Dylan signed his first recording contract. His debut album, self-titled, featured both traditional and original folk songs, including a tribute to Guthrie.

As Dylan prepared to release a second album, *The Freewheelin' Bob Dylan* (1963), a song written as political satire stirred controversy. When Dylan was invited to perform on the enormously popular television variety program, *The Ed Sullivan Show*, he was told not to perform "Talkin' John Birch Paranoid Blues." Dylan refused to cut the song, and canceled his appearance. The incident actually increased young people's interest in Dylan. The album itself was a critical and commercial success. It included the John Birch song (which was cut from subsequent pressings); "Don't Think Twice, It's Alright" about a recent breakup with on-again, off-again girlfriend Suze Rotolo; and a song that would become an anthem in the antiwar movement, "Blowin' in the Wind." The lyrics were haunting, posing questions as a set of lyrical and philosophical challenges.

Dylan was introduced to beat poets Allen Ginsberg and Lawrence Ferlinghetti. Ferlinghetti saw Dylan as a poet, pointing out that Dylan's lyrics were basically surrealist poems set to melodies. Ferlinghetti signed Dylan to a publishing contract with his own press, City Lights Books. It would take a number of years for the project to reach completion.

In the summer of 1966, Dylan's career was interrupted when a motorcycle accident sidelined him. He chose to take an extended break from public appearances, instead spending time with his growing family. Along with his other commitments, Dylan stalled on delivering a manuscript for the book he'd agreed to publish, under the working title *Tarantula*. The publisher had already produced promotional merchandise in advance of the anticipated book release, and despite the fact that there was no book on the horizon, he found a market for the items, selling memorabilia emblazoned with Dylan's image.

Tarantula reached bookshelves in 1971. The book was a series of free verse pieces, written as stream of consciousness and modeled along the line of the Beat poets, who first encouraged Dylan to publish.

Dylan was diagnosed with and treated for a heart condition in 1997, and turned his energies to recording *Time Out of Mind*, which became a best seller and won three Grammy Awards, including one for Album of the Year. He toured, even playing for an audience that included Pope John Paul II. He won a Grammy Award for his 2002 folk album, and his songs were being used in such films as *Hurricane* and *The Wonder Boys*. The latter won Dylan an Academy Award for the song "Things Have Changed." The first in what is planned to be a series of memoirs, *Chronicles* (2004), received an excellent critical reception and became a bestseller.

Dylan continues to tour and to produce new music. His lyrics are studied as poetry, even in colleges. His work is considered both a natural progression from the amalgamation of music and beat poetry which inspired him, and a study of an artist testing the boundaries of art forms—from the day he brought his electric guitar onstage at a folk concert to his beat poetry. His categorical refusal to be labeled or limited by fans or critics, his earnest pleas for geopolitical causes, and his very public quest to maintain his artistic integrity while guarding his privacy have drawn young people to explore him as an American original, one who remains contemporary and topical through lyrics that challenge and comfort, amuse and accuse.

Website

Bob Dylan official website: http://www.bobdylan.com/moderntimes/home/main.html

Poetry

Tarantula. New York: Macmillan, 1971.
Poem to Joanie. London: Aloes Press, 1972.

Prose

Writings and Drawings. New York: Knopf, 1973.
Renaldo and Clara (film script). Circuit Films, 1978.
Lyrics, 1962–1985. New York: Knopf, 1985.
Lyrics, 1962–1996. New York: Villard, 1997.
Lyrics, 1962–1999. New York: Knopf, 1999.
Man Gave Names to All the Animals. San Diego, CA: Harcourt Brace, 1999.
Lyrics: 1962–2001. New York: Simon & Schuster, 2004.
Chronicles: Volume One (memoir). New York: Simon & Schuster, 2004.

References and Suggested Reading

Younger Than That Now: The Collected Interviews with Bob Dylan. New York: Thunder's Mountain Press, 2004.

Ralph Waldo Emerson
(1803–1882)

Ralph Waldo Emerson was born on May 25, 1803, in Boston. The Emersons' fourth-born child was named Ralph in honor of his maternal uncle, but he made early attempts to shed this in favor of his middle name. There were six cousins named Ralph, and he did not savor being one of many sharing the name. By the age of three, Emerson was attending a private school; it was a disappointment to Emerson's father that the boy was not reading fluently by the age of four. Ralph did not take to schooling as enthusiastically as did his brother, and his lackluster academic performance remained a point of contention between father and son until the elder's death.

In 1812, when he was nine years of age, Emerson entered the Boston Public Library School, considered a college preparatory program. The education centered on the study of Latin and Greek, supplemented by outside tutoring in writing and arithmetic. Emerson began to exhibit a talent for working in rhyme, at first doing translations, then working elegies. The young Emerson practiced rephrasing family favorites found in his aunt's collections, and presenting them to his family when they were gathered. His family took pleasure in this talent, especially his Aunt Mary, who had a powerful influence on Emerson.

Emerson entered Harvard University on a scholarship in 1817, when he was fourteen years of age. He did not immediately distinguish himself in his studies. He read outside the curriculum, and he taught several winter terms at his uncle's school in Waltham. He graduated in the middle rank of his class, and he was elected class poet.

In 1825 he attended Harvard Divinity School and was licensed to preach by the Middlesex Association of Ministers. He was granted permission to preach in 1826.

A licensed minister, Emerson resumed teaching private students, subsequently taking positions at a public school, and finally teaching at his brother Edward's school. He preached even as he traveled south in search of weather better suited to his rheumatism and lung problems. He was reluctant to accept a permanent assignment because of the state of his health. In December 1828, while in Concord, New Hampshire, he met Ellen Louisa Tucker, a merchant's daughter, and they married in September, 1829 following Emerson's March ordination as pastor of the Second Unitarian Church of Boston. The rituals and responsibilities imposed by the church did not suit Emerson, and although he was a very strong orator, he was not successful in managing many of the other tasks required of him in the position.

In early 1831, Ellen died of consumption. Grief-stricken, and faced with his own declining health, Emerson sought respite in travel. He traveled throughout Europe in an effort to restore his health and overcome his grief. During his travels, he met and developed friendships with writers Thomas Carlyle, Samuel Coleridge, and William Wordsworth.

Emerson returned to the United States in restored health, and he attempted a return to the pulpit in the Unitarian church but demanded that he not be required to lead prayer or dispense communion. The church rescinded its offer of employment and Emerson turned to lecturing.

In 1835 Emerson became involved with a group called the Hedge, who espoused a movement called Transcendentalism. It was a philosophy and a cultural phenomenon that began as a debate within the Unitarian church but spread to a system that questioned the establishment as it was embodied in organized religion, social concerns, and academic philosophy. Transcendentalists embraced the spiritual and the natural worlds, rather than conventions or dogma. Emerson published his book *Nature* (1836), which read as a series of lectures or sermons. He continued to lecture on scholarly issues throughout the late 1830s. He was instrumental in editing *The Dial*, a periodical issued by the Transcendentalists—a group that included Henry David Thoreau. The publication lasted for only four years. One of Emerson's most memorable speeches, a treatise on business ethics, was among the pieces in the final issue of *The Dial*.

In December of 1845, Emerson's *Poems* was released. He had written about poetry in essays, embracing a style that reflected experiential poetry. Emerson saw the value of poetry not as the product of theory but rather as expressing life experiences and observations. His first collection featured fifty-nine poems and was universally received as being an unorthodox and exciting entry into the field. Emerson experimented with rhyme and meter to match his subjects, tone, or emotions rather than to conform to the styles of his contemporaries. Notably absent were references to Christianity, a common theme among poets of the time. At times satirical, Emerson addressed social concerns and intellectual issues. The collection opens with "The Sphinx," which invites readers to find their own meanings in the poems. The poems are heavily influenced by Transcendentalist thinking, especially in the themes of nature and of humanity, and they discuss diverse topics from truth to petty crime. There are some emotional pieces, notably his "Threnody," written about the loss of his son. The poem goes from a father's deepest grief to a voice of admonition against becoming lost in mourning, ending with lines about Providence and acceptance.

By 1870, Emerson's mind was declining, though he continued to deliver addresses. He was not writing with regularity. Two years later, his house burned down. Emerson and his neighbors were able to save his books, manuscripts, and some personal effects, and many contributed to the construction of a new home. Emerson traveled to Egypt, England, and Italy during the rebuilding. His collection of poems, *Parnassus*, was published. He had anthologized works by an array of authors, primarily English, but also by writers from America as well as Greek and Hindu authors. His own works were not represented in the volume.

Emerson spent the last years of his life making occasional appearances to read from his old lectures, enjoying life in his restored home. He died on April 27, 1882, of pneumonia. His work is a standard in the English Language Arts curriculum in secondary schools and in many universities, respected for the poet's clarity of language and imagery. Emerson's body of work, and its place in the unique Transcendentalist movement, is a nonexhaustive subject of study.

Website

"American Transcendentalism." http://www.vcu.edu/engweb/transcendentalism/authors

Poetry

Poetry. London: Chapman, 1847; Boston: Munroe, 1847.

Nonfiction

Nature. Boston: Munroe, 1836.
Essays: Second Series. Boston: Munroe, 1844.
Letters and Social Aims. Boston: Osgood, 1876.
The Works of Ralph Waldo Emerson. 3 vols. London: Bell, 1883.

Miscellanies. Boston: Houghton, Mifflin, 1884.

Lectures and Biographical Sketches. Boston and New York: Houghton, Mifflin, 1884.

Natural History and Intellect and Other Papers. Boston and New York: Houghton, Mifflin, 1893.

Uncollected Writings: Essays, Addresses, Poems, Reviews, and Letters. New York: Lamb, 1912.

Young Emerson Speaks: Unpublished Discourses on Many Subjects. Boston: Houghton, Mifflin, 1938.

The Early Lectures of Ralph Waldo Emerson. 16 vols. Cambridge, MA: Harvard University Press, 1959.

The Journals and Miscellaneous Notebooks of Ralph Waldo Emerson. 16 vols. Cambridge, MA: Harvard University Press, 1960–1983.

References and Suggested Reading

Allen, Gay Wilson. *Waldo Emerson: A Biography.* New York: Viking Press, 1981.

Barish, Evelyn. *Emerson: The Roots of Prophecy.* Princeton, NJ: Princeton University Press, 1989.

Porte, Joel, ed. *Emerson in His Journals.* Cambridge, MA: Harvard University Press, 1982.

"Ralph Waldo Emerson." In *Dictionary of Literary Biography, Volume 270: American Philosophers Before 1950.* Ed. Richard A. Hutch. A Bruccoli Clark Database, 2006.

"Ralph Waldo Emerson." In *Dictionary of Literary Biography, Volume 59: American Literary Critics and Scholars, 1800–1850.* Ed. Robert D. Richardson. A Bruccoli Clark Database, 2004.

Louise Erdrich
(1954–)

Louise Erdrich. Courtesy of Photofest.

Louise Erdrich was raised among the Turtle Mountain Chippewa People, a community rich in storytelling traditions. Her early life in a culture in which stories both illustrated and illuminated people's lives would be among the heaviest influences in both her choice of a career and in her sense of narrative. As she has created a body of work that includes poetry and fiction for readers of various ages, Erdrich has become recognized as a major force in popularizing Native American voices in contemporary literature.

Karen Louise Erdrich was born in Little Falls, Minnesota, on June 7, 1954, the oldest of seven children born to a German American father and a French Ojibwe (Chippewa) mother. The Erdrichs raised their family in Wahpeton, North Dakota, as they taught at a boarding school. Louise's father read Shakespeare to his children and paid his daughter a nickel for each story she wrote; Louise's mother created covers for the books. Erdrich was surrounded by stories in the Chippewa oral tradition, including those of her grandfather, a tribal leader with a special gift for storytelling and a determination to preserve the Native culture.

Erdrich attended a series of public schools and one parochial school, St. John's. She enrolled at Dartmouth College in 1972 as a member of the school's inaugural coeducational class. Erdrich had pieces published in the

Dartmouth literary magazine and in *Ms.*, and received the American Academy of Poets Prize as an undergraduate. She worked throughout and between her school terms at an eclectic variety of jobs, including library work, teaching, serving as a lifeguard, and putting in time as a signal flagman at a construction site. Erdrich later claimed that she was able to use some of her work experiences in her writing. She became immersed in studies of her culture and ancestry, and she edited an Indian Council newspaper called *Circle.*

After graduating with a bachelor's degree in English in 1976, Erdrich worked as a poet in schools as part of the grant from the State Arts Council of North Dakota. She taught children as well as patients at rehabilitation and substance abuse treatment programs. Erdrich pursued her master's degree in writing as a fellowship student at Johns Hopkins University. She wrote a good deal of poetry and submitted a series of poems as her thesis.

Erdrich took a position as writer in residence at Dartmouth. She renewed her friendship with Michael Dorris, an anthropologist and writer she met while a graduate student, and the two began collaborating, sending one another works in progress. They wrote a story that won the Nelson Algren fiction competition; they later expanded "The World's Greatest Fisherman" into the novel *Love Medicine.* Erdrich and Dorris married in 1981, and Erdrich adopted Dorris's three children. Throughout their marriage, which would end shortly before Dorris committed suicide in 1997, Erdrich and Dorris worked together on projects eventually attributed to one or the other.

Erdrich's first published book of poetry, *Jacklight*, and her first novel, *Love Medicine*, were published within a year of each other. *Jacklight*, her first full-length poetry collection, featured poems steeped in images of Native American people, including their customs and rituals. The title poem uses the image of an illegal hunting light as a metaphor for the destructive lure of European American culture. Erdrich would revisit this theme frequently in her writing, notably in her works for younger readers. Some of the poems in *Jacklight* are prefaced with quotes from other sources: a medicine woman, a woman held captive by Native Americans. The quotes frame the pieces, and Erdrich's voices, in verse, range from those of children deposited in boarding school to a contemporary Native American speaker's biting retort to a popular hero in a Hollywood Western. Erdrich also includes poems about the Native American trickster Potchikoo, a character who would appear in later writings.

The novel *Love Medicine*, released in 1984, became a bestseller. The book could be seen as a series of short stories; three of the chapters had already been published as short fiction. The work featured characters on a reservation in North Dakota and depicted several generations of its residents, a group of full-blooded and mixed-parentage Native Americans.

The relationships among its characters are complex. Families are built by circumstance as much as by blood, and in some cases, there are tremendous frictions and resentments among those who are related. One of the real-life issues Erdrich addressed in her fiction was alcohol abuse in the Native community. Erdrich and her husband dealt with the tragic consequences of alcohol. Their oldest son, whom Dorris adopted before the marriage, had been diagnosed with fetal alcohol syndrome. Dorris would chronicle the experience in an award-winning nonfiction book, *The Broken Cord: A Family's Ongoing Struggle with Fetal Alcohol Syndrome* (1989).

By 1996, Erdrich's novels and poetry had found an eclectic audience, including young adult readers, and in this year she released her first picture book, *Grandmother's Pigeon*. In a story that weaves elements of generational love, a mystical grandmother journeys to Greenland on a dolphin, leaving a set of children to raise her pigeons.

Erdrich launched a series of books for intermediate readers in 1999 with the historical novel *The Birchbark House*, the story of Omikayas, a young Ojibwe girl living on an island in Lake Superior as the lives of her people are threatened by European settlers. The book was a National Book Award finalist, and Omikayas's story is continued in the 2004 sequel *The Game of Silence*, which heightens the conflicts between the Ojibwe and the outsiders. Erdrich also did the artwork for the two books.

Erdrich's novel *Last Report of the Miracles at Little No Horse* (2001) told the story of the enigmatic reservation priest Father Damien, tacking themes of the parallels and disparities between Native beliefs and Catholicism. *The Master Butchers Singing Club* (2003), another National Book Award nominee, marks a departure from Erdrich's usual focus on Native American lead characters; while it takes place in the familiar setting of North Dakota, Erdrich's novel centers around a cast of German Americans. In *Four Souls* (2004), she returned to characters from *Last Report*, with themes of revenge and its consequences.

Erdrich's *Original Fire: Selected and New Poems* (2003) brought together themes and characters from most of her previous works, including her fiction. The poems include sequences about Potchikoo the trickster, original storylines about a traditional Native American character. There are poems about "The Seven Sleepers," legendary Christian youths who fall asleep for two hundred years as they hide from persecution. Erdrich provides a brief text to introduce such subjects. Poems in "The Butcher's Wife" hint at stories told in *Master Butcher's Singing Club*. Many of the poems in the section "Original Fire" consider themes of the ordinary and the extraordinary in everyday life. In "Asiniig," stones, viewed as grandparents, ponder the wisdom of allowing humanity to occur. Many of the poems are deeply personal as Erdrich speaks to us about children, identity, love, and life itself, in intimate rather than in epic tones.

Erdrich's works reach young audiences through their rich detail, their dramatic themes and storylines, and their explorations of identity through and beyond culture. Her writing is passionate, topical, and universal. Currently she lives in Minnesota with her daughters; she spends her time writing, quilting, and running a bookstore.

Website

"Native American Authors Project: The Internet Public Library." http://ipl.si.umich.edu/div/natam/

Poetry

Jacklight. New York: Holt, 1984.
Baptism of Desire. New York: Harper, 1989.
Original Fire: New and Selected Poems. New York: HarperCollins, 2003.

Novels

The Beet Queen. New York: Holt, 1986.
Tracks. New York: Harper, 1988.
(With husband, Michael Dorris) *The Crown of Columbus.* New York: HarperCollins, 1991.
Love Medicine. New York: Holt, 1984; expanded edition, 1993.
The Bingo Palace. New York: HarperCollins, 1994.
Tales of Burning Love. New York: HarperCollins, 1996.
The Antelope Wife. New York: HarperFlamingo, 1998.
The Last Report on the Miracles at Little No Horse. New York: HarperCollins, 2001.
The Master Butchers Singing Club. New York: HarperCollins, 2003.
Four Souls. New York: HarperCollins, 2004.

For Children

Grandmother's Pigeons. Illustrated by Jim LaMarche. New York: Hyperion, 1996.
(And illustrator) *The Birchbark House.* New York: Hyperion Books for Children, 1999.
(And illustrator) *The Game of Silence.* New York: HarperCollins, 2004.

References and Suggested Reading

Charkin, Allan. *The Chippewa Landscape of Louise Erdrich.* Tuscaloosa: University of Alabama Press, 1999.
Scott, Steven D. *The Gamefulness of American Postmodernism: John Barth and Louise Erdrich.* New York: Peter Lang, 2000.

Paul Fleischman
(1952–)

Although he grew up in a home where imaginative language and creative ability were prized, Paul Fleischman, the son of author Sid Fleischman (a writer of books for children and young adults), had no intention of becoming a writer until his college years. After working at several jobs, he wrote his first picture book, then completed several works of fiction, as his father continued to write. Several years later, the American Library Association affirmed that for the Fleischmans, literature would continue to be a family affair. Two years after his father won a Newbery Award for his historical novel *The Whipping Boy*, the young Fleischman received the same medal for his poetry collection *Joyful Noise: Poems for Two Voices.* In addition to poetry, Fleischman has written picture books, fiction for both juvenile readers and young adults, and nonfiction.

Paul Fleischman was born in California on September 5, 1952, to Albert Sidney Fleischman and Beth Fleischman. Paul's childhood in Santa Monica, in a home only blocks from the Pacific, was spent not in libraries or even doing heavy reading. Paul spent his time at the beach, on the playgrounds, in alleys, and riding his bike, yet he was immersed in both music and the spoken word. Sid Fleischman read chapters of works in progress aloud, inviting suggestions from his sons and daughters. This gave Paul a special appreciation for theater; several of his books are structured for readers' theater productions. A picture of ten-year-old Paul listening to the family's shortwave radio adorns the cover of his novel *Seek*; the book centers around the power of voices. An awareness of sound, meter, and rhythm was nurtured by the Fleischman family's collective interest in music. Paul and his mother played piano, his sisters played the flute, his father played the guitar. Paul would go on to become proficient at playing several other instruments; as an adult he claimed that he would have pursued a career in music if he'd had any genuine talent. Evenings were family time, and the Fleischman parents were fond of games such as cryptograms. Fleischman remembers little time being set aside for television viewing; he has recalled that he and his sisters created their own stationery, business cards, and a code they called "printer esoterica." The family enjoyed sharing music and listening to the elder Fleischman read aloud; from these activities, the young Paul gained a deep respect for the bonds of family.

Fleischman enjoyed collecting scrap items, sometimes as materials for sculptures. He developed a great respect for nature, a theme that recurs in many of his books. It was during his high-school years that Fleischman found himself drawn to classical music, an interest that led him to spend long hours trying to put words to the music he heard.

Fleischman studied botany, philosophy, and folk dancing at the University of California at Berkeley, which he attended from 1970 through 1972. During the summer after his sophomore year, Fleischman embarked on a cross-country trip, traveling by bicycle and train. He took residence in a 200-year-old house in New Hampshire, one with few modern conveniences, and lived there for two years. The setting rekindled his interest in the past and it provided a backdrop for a number of his books.

Fleischman completed his bachelor's degree in 1979 at the University of New Mexico. He spent time working at a bagel shop, as a bookstore clerk, at a library, and as a proofreader before taking up full-time writing. He wrote his first picture book, *The Birthday Tree* (1979), as he prepared to leave college, with no firm plans in mind. He went on to write several works of children's and young adult fiction before returning to picture books with *The Animal Hedge* in 1983.

In his work, Fleischman effectively re-creates the past while maintaining a lyrical, contemporary voice. It is voice that drives all of his work. His love of language is clear in his humor. One of his more celebrated works, *Bull Run* (1993), tells stories of the Civil War in sixteen distinct voices, bringing a sense of intimacy and immediacy to historical events that happened long before many of his readers were born.

There may be no better litmus test to measure Fleischman's gift for voice than in his choral poetry collections. In *I Am Phoenix* (1985), Fleischman presents the narratives of birds, each piece designed to be read by two voices. In his Newbery Award–winning *Joyful Noise* (1988), Fleischman invites readers to perform duets taking the points of view of insects in alternating rounds, cadences, and rhythms. Lines overlap; some read simultaneously, others in turn. In one poem, two bees, one a queen and the other a worker, respectively celebrate and lament their roles. "Whirligig Beetles" features an almost hypnotic drone, drawing the listener in to the movements of the insects. The book has been embraced by teachers, students, and theatrical troupes alike. Fleischman doubles the oratorical challenge in *Big Talk: Poems for Four Voices* (2000), a series of poems with complex rhythms and homey themes.

Although Fleischman's work is perfectly suited for children and young adults, he does not target a specific audience when he writes. He is married and the father of two adult sons, Seth and Dana. Fleischman and his wife, Patty, live in Aromas, Monterey County, California. He divides time between his professional obligations—writing and speaking commitments—and his hobbies, which include writing and performing music, playing bocce (a kind of street bowling), and participating in such art projects as constructing matchbox theaters.

Websites

Paul Fleischman's official website: http://www.paulfleischman.net/

Poetry

I Am Phoenix: Poems for Two Voices. Illustrated by Ken Nutt. New York: Harper, 1985.
Joyful Noise: Poems for Two Voices. Illustrated by Eric Beddows. New York: Harper, 1988.
Big Talk: Poems for Four Voices. Illustrated by Beppe Gioacobbe. Cambridge, MA: Candlewick Press, 2000.

Juvenile Fiction

The Half-a-Moon Inn. Illustrated by Kathy Jacobi. New York: Harper, 1980.
Phoebe Danger, Detective, in the Case of the Two-Minute Cough. Illustrated by Margot Apple. Boston: Houghton, 1983.
Finzel the Farsighted. Illustrated by Marcia Sewall. New York: Dutton, 1983.

Young Adult Fiction

Bull Run. Illustrated by David Frampton. New York: HarperCollins, 1993.
A Fate Totally Worse Than Death. Cambridge, MA: Candlewick Press, 1995.
Seedfolks. New York: HarperCollins, 1997.
Mind's Eye. New York: Holt, 1999.
Seek. Chicago: Cricket Books, 2001.
Breakout. Chicago: Cricket Books, 2003.
Zap. Cambridge, MA: Candlewick Press, 2005.

Picture Books

The Birthday Tree. Illustrated by Marcia Sewall. New York: Harper, 1979.
The Animal Hedge. Illustrated by Lydia Dabcovich. New York: Dutton, 1983.
Rondo in C. Illustrated by Janet Wentworth. New York: Harper, 1988.
Shadow Play. Illustrated by Beddows. New York: Harper, 1990.
Time Train. Illustrated by Claire Ewart. New York: HarperCollins, 1991.
Weslandia. Illustrated by Kevin Hawkes. Cambridge, MA: Candlewick Press, 1999.
Lost!: A Story in String. Illustrated by C. B. Mordan. New York: Holt, 2000.
The Animal Hedge. Illustrated by Bagram Ibatoulline. Cambridge, MA: Candlewick Press, 2003.
Sidewalk Circus. Illustrated by Kevin Hawkes. Cambridge, MA: Candlewick Press, 2004.

Nonfiction

Townsend's Warbler. New York: HarperCollins, 1992.
Copier Creations. Illustrated by David Cain. New York: HarperCollins, 1993.
Dateline: Troy. Illustrated by Gwen Frankfeldt and Glenn Morrow. Cambridge, MA: Candlewick Press, 1996.

References and Suggested Reading

Chevalier, Tracy, ed. *Twentieth Century Children's Writers, 3rd Edition.* Detroit: St. James Press, 1989.
Cole, Pam B. "Paul Fleischman." In *Writers for Young Adults, Supplement I.* Ed. Ted Hipple. New York: Charles Scribner's Sons, 2000.

Ralph Fletcher
(1953–)

Ralph Fletcher has made a career of working in several genres of young adult literature. He has written poetry, fiction, and nonfiction for young readers; books about writing directed toward the same age group; professional works for educators; and memoirs. A popular speaker in schools and at conferences for librarians and teachers, Fletcher has produced a body of work keenly tuned to contemporary intermediate readers and teen audiences.

Ralph Fletcher was born on March 17, 1953 in Marshfield, Massachusetts, the first child of Ralph Fletcher and Jean Collins Fletcher. His father worked in the publishing industry and often traveled. The Fletcher family grew quickly over the first years of Ralph's life: brother Jimmy, just a year younger than Ralph; Elaine two years younger; followed by Tommy, Bobby, Johnny, Joey, and Kathleen. Ralph was especially close with Jimmy, and the children spent much of their free time exploring the family's seven wooded acres, playing with the many children in their small town, even raising a flock of fractious roosters. There was also a large extended family, and the Fletcher children were surrounded by stories and storytellers. Ralph was a good student; he enjoyed reading, especially adventure stories and mysteries.

When Fletcher was thirteen, his father received a promotion, and the family relocated to a suburb of Chicago. Less than ten years later, Fletcher enrolled at Dartmouth College, and as a student was able to travel to the South Pacific and to Sierra Leone, Africa. His life and his creative energies took a dramatic turn following a family tragedy. When Fletcher was twenty-one, his seventeen-year-old brother Bob was killed in a car accident. As the Fletchers coped with their grief, Ralph found solace in reading poetry. Since childhood, Fletcher had enjoyed writing, but now was drawn to poems because of their brevity and their intensity. He started writing more in verse.

Fletcher graduated from Dartmouth in 1975, and in 1981 he matriculated in the master's degree program in fiction writing at Columbia University in New York City, where he worked alongside such writers as Gail Godwin and Richard Price. He was recruited by Columbia's Teachers College to teach writing to teachers. Fletcher traveled throughout New York City, sharing children's books with students and their instructors as he visited classrooms, using the books as models and prompts for student writing. He grew to appreciate the works of such writers as William Steig, Cynthia Rylant, Katherine Paterson, Gary Soto, and John Steptoe, and he was inspired by their work to try his own hand at writing for young audiences.

Fletcher married JoAnn Portalupi in May 1989. His wife is also a writer. Together, they have collaborated on three or more projects designed to help teachers become better instructors of writing. In addition to the collaborations with his wife, Fletcher continued his work as a writing coach while sending out manuscripts. The first book that was accepted for publication was a set of short pieces, *Water Planet: Poems About Water* (1991), an ecologically themed collection. Also in 1991, Fletcher released the first among his professional publications, *Walking Trees: Teaching Teachers in the New York City Schools*, later issued as *Walking Trees: Portraits of Teachers and Children in the Culture of Schools*. As was clear in his approach as he made visits to schools, Fletcher's book proved how firmly he believed that all children are natural writers. He was determined to assist teachers in tapping the potential of each young person and developing a sense of voice in each one. His next book reinforced that conviction. In 1993, Fletcher's *What a Writer Needs* was released, and was immediately a popular choice among teachers and in graduate programs.

The 1990s proved to be watershed years in Fletcher's emergence as an author of books for young adults. His collection *I Am Wings: Poems About Love* (1994) quickly garnered strong reviews. All of the poems are centered around the experiences of falling into and out of love. Arranged in a sequence of before, during, and after the ardor, Fletcher effectively captures the intensity of the experiences of young love in his subjects (and audience), from first infatuation to later disenchantment—even, at times, betrayal.

In 1996 he released a poetry collection that is a companion piece to *I Am Wings*. *Buried Alive: The Elements of Love* features another series of pieces about young romance, including the voices of some teens in transition, engaged in self-discovery. The poems were later combined with those from *I Am Wings* in an edition entitled *Room Enough for Love* (1998).

Fletcher again worked with his wife, JoAnn Portalupi, on the 1998 release *Craft Lessons: Teacher Writing K–8*; The two also wrote *Nonfiction Craft Lessons: Teaching Information Writing K–8* (2001) and *Writing Workshop: The Essential Guide* (2001). He returned to poetry with the 1999 collection *Relatively Speaking*, a work that weaves the voices and experiences of many members of a family, seeing the interrelationships from the points of view of different narrators, introduced by the youngest family member. Fletcher captures the exuberance of shared games, the exasperations and joys of siblings, the constants of shared meals and shared understanding. The book covers the full gamut of emotions from joy to grief, and portrays its characters' attempts to establish a sense of self while surrounded by others. Fletcher explored many of the same themes in his later autobiographical work, *Marshfield Dreams* (2005).

Fletcher's next poetry collection, aimed at younger readers, *Grandpa Never Lies* (2000) was followed quickly by two intermediate novels: *Tommy Trouble and the Magic Marble* (2000) and *The Circus Surprise* (2001). His next work of fiction, *Uncle Daddy* (2001), tells the story of Rivers, a boy who must deal with the return of a father who abandoned his family while Rivers was just a toddler. The book earned a Christopher Medal.

Fletcher claims to have a simple work routine, one that allots an amount of structured time to write, typically three to four hours a day. His ability both to create a body of work in his own voice and to act as an ardent advocate for encouraging young people to explore their own gifts has established him as a major force in contemporary publishing and as a respected speaker, poet, and educator.

Websites

Author's website: http://www.ralphfletcher.com/

Poetry

Water Planet: Poems about Water. Paramus, NJ: Arrowhead Books, 1991.
I Am Wings: Poems about Love. Photographs by Joe Baker. New York: Atheneum, 1994.
Ordinary Things: Poems from a Walk in Early Spring. Illustrated by Walter Lyon Krudop. New York: Atheneum, 1997.
Twilight Comes Twice. Illustrated by Kate Kiesler. New York: Clarion, 1997.
Buried Alive: The Elements of Love. Photographs by Andrew Moore. New York: Atheneum, 1996.
Room Enough for Love. New York: Aladdin, 1998.
Relatively Speaking: Poems about Family. New York: Orchard Books, 1999.
Grandpa Never Lies. Illustrated by Harvey Stevenson. New York: Clarion, 2000.

Have You Been to the Beach Lately? Illustrated by Andrea Sperling. New York: Orchard Books, 2001.

Hello, Harvest Moon. Illustrated by Kate Keisler. New York: Clarion, 2003.

Juvenile Fiction

Fig Pudding. New York: Clarion, 1995.

Spider Boy. New York: Clarion, 1997.

Flying Solo. New York: Clarion, 1998.

Tommy Trouble and the Magic Marble. New York: Holt, 2000.

The Circus Surprise. Illustrated by Vladimir Vagin. New York: Clarion, 2001.

Uncle Daddy. New York: Holt, 2001.

Juvenile Nonfiction

A Writer's Notebook: Unlocking the Writer Within You. New York: Avon, 1996.

Live Writing: Breathing Life into Your Words. New York: Avon, 1999.

How Writers Work: Finding a Process That Works for You. New York: HarperCollins, 2000.

Poetry Matters: Writing a Poem from the Inside Out. New York: HarperCollins, 2002.

References and Suggested Reading

Atwell, Nancie. *In the Middle: New Understanding about Writing, Reading, and Learning,* 2nd ed. Portsmouth, NH: Heinemann, 1998.

Blau, Sheridan. *Literature Workshop.* Portsmouth, NH: Heinemann, 2003.

Fleming, Gerald. *Keys to Creative Writing Activities to Unlock Imagination in the Classroom.* Boston: Allyn & Bacon, 1991.

Harvey, Susan. *Strategies That Work.* Portland, ME: Stenhouse, 1997.

———. *Nonfiction Matters: Reading, Writing, and Research in Grades 3–8.* Portland, ME: Stenhouse, 1998.

Miller, Debbie. *Reading with Meaning.* Portland, ME: Stenhouse, 2000.

Ray, Katie. *The Writing Workshop: Working Through the Hard Parts (And They're All Hard Parts).* Urbana, IL: National Council of Teachers of English, 2001.

Carolyn Forché
(1952-)

Forché (pronounced for-SHAY) is from Detroit, Michigan; she is one of seven children born into a Catholic family headed by her father, who worked as a tool and die maker, and her mother, a Czech American housewife who encouraged her daughter to write poetry. As a school girl, Forché was also supported in her efforts to create poetry by the nuns at her parochial school, who also encouraged her to read interpretively. About the part she played in her own development as a poet, Forché has observed that she never felt she had a choice regarding whether she would write. She has always been a writer; the task for her has been to find the place where she fit, the niche from which her voice would be most effective. She found that niche by writing in a tradition of literature that is described as poetry of witness.

As a youngster, Forché was curious about world events. She discovered photographs of a Nazi concentration camp in a magazine and promptly sought her mother's explanation of the events depicted in the pictures. Perhaps because of her own memories of friends and family members who suffered under a Communist regime, Forché's mother confiscated the magazine and hid it from the girl in an attempt to dissuade her daughter from viewing the photographs. However; the young poet would not be deterred; she discovered the hiding place and reclaimed possession of the magazine. Her curiosity about the human condition and her desire to unmask the extremes of human suffering, whether as a result of war, of famine, or of poverty, are consistent themes in her work. Like another Detroit poet, Phillip Levine, Forché's work often exposes the atrocities that result from man's inhumanity to man.

Forché received the Yale Younger Poets Prize for her collection of poetry, *Gathering the Tribes*, published in 1976. The predominant themes in this early work focus on the bonds of family and community. In this collection, she recalls her childhood and adolescence, calls upon her ancestors, and explores topics ranging from rituals in Native American culture to her own evolving sexual self. Her work is appropriate for young readers who are growing into adulthood and dealing with the physical, emotional, and spiritual changes that accompany such growth.

After completing her first collection of poetry, Forché received a Guggenheim Fellowship, which led to her completing human rights work in El Salvador. She spent a year there working with an archbishop who was also a human rights activist. Forché's collection, *The Country Between Us*, evolved beyond themes of community bonds that were apparent in her first book to themes that reveal the bonds between individuals, regardless of geography, ethnicity, gender, or class.

The Country Between Us, considered controversial because of its realistic portrayals of the result of North American intervention in Central America, was published when Forché was twenty-nine years old. This book of poems was a product of the year she spent in El Salvador, and it contains haunting word images of that war-torn country. One of the more disturbing yet memorable images of El Salvador in the volume may be seen in a prose poem titled "The Colonel." Here, the speaker calmly recites an army officer's delivery of the mutilated ears of citizens. This macabre offering is presented during a dinner-time gathering, and the body parts of the war's victims are described by the narrator as resembling dried peach halves. The poem is a testament to the brutality and horror of the lived experiences of many communities of people in Central America.

In addition to her poems that present images of a clear and present danger to humankind, Forché has used her imaginative verse as a lens to explore a historical context of human pain and suffering. The collection *The Angel of History* is a poetic meditation that examines an accumulation of human misconduct. The collection is divided into three sections; the first section maps the speaker's journey through Europe, offering stark images of death camps and of the Chernobyl disaster. Subsequent sections imagine the possibility of history repeating itself. In these, the speaker is analogous to the canary that early miners used to determine whether shafts contained poisonous gases; she warns humans of the logical, unfortunate ends that follow from their actions. Forché, as poet, calls on world citizens to remember and, when appropriate, to atone, or else risk the worst that is "yet to come."

This American poet's commitment to depict the individual's struggle with the results of social upheaval and political turmoil has taken her from El Salvador to the occupied West Bank, to Lebanon, and to South Africa. Her poetry reflects her persistent and enduring efforts to document human tragedy at its core and thereby to reveal the horrifying reality of political decisions made in boardrooms and at the ballot box. Because the ordinary citizens who become the victims of those political decisions are silenced, Forché's imaginative verse bears witness both to the indignity of their experiences and to the dignity of their lives. In a poem from *The Angel of History*, the poet writes of a world that has lost its soul. Forché's work is more than a search for that lost soul; it is reclamation of the souls of the innocent.

Website

Poet's website at George Mason University: http://mason.gmu.edu/~cforchem

Poetry

The Recording Angel. 1994.
Against Forgetting: Twentieth-Century Poetry of Witness. New York: W.W. Norton, 1991.
"A Lesson in Commitment." *Tri-Quarterly* (Winter 1986).
El Salvador: Work of Thirty Photographers (text). Ed. Harry Mattison and Susan Meiselas. New York: Writers and Readers, 1983.
The Country Between Us. Port Townsend, WA: Copper Canyon Press, 1981.
"El Salvador: An Aide Memoire," *American Poetry Review* (July/August 1981).

Translations

Flowers from the Volcano. Translations of the poetry of Claribel Alegría. Pittsburgh: University of Pittsburgh Press, 1982.
The Selected Poems of Robert Desnos. Trans. Carolyn Forché and William Kulik. New York: Ecco Press, 1991.

References and Suggested Reading

Montenegro, David. "Carolyn Forché: An Interview." In *Points of Departure: International Writers on Writing and Politics.* Ed. David Montenegro. Ann Arbor: University of Michigan Press, 1992.
Shayne, Julie D. *The Revolution Question: Feminisms in El Salvador, Chile, and Cuba.* New Brunswick, NJ: Rutgers University Press, 2004.
"Yale's Younger Poets: Chester Kerr, Stanley Kunitz, Carolyn Forché." *Book Forum 2* (1976): p. 3

Robert Frost
(1874–1963)

Robert Frost. Courtesy of Photofest.

When Frost was eleven years old, his father died, and the family relocated from the moderate, cosmopolitan temperature and environment of San Francisco, California, to the harsh winters and rural environment of Lawrence, Massachusetts. It was during his high-school years that Frost began to explore his interest in poetry. That interest continued throughout his period of study at Dartmouth and at Harvard. However, Frost left both institutions without earning a degree from either. After leaving college, he gained employment as a teacher, as a cobbler, and as editor of the Lawrence *Sentinel*. He also operated a farm in Derry, New Hampshire, and taught at Derry's Pinkerton Academy. His first poem, "My Butterfly," was written during this period and subsequently published in a New York journal, *The Independent*. Although Frost wrote other poetry at this time during his various stints at odd jobs, with few exceptions he rarely published his work.

However, in 1912, at the age of thirty-eight, he sold the farm bequeathed him by his paternal grandparents and used the proceeds from the sale to relocate to London. *A Boy's Will* was accepted by a London publisher within a year of his relocation; the following year, Frost released *North of Boston*. Frost's relocation to London was temporary; however, while in London, he established a friendship with the poet and essayist Ezra Pound, who helped Frost to promote and publish his work. Frost received favorable reviews for his work both in England and in America, thereby establishing his transatlantic reputation. Immediately after the publication of *North of Boston*, Frost purchased a farm in Franconia, New Hampshire, and from this location continued to write and publish poetry before moving on to South Shaftsbury, Vermont. In 1924, Frost received a Pulitzer Prize in poetry for *New Hampshire*, and between 1930 and 1942 he received the Pulitzer three more times, for *Collected Poems, A Further Range*, and *A Witness Tree.* During this period, he also received other literary, academic, and public honors.

The depth and breadth of Frost's contributions to American literature secure his place as one of America's leading poets of any century. Indeed, a new museum that opened in South Shaftsbury in 2002 to honor Frost attests to his popularity as an American poet. Frost lived in South Shaftsbury for approximately nine years; there he composed many of the pieces that became part of his first Pulitzer Prize–winning volume *New Hampshire*, including the widely read poem "Stopping by Woods on a Snowy Evening." Permanent as well as special educational and literary exhibits housed at the museum offer visitors a chance to discover Frost's varied interests and to relate those interests to themes found in his poetry. For example, a special exhibit, titled "The Flowers of Robert Frost," explores the poet's interest in botany; another exhibit, "Robert Frost: Poetry, Prowess and Play," explores Frost's interest in sports.

Frost is often described as a pastoral poet who uses traditional verse forms to display a genuineness of thought and feeling as well as a longing for the simple, or country, life as opposed to a desire for the city life. Frost's poetry is described as visionary for its focus on future possibilities rather than on present impossibilities. The poet uses conventional rhyme and meter coupled with everyday speech to produce poems that are at once traditional and avant-garde; Frost often infuses his poetry with lyrical verse, dramatic conversation, and ironic commentary. Although Frost may be better known for certain celebrated poems, his work is not limited to a single theme or context. Frost wrote as a poet possessed of a keen eye, a steady hand, and an unwavering commitment to discovery.

Website

"Academy of American Poets." http://www.poets.org

Poetry

Robert Frost's Poems. New York: Henry Holt, 1971.
The Poetry of Robert Frost. New York: Henry Holt, 1979.

References and Suggested Reading

Brunshaw, Stanley, *Robert Frost Himself.* New York: George Braziller, 1989.

DeFusco, Andrea, ed. *Readings on Robert Frost.* San Diego, CA: Greenhaven, 1999.

Faggen, Robert. *Robert Frost and the Challenge of Darwin.* Ann Arbor: University of Michigan Press, 1997.

Fleissner, Robert F. *Frost's Road Taken.* New York: Peter Lang, 1996.

Hall, Dorothy J. *Robert Frost: Contours of Belief.* Athens: Ohio University Press, 1984.

Kilcup, Karen L. *Robert Frost and Feminine Literary Tradition.* Ann Arbor: University of Michigan Press, 1998.

Lakritz, Andrew M. *Modernism and the Other in Stevens, Frost, and Moore.* Gainesville: University Press of Florida, 1996.

Meyers, Jeffrey. *Robert Frost: A Biography.* Boston: Houghton, Mifflin, 1996.

Monteiro, George. *Robert Frost & the New England Renaissance.* Lexington: University Press of Kentucky, 1988.

Oster, Judith. *Toward Robert Frost: The Reader and the Poet.* Athens: University of Georgia Press, 1991.

Parini, Jay. *Robert Frost: A Life.* New York: Holt, 1999.

Potter, James L. *Robert Frost Handbook.* University Park: Pennsylvania State University Press, 1980.

Pritchard, William H. *Frost: A Literary Life Reconsidered.* New York: Oxford University Press, 1984.

Rotella, Guy. *Reading and Writing Nature: The Poetry of Robert Frost, Wallace Stevens, Marianne Moore, and Elizabeth Bishop.* Boston: Northeastern University Press, 1991.

Van Egmond, Peter. *The Critical Reception of Robert Frost.* Boston: G. K. Hall, 1974.

Wagner-Martin, Linda, ed. *Robert Frost: The Critical Reception.* New York: B. Franklin, 1977.

Nikki Giovanni
(1943–)

Nikki Giovanni. Courtesy of Photofest.

The writer affectionately known as Nikki Giovanni was born Yolande Cornelia Giovanni, Jr., on June 7, 1943, in Knoxville, Tennessee, the daughter of Yolande Cornelia and Jones Giovanni. Her sister, Gary Ann, was approximately three years old at the time of Yolande's birth. Knoxville was the home of Giovanni's maternal grandparents, and when she was two months old, her immediate family relocated to her father's hometown, Cincinnati, Ohio, where her parents were employed as house parents at Glenview School, a home for black boys. During this time, Gary Ann Giovanni began calling her younger sister *Nikki*, the name that would one day introduce this American poet to the world.

Soon after the family moved to Cincinnati, they relocated again to Woodlawn, a suburb of Cincinnati that did not permit black children to enroll in its schools. At this time, Gary Ann was sent to live with her uncle in Columbus, where she attended second grade. However, by the time Nikki was to begin kindergarten, her family moved again, this time to Wyoming, another suburb of Cincinnati. Nikki began kindergarten and her sister began third grade in Wyoming, but by the time Nikki matriculated to third grade, her family moved yet again. Her parents purchased a home in the black suburb of Lincoln Heights, where her mother had accepted a position teaching third grade at an all-black Episcopal school. Readers may well suppose that the frequent relocations that characterized Giovanni's early years resulted in her tendency to act out. In an admittedly autobiographical poem titled "Nikki Rosa," the poet pleads with biographers not to try to interpret her young life, admonishing them that many of the events in her life could not be understood from the perspective of one outside her close-knit family.

Whatever turmoil the frequent relocations may have caused the young Giovanni were more than mitigated by the supportive and nurturing relationships the young poet shared with her immediate family and with her maternal grandparents, all of whom encouraged the sisters to be self-determining. When Nikki was twelve years old, she walked out of class in protest after a teacher made a negative comment on the death of Emmett Till. About the same time, her sister Gary became one of three black students to desegregate a previously all-white school. Still, there may be evidence that Nikki sought a calmer, friendlier environment than the one she found in Lincoln Heights. When she was ready to enter high school, the young woman returned to Knoxville to live with her grandparents and enrolled in the same high school where her grandfather had once taught. Giovanni's grandparents both stabilized her world and nurtured her blossoming knowledge regarding her own duty to work against social injustice. While a student in high school, Giovanni secured her grandparents' permission to participate in a protest against segregated dining facilities at a Knoxville department store.

Giovanni's intellect, compassion, and commitment soon came to the attention of her teachers. An English teacher persuaded her to apply for early admission to college and she was accepted into Fisk University at age seventeen. However, Giovanni was not the model student that the Dean had in mind. While her academic achievement was never a problem for administrators, her ideas about the behavior and attitudes appropriate for young women were in direct opposition to those fostered by at least one Dean, and after a few incidents in which she expressed her personal independence, she was expelled.

After leaving Fisk, Giovanni returned to her parents' home, took a job at Walgreens, enrolled in classes at the University of Cincinnati, and otherwise occupied herself with volunteer work. Her grandfather died when she was nineteen years old, and soon afterward her grandmother was forced to move from her home. About this time, Giovanni returned to Fisk to determine her eligibility for reenrollment. She was reaccepted at the school in the fall of 1964 when she was twenty-one years old. At Fisk the second time

around, the young woman majored in history, and not only did she perform well academically, she also became a leader on campus. In addition to
attending writers' workshops where she met the poets Dudley Randall,
Melvin Tolson, Margaret Walker, and Amiri Baraka, Giovanni edited a student literary journal, published an essay on gender and the civil rights
movement in the *Negro Digest*, and reestablished the campus chapter of the
Student Nonviolent Coordinating Committee (SNCC).

Giovanni graduated from Fisk with honors; shortly after her graduation, Giovanni's grandmother died. This American poet's young life was
punctuated in equal measure by joy and grief, failure and accomplish-
ment. In this regard she is no different from any of us. Still, poets often
subsume grief in the craft, in the comfort verse affords. Poets often
attempt to drown the self in the page and thus imagine recovery of what
has been lost. Indeed, Giovanni responded to her grandmother's death
by writing poetry; she completed most of the poems that made up her
first volume, *Black Feeling, Black Talk*, a repository of her childhood, its
dreams as well as its visions. During this period, Giovanni also edited
Conversation, a Cincinnati revolutionary art journal, and attended the
Detroit Conference of Unity and Art, where she met Jamil Abdullah Al-
Amin, formerly H. Rap Brown. She organized Cincinnati's first Black
Arts Festival and then relocated to Wilmington, Delaware, and enrolled
in the University of Pennsylvania's School of Social Work. However,
within a year, Giovanni had dropped out of college, and she began to
focus her energies on publishing the text she completed after her grandmother's death.

Giovanni received a grant from the National Endowment for the Arts
and moved to New York City, where she enrolled in an Master of Fine Arts
program at Columbia University. At the conclusion of her first year in New
York, Giovanni used the money she made from sales of *Black Feeling, Black
Talk* and a grant from the Harlem Arts Council to publish her second volume of poetry, *Black Judgment*. In 1970, she established a publishing company, NikTom, Ltd, and published *Night Comes Softly*, an early anthology
highlighting poetry by black women; soon afterward *Ebony Magazine*
named her its Woman of the Year.

Giovanni continued to write and publish poetry, and she began as well
to collaborate with other artists to produce recordings of poetry. Her collection of poems for children, *Spin a Soft Black Song*, was published in 1971,
about the same time that she recorded *Truth Is on Its Way* with the New
York Community Choir. Boston University approached her about housing
her papers and she accepted; currently all of her papers and memorabilia
are housed at the Mugar Library on the Boston campus.

In 1989, Giovanni accepted a position as tenured Full Professor of English at Virginia Tech. In an effort to help students at the school to understand the social, political, and aesthetic importance of the Harlem Renaissance, rather than simply introducing her students to the literature and authors of the period, she taught them to organize a rent party, a community event routinely held during the Harlem Renaissance as a way to raise rent for a deserving, but out of luck, person. Giovanni continues to lecture on campuses across the country.

Websites

Nikki Giovanni's home page: http://nikki-giovanni.com
An interview with the poet: http://www.writerswrite.com

Poetry

Black Judgment. Detroit: Broadside Press, 1968.
Re: creation. Detroit: Broadside Press, 1970.
Spin a Soft Black Song; Poems for Children. Illustrated by Charles Bible. New York: Hill and Wang, 1971.
My House. New York: William Morrow, 1974.
Black Feeling, Black Talk. New York: William Morrow, 1980.
Cotton Candy on a Rainy Day. New York: William Morrow, 1980.
Ego-Tripping and Other Poems for Young People. Chicago: Lawrence Hill Books, 1993.
The Selected Poems of Nikki Giovanni: 1986–1995. New York: William Morrow, 1996.
Love Poems. New York: William Morrow, 1997.
Blues: For All the Changes. New York: William Morrow, 1999.

Nonfiction

Gemini: An Extended Autobiographical Statement on My First Twenty-Five Years of Being a Black Poet. Indianapolis: Bobbs-Merrill, 1972.
A Poetic Equation: Conversations between Nikki Giovanni and Margaret Walker. Washington, DC: Howard University Press, 1974.
The Women and the Men. New York: William Morrow, 1975.
Those Who Ride the Night Winds. New York: William Morrow, 1983.
Knoxville, Tennessee. Illustrated by Larry Johnson. New York: Scholastic, 1994.
Racism 101. North Hampshire: Quill, 1995.
The Genie in the Jar. Illustrated by Chris Raschka. New York: H. Holt, 1996.

Recordings

The Reason I Like Chocolate and Other Children's Poems. Washington, DC: Smithsonian Folkways Records.

References and Suggested Reading

Adoff, Arnold, and Benny Andrews. *I Am the Darker Brother: An Anthology of Modern Poems by African Americans.* New York: Simon & Schuster, 1997.

Gibson, Donald B., ed. *Modern Black Poets; A Collection of Critical Essays.* Englewood Cliffs, NJ: Prentice Hall, 1973.

King, Woodie., ed. *BlackSpirits: A Festival of New Black Poets in America.* Artistic consultant Imamu Amiri Baraka, foreword by Nikki Giovanni, introduction by Don L. Lee. New York: Random House, 1972.

Smith, Jessie C., ed. *Images of Blacks in American Culture: A Reference Guide to Information Sources.* Foreword by Nikki Giovanni. Westport, CT: Greenwood Press, 1988.

Mel Glenn
(1943-)

If the voices of the characters in Mel Glenn's poetry are convincing, it may be because Glenn himself considers his thirty-one years as a high-school English teacher in Brooklyn as the training ground for his literary career. In his nine full-length works of poetry, Glenn captures the tone and the spirit of young people entering adulthood, and all the delight and misery of that growth.

Glenn was born Melvyn Haskell Glenn in May 1943 in Zurich, Switzerland, to Jacob and Elizabeth Glenn. The family moved to New York City in 1946 and settled in Brooklyn. Throughout his childhood, Glenn saw his father, a physician, write. The senior Glenn was also a Biblical scholar and wrote articles in Yiddish for a local periodical.

Growing up in the shadow of Coney Island, playing baseball, stickball, and basketball on local fields and courts, Glenn developed an early love for sports. He has described himself as a teen as being serious and quiet. He spent summers working at Coney Island and played high school tennis. After Glenn graduated from Brooklyn's Abraham Lincoln High School, where he would later teach for more than three decades, he matriculated in English at New York University, where he also wrote sports columns for the school newspaper. He enjoyed journalism and traveling with the sports teams to cover events.

Inspired by the words of the late President John F. Kennedy and by his burgeoning interest in travel, Glenn joined the Peace Corps following his college graduation in 1964. He taught English and history classes in Sierra Leone from 1964 through 1966, living in sparse quarters and impressed by the respect and passion for education he found among the local youth. Once back in the United States, Glenn completed his master's degree at New York's Yeshiva University. He spent a few years teaching middle school, then returned to Lincoln High, where he remained until his retirement in June 2001. Since leaving the public school system, Glenn has focused on full-time writing and speaking engagements and has taught at Vermont College's summer writing program.

Although Glenn always had an interest in writing, it was a dare posed by his wife that got him to seriously consider pursuing publication. Upon hearing her husband criticize a colleague's manuscript, Elyse Glenn asked whether he could do better. A 1979 New Year's resolution followed, and Glenn began writing a poem or two each day. The result was *Class Dismissed!* (1982), which featured seventy poems, each in the voice of a different high-school student. Together, the poems formed a composite of verbal snapshots in a cross section of a fictional inner-city high school. Tower High is the setting of nearly all of Glenn's poetic works. The book was awarded the Society of Children's Book Writers and Illustrators Golden Kite Award, and it appeared on the American Library Association's short list of Best Books for Young Adults.

Glenn went on to write two novels for intermediate readers before returning to poetry with the 1986 collection *Class Dismissed II*, which followed the same format as its predecessor. *Class Dismissed II* received the Christopher Award and was chosen as one of *School Library Journal's* Best Books of 1986 as well as for another American Library Association (ALA) posting. *Back to Class* (1988) and *My Friend's Got This Problem, Mr. Candler* (1991) added the voices of teachers to those of students.

In his work, Glenn reaches out to young people, expressing both the uniqueness of individuals and the universalities of the high-school experience. A sense of longing pervades all of his works, expressing the needs of young people to be noticed, to blend in, to be affirmed. As in the lives of real teens, the characters' worlds are dramatic and immediate. Through tightly worded poems that blend poignancy and humor, Glenn strips away the swagger and bravado of some and gives voice to others whose voices are layered in insecurities; he never compromises in showing the underside of being young in a time and place where messages can be mixed and expectations high. The voices of parents range from overprotective to abusive.

It is this recognition that, even at the age of fifteen or sixteen, young peoples' lives already have such intricacy—and that they sometimes already bear scars—that makes Glenn such a credible voice for this age group, allowing readers to recognize themselves in clear and startling ways. Glenn chips away at labels, those assigned to students and teachers alike. His poems show compassion and sensitivity and assure young readers that they are not alone in their frustrations, their dreams, and their struggles with the mundane and the remarkable.

Website

"Mel Glenn." *Authors4Teens*, http://www.authors4teens.com

Poetry

Class Dismissed! High School Poems. Michael J. Bernstein, photographer. Boston: Clarion, 1982.

Class Dismissed II: More High School Poems. Michael J. Bernstein, photographer. Boston: Clarion, 1982.

Back to Class. Michael J. Bernstein, photographer. Boston: Clarion, 1989.

My Friend's Got This Problem, Mr. Candler: High School Poems. Michael Bernstein, photographer. Boston: Clarion, 1991.

Foreign Exchange: A Mystery in Poems. New York: Morrow Junior, 1999.

Split Image: A Story in Poems. New York: HarperCollins, 2000.

Fiction

One Order to Go. Boston: Clarion, 1984.

Play-by-Play. Boston: Clarion, 1986.

Squeeze Play: A Baseball Story. Boston: Clarion, 1989.

References and Suggested Reading

Lesesne, Teri S. "Mel Glenn." In *Writers for Young Adults, Supplement I.* Ed. Ted Hipple. New York: Charles Scribner's Sons, Literature Resource Center, 2000.

Nikki Grimes
(1950–)

Nikki Grimes is the quintessential village griot, or storyteller; but her village is global and its citizens a multihued populace. And not unlike the oral poetry of the traditional village, Grimes's verse reflects far more than simple recitations of a humorous event; her efforts fix her in the tradition of poets who function equally as storytellers and as historians. Of course, most imaginative verse has its roots in oral traditions. Once written, imaginative verse contains both the contradiction and the beauty of language. The work of poets such as Grimes points to the existence of an oral literature and to words that remain unwritten and thus changeable, making their verse as much malleable as it is an instance of historical recording. In this way, poets encourage their audiences to join in a recreation both of history and of their place in its making.

In her role as oral historian and poet, Grimes records the daily events in the lives of the people she observes and relates those events to larger themes of community, family, and personal relationships. Grimes has produced more than thirty children's books, whose themes, for the most part, reflect the importance of literacy as well as family values. Perhaps it is for this reason that Grimes's verse is immediately familiar to readers. And although her work is uplifting, Grimes's verse is just as often didactic in its recitations of loss, renewal, despair, and joy. Grimes records the child's song; its cadences and its dreams of becoming are reflected in verse that, while dealing with moments of heartbreak, is never remorseful but is often both poignant and magical.

Born in Harlem, the young poet wrote her first poem when she was approximately six years old. At that time, she lived with a foster family in Ossining, New York, after having been removed from her mother's supervision. In recounting her stays with various foster families with whom she lived for approximately four years, Grimes recalls her Ossining family with gratitude and joy. And although she rejoined her mother when she was ten years old, Grimes keeps in touch with members of her Ossining foster family. Her experiences as a foster child no doubt influenced the focus of her work: Grimes's poetry is concerned with things that are important to all children, whether the issue is what it means to be the new kid on the block or what it means to receive a longed-for gift on one's birthday.

An accomplished poet and storyteller, Grimes is internationally recognized and has presented poetry readings and lectures to audiences in the United States, Russia, China, Sweden, Tanzania, and Haiti. Her collections of poetry include *Is It Far to Zanzibar?: Poems About Tanzania; It's Raining Laughter: Poems; A Pocketful of Poems; Under the Christmas Tree;* and *Meet Danitra Brown.* Grimes has been winning awards for her poetry since she was a little girl. In addition to early awards for poetry, Grimes has also received an American Library Association Notable Book Award and a Coretta Scott King Award. Grimes has also won several awards for her fiction; she received an American Bookseller Pick of the List for *Aneesa Lee and The Weaver's Gift,* and she received a National Association for the Advancement of Colored People (NAACP) award for her young adult biography of Malcolm X.

A gifted and talented writer who works in several genres, Grimes has written a collection of children's prayers and has co-produced and hosted a children's television show, *The Kid's Show,* in New York. During a six-year stay in Sweden, where she is referred to as a singer who also writes, Grimes hosted a radio program for immigrants, and she hosted a second program for Swedish Educational Radio. More recently, in November 2005, Nikki Grimes was honored for her work at the Books for Children Luncheon sponsored by the National Council for the Teachers of English during its annual convention.

Website

Poet's home page: http://www.nikkigrimes.com

Poetry

Pooh: Oh, Brother! Someone's Fighting. New York: Golden Books, 1991.
Minnie 'n Me: Minnie's New Friend. New York: Western, 1992.
Pooh: Oh, Brother! Someone Won't Share. New York: Golden Books, 1993.
Cinderella. New York: Western, 1993.
Something on My Mind. New York: Penguin Group, 1995.

Growin'. New York: Penguin Group, 1995.
Baby's Bedtime. New York: Golden Books, 1996.
Come Sunday. Grand Rapids, MI: Eerdman's Books for Young Children, 1996.
A Dime a Dozen. New York: Dial Books for Young Readers, 1998.
Hopscotch Love. New York: Lothrop, Lee, & Sheppard, 1998.
At Break of Day. Grand Rapids, MI: Eerdman's Books for Young Children, 1999.
My Man Blue. New York: Dial Books for Young Readers, 1999.
Jazmin's Notebook. New York: Puffin, 2000.
Portrait of Mary. New York: Diane, 2001.
Danitra Brown Leaves Town. New York: HarperCollins, 2001.
Masquerade. New York: Dial Books for Young Readers, 2002.
Talkin' about Bessie. New York: Scholastic, 2002.
What Is Goodbye? New York: Hyperion Books for Young Children, 2002.
When Daddy Prays. Grand Rapids, MI: Eerdman's Books for Young Children, 2002.
Wild, Wild Hair. New York: Book Wholesalers, 2002.
Shoe Magic. New York: Scholastic, 2002.
On the Road to Paris. New York: Penguin Group, 2003.
C Is for City. Honesdale, PA: Boyds Mills Press, 2003.
Just for You!: A Day with Daddy. New York: Scholastic, 2004.
Tai Chi Morning: Snapshots of China. New York: Cricket Books, 2004.
At Jerusalem's Gate. Grand Rapids, MI: Eerdman's Books for Young Children, 2004.

References and Suggested Reading

Avery, Gillian. *Everyman Anthology of Poetry for Children.* New York: Everyman's Library, 1994.
Brinnin, John Malcolm. *Twentieth Century Poetry: American and British: 1900–1970, An American British Anthology.* New York: McGraw-Hill, 1970.
Hall, Donald. *Contemporary American Poetry: Revised and Expanded Second Edition.* New York: Penguin, 1989.
Harrison, Michael, and Christopher Stuart-Clark. *One Hundred Years of Poetry for Children.* New York: Oxford University Press, 2000.
Hoover, Paul. *Postmodern American Poetry: A Norton Anthology.* New York: W.W. Norton, 1994.
Hudson, Wade, and Floyd Cooper. *Pass It On: African American Poetry.* New York: Scholastic Press, 1993.
Koch, Kenneth. *Rose, Where Did You Get That Red? Teaching Great Poetry to Children.* New York: Vintage Books, 1974.
Miller, E. Ethelbert. *Beyond the Frontier: African American Poetry for the 21st Century.* Baltimore, MD: Black Classic Press, 2002.
Prelutsky, Jack, ed. Illustrated by Arnold Lobel. *The Random House Book of Poetry for Children.* New York: Random House Books for Young Readers, 2000.
Rampersad, Arnold, and Hilary Herbold. *The Oxford Anthology of African-American Poetry.* New York: Oxford University Press, 2005.

Jessica Tarahata Hagedorn (1949-)

Hagedorn is an American poet who also finds expression for her creativity in the multimedia and performing arts. A mixed-race woman of Filipino, Latino, and Asian ancestry, she immigrated to the United States from the Philippines when she was thirteen years old. Both Spanish and Asian influence on Filipino culture can be found in that country's music, dance, language, and cuisine. In fact, Hagedorn reports being pleased to discover as an adult that a Filipino dance she learned as a child was still being practiced in some rural areas of Spain. The mixtures of cultures, languages, and identities amuse and amaze Hagedorn. She attempts to explore the particulars of each of her cultural and ethnic identities and to synthesize them in her work. And she often does so in remarkably inventive ways: her poetry is an eclectic concoction of Latin and African beats with haiku-like verses interspersed among free verse and the jagged rhythm of a rock and roll beat.

By the time Hagedorn was sixteen, she had come to the attention of an artist in San Francisco, who helped her to find outlets for her work and who subsequently edited the first anthology featuring her poetry. However, Hagedorn began writing long before she was a teenager. In interviews, she has described herself as a "dramatic" child who wrote poems and created comic books that she also illustrated. Her mother gave the young Hagedorn a typewriter when she was fourteen, shortly after the girl had been uprooted in the middle of the school year to immigrate to the United States. Hagedorn's mother, aware of her daughter's love affair with language, no doubt gave her the typewriter both in an effort to encourage the blossoming poet and to ease the disruption of her life and the subsequent adjustment to a new life in an unfamiliar country.

However; Hagedorn does not appear to have had any problems acclimating to life in the United States. Her interest in films was ignited in the Philippines, where she was a frequent patron of the movie houses. Once in San Francisco, her interest in the performing arts led her to take acting lessons. Hagedorn also wrote song lyrics for a band, and she performed with that band for several years. Not surprisingly, she also collaborated with Ntozake Shange to produce *Where the Mississippi Meets the Amazon*, a union of poetry and theater.

Hagedorn's work has broad appeal, reflected in its acceptance by African American, Latino, Asian, and mainstream audiences. Young readers discover themselves, or a neighbor, in Hagedorn's imaginative verse. And although she uses a language that is often so specific and contextual as to require a footnote, the intent of her language usage is always clear. Her work is often coded in the hybrid language she calls Tag-lish, which is a combination of her first language, Tagalog, and of her second language, English; however, young readers quickly decipher the code because the verse this poet writes transforms into stories that incite her readers' imagination.

Hagedorn's imaginative verse is a creative exploration embracing themes of racial, ethnic, and cultural identities, and her observations are often humorous and set to a jazz beat reminiscent of the poetry of the Black Arts movement of the 1960s. Hagedorn's poetry is both contemporary and hip; her poems are contradictions set to rhyme that embody a glorious mixture of cultures, languages, and identities.

Hagedorn is one of several distinguished American poets who elected not to attend college. In Hagedorn's case, she has opted thus far to forgo university training in lieu of practical training in her art forms. In this regard, she is similar to the poet Carl Sandburg, who worked a host of jobs in an effort to broaden his experiences and thereby inform his craftsmanship. Certainly, the practical education Hagedorn gained at the American Conservatory Theater, where she completed a two-year acting and theater arts program, finds ready expression in her poetry.

Website

"Voices From the Gaps, Women Artists and Writers of Color." http://voices.cla.umn.edu/VG/index.html

Poetry

Danger and Beauty. New York: Penguin, 1993.

Fiction

Dogeaters. New York: Penguin, 1990.
The Gangster of Love. New York: Penguin, 1996.
Dream Jungle. New York: Viking, 2003.

Nonfiction

Charlie Chan Is Dead: An Anthology of Contemporary Asian American Fiction (editor). New York: Penguin, 1993.
"Music for Gangsters and (Other) Chameleons." *Stars Don't Stand Still in the Sky: Music and Myth* (1999).
Burning Heart: A Portrait of the Philippines. Photographs by Marissa Roth. New York: Rizzoli, 1999.

References and Suggested Reading

Bloom, Harold, ed. *A Review of Asian American Women Writers.* Philadelphia: Chelsea House, 1997.
Bonetti, Kay. "An Interview with Jessica Hagedorn." *Missouri Review 18.1* (1995).
Davidson, Cathy N., and Linda Wagner-Martin, eds. *The Oxford Companion to Women's Writing in the United States.* New York: Oxford University Press, 1995.
Doyle, Jacqueline. "'A Love Letter to My Motherland': Maternal Discourses in Jessica Hagedorn's Dogeaters." *Hitting Critical Mass: A Journal of Asian-American Cultural Criticism 4.2* (Summer 1997): pp. 1–25.
Francia, Luis H., and Eric Gamalinda. "A Review of Flippin': Filipinos on America." New York: Asian American Writers' Workshop, 1996.
Geok-lin Lim, Shirley, ed. *The Forbidden Stitch: An Asian American Women's Anthology.* Corvallis, OR: Calyx, 1989.
Hongo, Garrett. *The Open Boat: Poems from Asian America.* New York: Anchor, 1993.

Donald Hall
(1928-)

Donald Hall. Courtesy of Photofest.

Donald Hall was born in New Haven, Connecticut, the only child of businessman Donald Andrew Hall and his wife, Lucy. He began writing poems and short stories before his teens; later he began to write novels and dramatic verse. An introspective and quiet young man, Hall was influenced by the nineteenth-century poet Edgar Allan Poe; he has described Poe as the poet he most wanted to emulate in his own verse.

As a young man, Hall was presented with several opportunities to have his efforts recognized and encouraged. When he was only sixteen years old, Hall attended the Bread Loaf Writers' Conference, which is renowned for its annual gathering of well-known and respected writers. There he met the poet Robert Frost. After high school, Hall attended Harvard University, where he served on the editorial board of *The Harvard Advocate*. There he met writers John Ashbery, Robert Bly, Kenneth Koch, Frank O'Hara, and Adrienne Rich.

Hall earned a BA from Harvard in 1951 and a B. Litt. from Oxford in 1953. While at Oxford, he edited *The Fantasy Poets*, in which he published the work of poets Thom Gunn and Geoffrey Hill. He also served as editor of the Oxford Poetry Society's journal and as poetry editor of *The Paris*

Review. Hall received Oxford's prestigious Newdigate Prize for his poem "Exile."

Upon returning to the United States, Hall spent one year as a Creative Writing fellow at Stanford University. Following that year, he returned to Harvard and spent the next three years editing an anthology, *The New Poets of England and America*, and putting together his collection of poetry, *Exiles and Marriages*. Shortly afterward, in 1957, Hall was appointed to the faculty of the University of Michigan at Ann Arbor. While teaching at the University of Michigan in Ann Arbor, Hall met the poet Jane Kenyon, whom he married in 1972. Within three years after they married, the couple moved to Hall's maternal grandparent's former home, Eagle Pond Farm, located in Wilmot, New Hampshire. Unfortunately, life on his ancestor's homeland was colored by illnesses—both his own and Jane's. In 1989, Hall was diagnosed with colon cancer; by 1992 the cancer had invaded his liver. After a series of operations, his cancer went into remission; however, Jane died of complications from leukemia during the same time.

Hall is one of America's leading poets, and he has written not only several books of poetry but also twenty-two books of prose. Many of his publications have been with academic presses, making his texts readily accessible to students and teachers at the primary, secondary, and tertiary levels of education. Furthermore, his poems appeal to a wide audience. In addition to his poems about loss, such as those included in *Without*, published on the third anniversary of the death of his wife, Jane. Hall also writes about nature, about the human experience, and about the relationship between the two in poems such as "Sudden Things".

Hall's poetry and prose have garnered recognition and awards. *The One Day*, published in 1988, won the National Book Critics Circle Award, the Los Angeles Times Book Prize, and a Pulitzer Prize nomination. *The Happy Man*, published in 1986, won the Lenore Marshall Poetry Prize, and *Exiles and Marriages*, published in 1955, won the Lamont Poetry Selection Prize. His more recent publications include *The Painted Bed*, which was published by Houghton Mifflin in 2002.

In addition to poetry and prose, Hall has published several autobiographical works, including *Life Work* which won the 1993 New England Book Award for nonfiction. From 1957 until 1990, he edited more than two dozen textbooks and anthologies, including *The Oxford Book of Children's Verse in America*, *The Oxford Book of American Literary Anecdotes*, *The New Poets of England and America*, and *Contemporary American Poetry*. Hall's dedication to producing quality texts for readers has resulted in stints as the poetry editor of *The Paris Review* and as a member of the editorial board for poetry at Wesleyan University Press.

Hall is a prolific author who has supported himself most of his life by writing. He has written poetry, reviews, criticism, textbooks, sports journalism, memoirs, biographies, children's stories, and plays. He has also devoted time to editing; between 1983 and 1996 he oversaw publication of more than sixty titles for the University of Michigan Press alone. At one point in his career, biographers estimated that Hall was publishing a minimum of one item per week and four books a year, securing his place as one of the more widely read writers in American letters.

Websites

"Academy of American Poets." http://www.poets.org
"Poem Hunter." http://www.poemhunter.com

Poetry

Exiles and Marriages. New York: Viking, 1955.
A Roof of Tiger Lilies. New York: Viking, 1964.
The Alligator Bride: Poems, New and Selected. New York: Harper & Row, 1969.
A Blue Wing Tilts at the Edge of the Sea: Selected Poems, 1964–1974. New York: Random House, 1975.
The Museum of Clear Ideas. Boston: Houghton Mifflin, 1996.
The Old Life. New York: Mariner, 1996.
Without. New York: Mariner, 1998.
The Painted Bed. Boston: Houghton Mifflin, 2002.

References and Suggested Reading

Braham, Jeanne. *Light Within the Light: Portraits of Donald Hall, Richard Wilbur, Maxine Kumin, and Stanley Kunitz.* Boston: David R. Godine, 2005.
Hamilton, Ian. *Donald Hall in Conversation with Ian Hamilton.* London: Between the Lines, 2000.
Ratiner, Steven. "Work That Builds a Sense of Home: An interview with Donald Hall." *Christian Science Monitor* (November 6, 1991).
Rector, Liam. *The Day I Was Older: On the Poetry of Donald Hall.* Santa Cruz, CA: Story Line Press, 1989.

Sara Holbrook
(1949–)

Sara Holbrook's poetry began with the simplest of inspirations: writing for her two daughters. Holbrook worked as a part-time teacher and as a writer in the public relations field before finding a new passion in poetry, both in print and in performance. Her books, which divide her poems by age and interest, appeal to the reluctant young reader as well as to those who are interested in dynamic pieces for slams. A noted public speaker, Holbrook manages to find the humor and pathos in the everyday sights and sounds of home, school, and young people's forays into the wider world.

Sara Holbrook, the older of two sisters, grew up in Berkley, Michigan, a suburb of Detroit. She attended school at Berkley Elementary, Anderson Junior High, and Berkley High School. Holbrook describes herself as having been a voracious reader but not a straight-A student, more a daydreamer than a young scholar. She went on to earn a B.A. in English at Mount Union College in Ohio, planning at the time to work as a reporter; her interest and training in journalism continues to influence her writing. Holbrook claims to use this approach to gather data, to report almost objectively, even in her poetry.

Holbrook began writing as a means of storytelling. Her first venture into poetry was writing in blank books for her daughters, Kelley and Katie, who then illustrated the poems. As Holbrook's children grew, so did the subject matter and sophistication of her poems. With her daughters approaching adulthood, Holbrook found that she had an impressive back-list of original work and decided to try self-publishing. Within a few years, Holbrook sold over 40,000 books in this way. Some of her works, such as *Feelings Make Me Real, The Dog Ate My Homework,* and *Some Families,* were published exclusively through private publications in 1990.

In 1995, Boyds Mills Press released *Nothing's the End of the World*, followed quickly by *Am I Naturally This Crazy?* and *Which Way to the Dragon! Poems for the Coming-on-Strong*. The poems in *The Dog Ate My Homework*, and *Nothing's the End of the World* center on the trials and triumphs of children in elementary school, written in accessible verse.

Which Way to the Dragons! handles many of the same issues, including friendships, anxieties, embarrassments, and frustrations, all in straightforward poems directed at a first through third grade audience, when the main frustration in a child's life is just getting adults to listen. *Am I Naturally This Crazy?* was written for children from third grade up, those Holbrook describes as beginning to question the world.

Kid Poems for the Not-So-Bad, first privately published in 1992, was released by Boyds Mills Press in 1997 as *I Never Said I Wasn't Difficult*. The title of this reissue summarizes the collective theme: middle-grade and middle-school students working through issues of identity, emotion, and image. With titles like "I Hate My Body," "Wrong," "Losing It," "Violence Hurts," "Popular," and the title piece, narrators answer offstage authority figures and pose questions without providing pat answers. The uncertainties and insecurities of defining the self contrast with simple rhyme schemes and rhythms.

In 2002, Holbrook released *Isn't She Ladylike*, meant for older readers. Holbrook captures the angst of adult audiences with the same blend of sentiment, humor, and edgy observations as in her works for younger readers. *Wham! It's a Poetry Jam: Discovering Performance Poetry* was also published in 2002. In *Wham!*, Holbrook gives instructions, advice, and guidelines for conducting, participating in, and judging child-friendly competitions—whams or jams instead of slams. The book features tips on public speaking and speech techniques as well as lists suggested pieces. Holbrook encourages incorporating body movements, call-and-response, and merging poems. Activities and poems run a wide gamut, across grade and age levels.

2003's *By Definition: Poems of Feelings* looks at universal and personal issues, putting verse to such figures as the "Voice of Authority" (complete with "fiery-red neck, marble blue eyes, demanding") and a host of intangibles such as hope, honesty, anger, pouting, luck, love, and jealousy. The yearning for recognition is still strong, as in the plea "Labels," which warns against trying to assign identity by any known ethnic or demographic tag. The humor is clear as Holbrook depicts the range of emotions almost as a landscape to be navigated, proposing that words can provide some tools for the traveler.

Holbrook implores educators to keep poetry in the hands of children as a way to keep self-expression alive in a world of mass communication. She reaches out to adolescents, in print and by visiting schools, and by participating in poetry slams and competitions that attract young readers. Holbrook works to keep words alive; a dynamic speaker, she writes poetry that speaks honestly and directly to her audiences, always encouraging readers and listeners to meet the challenges that face them.

Websites

Author website: www.saraholbrook.com
"Sara Holbrook." *Authors and Illustrators.* www.boydsmillspress.com

Poetry

Nothing's the End of the World. Illustrated by J. J. Smith-More. Honesdale, PA: Boyds Mills Press, 1995.
Am I Naturally This Crazy? Honesdale, PA: Boyds Mills Press, 1996.
Which Way to the Dragon! Poems from the Coming-on-Strong. Honesdale, PA: Boyds Mills Press, 1996.
The Dog Ate My Homework. Village, OH: Privately published, 1990; Honesdale, PA: Boyds Mills, 1996.
Kid Poems for the Not-So-Bad. Bay Village, OH: Privately published, 1992. Republished as *I Never Said I Wasn't Difficult.* Honesdale, PA: Boyds Mills Press, 1997.
Walking on the Boundaries of Change: Poems of Transition. Honesdale, PA: Boyds Mills Press, 1998.
Chicks Up Front. Cleveland, OH: Cleveland State University, 1998.
Wham! It's a Poetry Jam: Discovering Performance Poetry. Honesdale, PA: Boyds Mills Press, 2002.
Isn't She Ladylike. Mentor, OH: Collinwood Media, 2002.
By Definition. Honesdale, PA: Boyds Mills Press, 2003.

Picture Books and Chapbooks

Feelings Make Me Real. Bay Village, OH: Privately published, 1990.
Some Families. Bay Village, OH: Privately published, 1990.
What's So Big About Cleveland, Ohio? Illustrated by Ennis McNulty. Cleveland, OH: Gray & Co., 1997.

Nonfiction

Practical Poetry: A Nonstandard Approach to Meeting Content-Area Standards. Portsmouth, NH: Heinemann, 2005.

References and Suggested Reading

"Sara Holbrook." In *Journal of Adolescent and Adult Literacy.* International Reading Association, 1996–2003.

Lee Bennett Hopkins
(1938–)

As a child, Lee Bennett Hopkins had a rabid dislike of poetry—or at least the way his teacher taught poetry, by rote and line-by-line analysis. When he began working in the field of education, he was determined to get teachers to work with poetry in a way that would make children want to embrace it. As a poet and anthologist, he has made it his purpose to write, and to compile, works that would inspire passion for poetry in young readers.

Lee Bennett Hopkins was born in Scranton, Pennsylvania, on April 13, 1938, to Leon Hopkins, a police officer, and Gertrude Thomas Hopkins. Gertrude's family was very much a part of Hopkins's earliest years, and his maternal grandmother's love of reciting nursery rhymes provided his earliest memories of poetry. When the economy of Scranton plunged into its own depression in the years immediately following World War II, the Hopkins family, which now included younger siblings Donald and Donna Lea, moved to Newark, New Jersey.

It was a middle-school teacher named Mrs. McLaughlin who saw potential in the teen-aged Hopkins's writing, and she inspired what would become a lifelong love of theater and of reading. Hopkins became especially enamored of the novel *Little Women*, reading it over and over for a year. He found high school less than inspiring and frequently cut classes. His grades were mediocre, and he tolerated school with one goal in mind: he wanted to become a teacher who would inspire young people to write in the same way Mrs. McLaughlin had inspired him.

In 1956, Hopkins entered Newark State Teachers College, only to find that he had to make up for his years of poor study habits by enrolling in remedial courses. Once Hopkins was able to specialize in education, he excelled. Hopkins graduated in 1960 and headed for his first teaching position as a sixth-grade teacher at the Westmoreland School in suburban Fair Lawn, New Jersey. Hopkins quickly distinguished himself as dedicated and enthusiastic, and within three years he was reassigned to work as a resource teacher. He quickly established a small library for the school, and spent his days gathering resources and developing thematic lessons for classes from kindergarten to sixth grade.

Hopkins was also writing articles for a number of professional journals. He was convinced that children made immediate emotional connections with good poems and wanted teachers to get students to embrace poetry, not dissect it. Hopkins's first books, *Let Them Be Themselves: Language Arts Enrichment for Disadvantaged Children in Elementary Schools* (1969) and *Creative Activities for Gifted Children* (1969), were compilations of his own teaching approaches. In 1968, Scholastic Publishers hired Hopkins as a curriculum specialist and an editor. For his next major writing project, Hopkins interviewed two hundred authors and artists from the field of children's literature, including such prominent figures as Theodor Seuss Geisel ("Dr. Seuss") and E. B. White. These interviews were collected as *Books Are by People* (1969) and *More Books Are by People* (1974).

Hopkins was, at the same time, continuing his mission to connect teachers and students with a wealth of poems that would be exciting and accessible, while challenging readers with more than the light verse that made up much of teachers' classroom collections. He began collecting poems by themes, placing works by contemporary and emerging talents alongside pieces by some of the most recognizable figures in literature. Hopkins believed that some teachers underestimated their students' abilities to appreciate works by Sandburg, Hughes, or even Shakespeare if the poems were placed in the context of an overriding theme.

Hopkins also invited poets to contribute to the collections he had built, filling in gaps in themes with new poems or using outside sources as inspiration. He turned his own efforts to writing and began submitting original poems to small magazines. By 1970, he had released these as *This Street's for Me!*, a series about the streets of Harlem, followed quickly by *Faces and Places: Poems for You*. His original 1972 compilations *When I Am All Alone: A Book of Poems* and *Charlie's World: A Book of Poems* featured poems more personal in tone as Hopkins assumed the voice of the fictional Charlie, chronicling a child's world in verse.

The collections Hopkins edited were finding broad audiences as he varied his topics to appeal to readers from elementary through high school. He compiled poems by recovering addicts in *I Really Want to Feel Good About Myself* (1974) and poems by Pulitzer Prize winners in *Take Hold!* (1974). His use of poems that varied greatly in structure and complexity allowed teachers to use the books across grade and ability levels, including reluctant readers.

Although he continued to work as a compiler, Hopkins was becoming more interested in writing his own poetry. He left his job at Scholastic in 1976, moved from New York City to Westchester County, and immersed himself in reading and in producing thematic collections. By this time, his own poems usually appeared in the collections he produced.

Hopkins's work has received numerous accolades in the literary community, and his career has been acknowledged with an honorary doctorate from his college and the University of Southern Mississippi's Medallion, granted for lifetime achievement. In 1993, Hopkins established an award in his own name, to be given annually to a new talent in the field of poetry, either for compiling anthologies or for original writing.

Hopkins continues to write, and to compile children's and teen collections. He currently lives in Cape Coral, Florida, and remains a powerful voice in literature, both as author and through his lifelong drive to invigorate the use of poetry in classrooms and in children's and young adults' lives.

Website

"Lee Bennett Hopkins." www.HarperCollins.com

Poetry

Circus! Circus! Illustrated by John O'Brien. New York: Knopf, 1982.

Rainbows Are Made: Poems by Carl Sandburg. Illustrated by Fritz Eichenberg. New York: Harcourt, 1982.

A Dog's Life. Illustrated by Linda Rochester Richards. New York: Harcourt, 1983.

The Sky is Full of Song. Illustrated by Dirk Zimmer. New York: Harper, 1983.

A Song in Stone: City Poems. Illustrated by Anna Held Audette. New York: Crowell, 1983.

Crickets and Bullfrogs and Whispers of Thunder: Poems and Pictures by Harry Behn. New York: Harcourt, 1984.

Love and Kisses. Illustrated by Kris Boyd. Burlington, MA: Houghton, 1984.

Surprises: An "I Can Read" Book of Poems. Illustrated by Meagan Lloyd. New York: Harper, 1984.

Creatures. Illustrated by Stella Ormai. New York: Harcourt, 1985.

Munching: Poems about Eating. Illustrated by Nelle Davis. Boston: Little, Brown, 1985.

Best Friends. Illustrated by James Watts. New York: Harper, 1986.

The Sea is Calling Me. Illustrated by Walter Gaffney-Kessel. New York: Harcourt, 1986.

Click, Rumble, Roar: Poems about Machines. Illustrated by Anna Held Audette. New York: Crowell, 1987.

Dinosaurs. Illustrated by Murray Tinkelman. New York: Harcourt, 1987.

More Surprises: An "I Can Read" Book. Illustrated by Meagan Lloyd. New York: Harper, 1987.

Side by Side: Poems to Read Together. Illustrated by Hilary Knight. New York: Simon & Schuster, 1988.

Still as a Star: Nighttime Poems. Illustrated by Karen Malone. Boston: Little, Brown, 1988.

Good Books, Good Times! New York: Harper, 1990.

On the Farm. Illustrated by Laurel Molk. Boston: Little, Brown, 1991.

Happy Birthday: Poems. Illustrated by Hilary Knight. New York: Simon & Schuster, 1991.

Questions: An "I Can Read" Book. Illustrated by Carolyn Croll. New York HarperCollins, 1992.

Through Our Eyes: Poems and Pictures about Growing Up. Illustrated by Jeffrey Dunn. Boston: Little, Brown, 1992.

To the Zoo: Animal Poems. Illustrated by John Wallner. Boston: Little, Brown, 1992.

Ring Out, Wild Bells: Poems of the Holidays and Season. Illustrated by Karen Baumann. New York: Harcourt, 1992.

Pterodactyls and Pizza: A Trumpet Club Book of Poetry. Illustrated by Nadine Bernard Westcott. New York: Trumpet Club, 1992.

Flit, Flutter, Fly! Poems about Bugs and Other Crawly Creatures. Illustrated by Peter Palagonia. New York: Doubleday, 1992.

Ragged Shadows: Poems of Halloween Night. Illustrated by Giles Laroche. Boston: Little, Brown, 1993.

Extra Innings: Baseball Poems. Illustrated by Scott Medlock. New York: Harcourt, 1993.

It's About Time: Poems. Illustrated by Matt Novak. New York: Simon & Schuster, 1993.

Hand in Hand: An American History through Poetry. Illustrated by Barry Root. New York: Simon & Schuster, 1994.

April, Bubbles, and Chocolate: An ABC of Poetry. Illustrated by Barry Root. New York: Simon & Schuster, 1994.

Weather: An "I Can Read" Book. Illustrated by Melanie Hill. New York: HarperCollins, 1994.

Blast Off: Poems about Space. Illustrated by Melissa Sweet. New York: HarperCollins, 1995.

Small Talk: A Book of Short Poems. Illustrated by Scott Medlock. New York: Harcourt, 1996.

School Supplies. Illustrated by Renee Flower. New York: Simon & Schuster, 1996.

Opening Days: Sports Poems. Illustrated by Karen Barbour. New York: Simon & Schuster, 1996.

Marvelous Math: A Book of Poems. Illustrated by Karen Barbour. New York: Simon & Schuster, 1997.

Song and Dance. Illustrated by Cheryl Munro Taylor. New York: Simon & Schuster, 1997.

All God's Children: A Book of Prayers. Illustrated by Amanda Schaffer. New York: Harcourt, 1998.

Climb into My Lap: First Poems to Read Together. Illustrated by Kathryn Brown. New York: Simon & Schuster, 1998.

Dino-Roars. Illustrated by Cynthia Fisher. New York: Golden Books, 1999.

Lives: Poems about Famous Americans. Illustrated by Leslie Staub. New York: HarperCollins, 1999.

Lee Bennett Hopkins

Spectacular Science: A Book of Poems. Illustrated by Virginia Halstead. New York: Simon & Schuster, 1999.

Sports! Sports! Sports! An "I Can Read" Book. Illustrated by Brian Floca. New York: HarperCollins, 1999.

My America. Illustrated by Stephen Alcorn. New York: Simon & Schuster, 2000.

Yummy! Eating through a Day. Illustrated by Renee Flower. New York: Simon & Schuster, 2000.

Hoofbeats, Claws, and Rippled Fins: Creature Poems. Illustrated by Stephen Alcorn. New York: HarperCollins, 2001.

References and Suggested Reading

Strong, Amy. *Lee Bennett Hopkins: A Children's Poet.* New York: Franklin Watts, 2003.

(James) Langston Hughes (1902–1967)

Langston Hughes. Courtesy of Photofest.

Langston Hughes is one of the most distinguished figures in both the literary and the cultural worlds of the twentieth century, he is recognized as a pioneer among American writers, and he was one of the more prolific writers of any generation. Hughes was also a focal figure in the Harlem Renaissance. Beyond the accolades is a body of work that speaks to young people in a tone and a style that connect to their own experiences, hopes, and aspirations. Writing of rapid social change, Hughes chose themes, characters, and settings to which he and his wider audience could relate.

James Langston Hughes was born on February 1, 1902, in Joplin, Missouri, the son of James Nathaniel and Carolina (Carrie) Mercer Hughes. He was descended from a family with roots in the abolitionist movement, including grandmother Mary Sampson Patterson Leary Langston. She and her first husband, Lewis Leary, worked as part of the Underground Railroad network, and Leary later fought at Harper's Ferry with John Brown, only to be fatally shot the day after the attack. Hughes's grandmother's second cousin, Charles Howard Langston, was the son of a white landowner and a former slave—a man whose own brother was the famous nineteenth-century author John Mercer Langston. Langston Hughes's mother, Carrie, grew up in Lawrence, Kansas. At first, she explored professional aspirations in education and a position in the literary community of the time, but was limited by her own mother's sensibilities and increased post-Reconstruction segregation in her home town. While teaching in Guthrie, Oklahoma, she met and subsequently married James Nathaniel Hughes, a law clerk, teacher, businessman, and surveyor, on April 30, 1899.

Langston spent much of his childhood being shuttled from Mexico City, where his father relocated to explore business opportunities, to Kansas City, to live under the care of his maternal grandmother. These early years greatly influenced the young Langston, who developed a love of musical theatre during his stay at his grandmother's house.

Hughes moved from Kansas City to Topeka with his mother after she found a job as a stenographer there. He entered a segregated school in Topeka, and he was often taunted and harassed by the other students, but he did not lose his love of learning or of books. This unfortunate experience was limited to one year, as his mother withdrew Hughes from the school to send him back to his grandmother.

During his preadolescent and teen years, Hughes developed interests in things both maudlin and grim, ruminating about mortality and loneliness. Occasionally rebellious, often melancholy, he received little warmth or support from his aging grandmother. Hughes sought independence, and by the age of twelve he had begun to work at odd jobs. In seventh grade, he was expelled (then later reinstated) for taking a stand against a teacher who segregated black students within her classroom.

Langston Hughes arrived in Harlem in September 1921 and found himself in America's largest black community. Although he enrolled at Columbia University, he did not adjust well to life at the school, and he gradually began completing fewer and fewer of his assignments; he left the school after his first year. He signed up to work on the galley of a ship, finding time to write works such as "The Weary Blues," a reflection on his love of blues music.

During a stint working as a busboy at the Wardman Park Hotel, he learned that poet Vachel Lindsay planned a reading at the property. Hughes was not permitted to attend the author's appearance, but slipped copies of three of his own poems next to Lindsay's plate, speaking briefly to the man. Lindsay announced to the local press that he had discovered a promising "busboy poet," and he left books and words of encouragement for Hughes. Hughes began entering literary competitions, winning first prize in a National Urban League contest. Langston decided to return to school, enrolling at Pennsylvania's Lincoln University in 1925. That same year, he won first prize in a competition sponsored by *Opportunity* magazine, and third prize in an essay contest. In 1926, Hughes published his first volume of poetry, *The Weary Blues*. A second volume, *Fine Clothes to the Jew*, was released the following year.

In 1953, Hughes was questioned by the House Un-American Activities Committee about his supposed Communist sympathies. During this period, he also wrote several children's histories: *Famous American Negroes* (1954), *First Book of Rhythms* (1954), *The First Book of Jazz* (1955), and *Famous Negro Music Makers* (1955), while continuing to chronicle Jesse Semple's fictional life, even adapting the stories for the stage. He published a second autobiography, *I Wonder as I Wander* (1956).

Throughout the 1960s, Hughes worked in virtually every genre; he also edited collections of imaginative verse and prose. He distinguished himself not only by the caliber of his work, but also by its appeal. Langston Hughes died on May 22, 1967, following abdominal surgery while being treated for cancer. His Harlem home has earned landmark status, and the street on which it is located has been renamed Langston Hughes Place.

Hughes's poetry is the subject of study in high schools, middle schools and universities. Organizations such as the Langston Hughes Society and those dedicated to the preservation of voices of the Harlem Renaissance provide resources for students and educators to explore Hughes's work. His spoken word recording "The Voice of the Poet" is used in high schools and in libraries, allowing new generations to hear Hughes in his own voice. His *The Dream Keeper and Other Poems* is filed among collections in children's rooms, young adult sections, and general poetry. Hughes's deft approaches to social issues and to the universal longing for self-realization make the poems "Let America Be America Again," "The Negro Speaks of Rivers," "A Dream Deferred," and "Mother to Son" among those most studied—and downloaded—by young adult and teen readers.

Website

"Langston Hughes." *The Black Renaissance in Washington, D.C., 1920s–1930s.*
   http://www.dclibrary.org.bikren.2003

Poetry

The Weary Blues. New York: Knopf, 1926; London: Knopf, 1926.
Fine Clothes to the Jew. New York: Knopf, 1927; London: Knopf, 1927.
The Negro Mother and Other Dramatic Recitations. New York: Golden Stair Press, 1931.
Dear Lovely Death. Amenia, NY: Privately printed at Troutbeck Press, 1931.
The Dream Keeper and Other Poems. New York: Knopf, 1932.

(James) Langston Hughes

Scottsboro Limited: Four Poems and a Play in Verse. New York: Golden Stair Press, 1932.

A New Song. New York: International Workers Order, 1938.

(With Robert Glenn) *Shakespeare in Harlem.* New York: Knopf, 1942.

Jim Crow's Last Stand. Atlanta: Negro Publication Society of America, 1943.

Freedom's Plow. New York: Musette, 1943.

Lament for Dark Peoples and Other Poems. New York: Holland Press, 1944.

Fields of Wonder. New York: Knopf, 1947.

One-Way Ticket. New York: Knopf, 1949.

Montage of a Dream Deferred. New York: Holt, 1951.

Ask Your Mama: 12 Moods for Jazz. New York: Knopf, 1961.

The Panther and the Lash. New York: Knopf, 1967.

The Collected Poems of Langston Hughes. Ed. Arnold Rampersad. New York: Knopf, 1994.

The Block: Poems. New York: Viking, 1995.

Carol of the Brown King: Poems. New York: Atheneum Press, 1997.

The Pasteboard Bandit. New York: Oxford University Press, 1997.

References and Suggested Reading

Haskins, James S. *Always Movin' On: The Life of Langston Hughes.* Trenton, NJ: Africa World Press, 1993.

Rampersad, Arnold. *The Life of Langston Hughes, Vol. 1: 1902–1941: I, Too, Sing America.* New York: Oxford University Press, 1986.

———. *The Life of Langston Hughes, Vol. II: 1941–1967: I Dream a World.* New York: Oxford University Press, 1986.

Paul Janeczko
(1945-)

Paul Janeczko is among the top anthologists in the field of poetry; he works both as a writer and as a collector of works that appeal to children and young adults. Born in Passaic, New Jersey, to Frank and Verna Janeczko, he seemed as a youth an unlikely candidate for a career in literature. Described as being a middling student, he came to his love of reading after being forced by his mother to read for at least twenty minutes each day. Janeczko at first resisted but then found himself engrossed in books such as those in the Hardy Boys series, and he began to read of his own volition.

Janeczko, one of four boys in the family, was interested in sports, and his interests in outdoor activities manifest as themes in several of his later writings and collections. He attended Catholic schools, including a high school where discipline was severely enforced—a painful experience he chronicled in the novel *Bridges to Cross*. It was during his years at St. Francis College in Maine that Janeczko became more engaged in his studies. During this period he discovered that school became more rewarding when he worked harder to fulfill his scholarly responsibilities. Janeczko majored in English at St. Francis College, and he wrote for the school's literary magazine, beginning to earnestly consider his worth as a poet. He earned his undergraduate degree in 1967, then completed graduate work at John Carroll University, receiving his master's degree in 1970. During his last two years at the university, he taught English at a high school in Parma, Ohio, remaining there until 1972. He moved to Massachusetts and taught in Topsfield, then relocated to Maine. He taught language arts at Gloucester High School in Gray, Maine, from 1977 through 1990, and still retains his position there as visiting writer. Originally meant as a leave of absence when Janeczko and his wife welcomed their firstborn daughter, his family leave became a retirement from teaching and a transition to full time-writing and anthologizing.

It was teaching and writing for professional journals that led Janeczko to his career as author and anthologist. During his early years in the classroom, he began collecting poetry to spark his students' interest. There was a scarcity of contemporary poetry in curricula, and Janeczko read avidly to introduce topical pieces into his own Language Arts program. The social upheavals of the latter several decades of the twentieth century had bred a rich panoply of writers and authors, and Janeczko believed that students would relate more to the works of these new voices than to those from earlier periods. He reasoned that once students were hooked on contemporary poetry, they would learn to understand and appreciate the classics.

In 1983, Janeczko published *Poetspeak: In Their Words, About Their Work*, which invited writers to speak directly to their audiences about their own inspirations, their careers, and their musings on creativity. One of the strengths of the book is its affirming tone, encouraging young people to find their own voices, to tap into their own experiences and to explore words. In 1984, Janeczko's *Strings: A Gathering of Family Poems* was released; originally envisioned as a collection about aging, it morphed into a series about the dynamics of family life. *Pocket Poems: Selected for a Journey* (1985) contains works about leaving home and returning.

In 1987, Janeczko published *Going Over to Your Place: Poems for Each Other* and *This Delicious Day: 65 Poems*, and in 1988, *The Music of What Happens: Poems That Tell Stories.* Throughout the 1990s, Janeczko published a series of well-received collections, including *The Place My Words Are Looking For: What Poets Say About and Through Their Work* (1990) and the extremely popular *I Feel A Little Jumpy Around You: A Book of Her Poems and His Poems Presented in Pairs* (1996), coedited by Naomi Shihab Nye. Janeczko's own poems are featured in 1998's *That Sweet Diamond: Baseball Poems*; *Favorite Lessons* was published the same year. Janeczko released *How to Write Poetry* in 1999, to wide circulation among schools. His 2000 collection *A Poke in the Eye: A Collection of Concrete Poems* was included on many "best of" lists for its year.

Janeczko's collections tackle themes that focus on the experiences of teens and young adults, as in *Preposterous* (1991), which features poems in many voices, expressing longing, frustration, loss, anger, resentment, and self-exploration. Although the subject matter crosses into adult themes, Janeczko sees the young adult audience as distinct from older readers, needing more guidance to frame their emerging convictions. While the works he chooses are clear and grounded in language and rhythms easily understood by preteens and teens, Janeczko avoids patronizing platitudes. Messages are clear and emotions are often left in flux, but to the young adult reader, the expression of those intense feelings can be more important than offering resolution. Some collections are arranged in what might best be described as cycles or progressions, others are clearly divided by subject matter within broader themes. His work tempers realistic situations and stories of young people in crisis with messages of hope. Janeczko does school, library, and conference visits, always emphasizing the need for students to stretch their minds through both reading and writing. His ongoing efforts bring fresh, exciting poetry, often by up-and-coming writers, to young readers. His collections and his own writings help those working in education to better serve young people, and they have made Janeczko's body of work an invaluable resource in the field of contemporary young adult literature.

Poetry

Brickyard Summer. Illustrated by Ken Rush. New York: Orchard Books, 1989.
Stardust Hotel. Illustrated by Dorothy Leech. New York: Orchard Books, 1993.
That Sweet Diamond: Baseball Poems. Illustrated by Carol Katchen. New York: Simon & Schuster, 1998.

Poetry Anthologies (as Editor and Compiler)

That Crystal Image. New York: Dell, 1977.
Postcard Poems. New York: Bradbury, 1979.
Don't Forget to Fly: A Cycle of Modern Poems. New York: Bradbury, 1981.
Poetspeak: In Their Words, About Their Work. New York: Bradbury, 1983.
Strings: A Gathering of Family Poems. New York: Bradbury, 1984.
Pocket Poems: Selected for a Journey. New York: Bradbury, 1985.
This Delicious Day: 65 Poems. New York: Orchard Books, 1987.
Going Over to Your Place: Poems for Each Other. New York: Bradbury, 1987.
The Music of What Happens: Poems That Tell Stories. New York: Orchard Books, 1988.
Preposterous: Poems of Youth. New York: Orchard Books, 1991.
Looking for Your Name. New York: Orchard Books, 1993.
Wherever Home Begins: 100 Contemporary Poems. New York: Orchard Books, 1995.
Home on the Range: Cowboy Poems. New York: Dial Books, 1997.
Very Best (Almost) Friends: Poems of Friendship. Cambridge, MA: Christine Davenier, 1999.
Stone Bench in an Empty Park. New York: Orchard Books, 2000.
A Poke in the I: A Collection of Concrete Poems. Illustrated by Chris Raschka. Cambridge, MA: Candlewick Press, 2001.
Dirty Laundry Pile: Poems in Different Voices. New York: HarperCollins, 2001.
Blushing: Expressions of Love in Poems and Letters. New York: Orchard Books, 2004.

Paul Janeczko

Nonfiction

Poetry from A to Z: A Guide for Young Writers. Illustrated by Cathy Bobak. New York: Scholastic, 1994.

Favorite Poetry Lessons. New York: Scholastic, 1998.

How to Write Poetry. New York: Scholastic, 1999.

Teaching 10 Fabulous Forms of Poetry: Great Lessons, Brainstorming Sheets, and Organizers for Writing Haiku, Limericks, Cinquains, and Other Kinds of Poetry Kids Love. New York: Scholastic, 2000.

How to Write Poetry, Grades 4 to 9. New York: Scholastic, 2001.

Writing Funny Bone Poems. New York: Scholastic, 2001.

Seeing the Blue Between: Advice and Inspiration for Young Poets. Cambridge, MA: Candlewick Press, 2002.

Good for a Laugh: A Guide to Writing Amusing, Clever, and Downright Funny Poems. New York: Scholastic, 2003.

Opening a Door: Reading Poetry in the Middle School Classroom. New York: Scholastic, 2003.

Writing Winning Reports and Essay. New York: Scholastic, 2003.

Top Secret: A Handbook of Codes, Ciphers, and Secret Writing. Illustrated by Jenna LaReau. Cambridge, MA: Candlewick Press, 2004.

Worlds Afire: The Hartford Circus Fire of 1944. Cambridge, MA: Candlewick Press, 2004.

References and Suggested Reading

Apollinaire, Guillaume. *Calligrammes: Poems of Peace and War.* Berkeley: University of California Press, 1980.

McCullough, Kathleen. *Concrete Poetry: An Annotated International Bibliography.* New York: Whitston, 1989.

Williams, Emmett. *An Anthology of Concrete Poetry.* New York: Something Else Press, 1967.

James Weldon Johnson
(1871–1938)

This American poet was a Renaissance man who was born during the promise of the period of Reconstruction in American history, after the end of slavery and the awaited beginning of equal opportunity for former slaves. In addition to writing poetry, Johnson was a novelist, a journalist, a writer of literary criticism, and an attorney. Born in Jacksonville, Florida, the son of James Johnson, a resort hotel headwaiter, and Helen Dillet, a schoolteacher, the multitalented Johnson grew up in a secure, middle-class home. After completing eighth grade at a segregated school for African Americans, Johnson attended preparatory school and subsequently enrolled in Atlanta University, where he honed his writing and speaking skills. Upon his graduation in 1894 at age twenty three, Johnson returned to Florida and accepted a position as principal of his former primary school.

However, public school administration did not quell Johnson's love of writing. While working as a principal, he started a newspaper and passed the examination for admission to the Florida state bar. He also continued to write poetry, and in the early 1900s he and his brother, J. Rosamond Johnson, collaborated to produce "Lift Every Voice and Sing," a poem set to music that was originally intended as a commemoration of Abraham Lincoln's birthday. However, African Americans around the country adopted the song, and by 1915 the National Association for the Advancement of Colored People (NAAACP) supported recognition of the song as the Negro National Anthem. From its debut until contemporary times, "Lift Every Voice and Sing" has been a staple at formal and informal gatherings of African Americans. The popularity of the piece, as well as the reverence paid to its author, is evident in the 1988 decision by

131

the U. S. Postal Service to honor Johnson by issuing a postage stamp bearing the phrase.

However; "Lift Every Voice and Sing" was not the only verse-song on which the Johnson brothers collaborated. The two sold their first song, "Louisiana Lize" in New York City in 1899, a year before they produced their more famous piece. In 1902, the brothers left Jacksonville to join a songwriter they had met in New York, and for the next few years, from 1901 until 1905, Johnson wrote the lyrics of several hit songs, including "Nobody's Lookin' but de Owl and de Moon,", "Under the Bamboo Tree," and "Congo Love Song."

Johnson also maintained his literary output during this period of writing lyrics. Several of his poems appeared in nationally circulated publications in the years from 1903 until 1912, and as a prominent voice in the literary debates of the day, Johnson edited or produced several significant texts from 1922 until 1930, including *The Book of American Negro Poetry* and two collections of spirituals. Johnson sought to establish a record of black literary achievement that was in contrast to the black literature characterized by the use of dialect. He sought to chronicle and thus safeguard depictions of black Americans that represented them as intelligent, articulate, and artistic beings. And although writers such as Zora Neale Hurston and Sterling A. Brown would chronicle a black experience characterized by the use of that same dialect, the efforts of all three writers were necessary to bring forth a black literary tradition that continues to be defined by its context, as well as by its many elements of content and form, rather than by a single element of construction. Johnson played an active role, as an author and as a supporter of young talent, in what came to be known as the Harlem Renaissance.

Throughout his life and many careers, Johnson was deeply committed to exposing the injustice and brutality imposed on African Americans throughout the United States, especially in the segregated South. And although he worked with considerable success to put the NAACP on secure financial ground, Johnson was probably better known in the 1920s for his literary efforts than for his leadership of the NAACP when he stepped down from that organization in 1931 to become a professor at Fisk University. For the remainder of his life, he divided the year between semesters spent in Nashville teaching creative writing and classes in American and African American literature and semesters spent in New York City where he remained active as a writer. An important, primary source for the study of this American poet's life and work, The James Weldon Johnson papers are housed in the Beinecke Library at Yale University. In addition, the Library of Congress is the repository for the NAACP Collection and the papers of Booker T. Washington, important secondary sources for the study of Johnson's life and work.

Website

"Strangers to Us All: Lawyers Who Were Poets."
    http://www.wvu.edu/~lawfac/jelkins/lp-2001/intro/contemp_pt2.html

Poetry

God's Trombones: Seven Negro Sermons in Verse. New York: Penguin, 1990 (reissue).
Saint Peter Relates an Incident. Reprint edition. New York: Penguin, 1993.
The Creation. Illustrated by James E. Ransome. New York: Holiday House, 1994.

Fiction

Autobiography of an Ex-Coloured Man. New York: Dover, 1995 (reprint).

Autobiography

Along This Way: The Autobiography of James Weldon Johnson (1933); New York: De Capo Press, 2002 (reprint).

References and Suggested Reading

Andrews, William L. *Classic Fiction of the Harlem Renaissance.* New York: Oxford University Press, 1994.

Bassett, John E. *Harlem in Review: Critical Reactions to Black American Writers, 1917–1939.* Selinsgrove, PA: Susquehanna University Press, 1992.

Bone, Robert A. *Down Home: A History of Afro-American Short Fiction from Its Beginnings to the End of the Harlem Renaissance.* New York: Putnam, 1975.

Bontemps, Arna W., ed. *The Harlem Renaissance Remembered: Essays.* New York: Dodd, Mead, 1972.

Boyd, Herb, ed. *The Harlem Reader: A Celebration of New York's Most Famous Neighborhood, from the Renaissance Years to the Twenty-first Century.* New York: Three Rivers, 2003.

Bronz, Stephen H. *Roots of Negro Racial Consciousness; the 1920's: Three Harlem Renaissance Authors: Johnson, James Weldon; Cullen, Countee; McKay, Claude.* New York: Libra, 1964.

Douglas, Ann. *Terrible Honesty: Mongrel Manhattan in the 1920s.* New York: Farrar, Straus & Giroux, 1995.

Jones, Gayl. *Liberating Voices: Oral Tradition in African American Literature.* Cambridge, MA: Harvard University Press, 1991.

Locke, Alain, ed. *The New Negro: An Interpretation.* New York: Arno, 1968.

Mitchell, Angelyn, ed. *Within the Circle: An Anthology of African American Literary Criticism from the Harlem Renaissance to the Present.* Durham, NC: Duke University Press, 1994.

Sundquist, Eric J. *To Wake the Nations: Race in the Making of American Literature.* Cambridge: Harvard University Press, 1993.

Wright, John S. *A Stronger Soul Within a Finer Frame: Portraying African-Americans in the Black Renaissance.* Minneapolis: University Art Museum, University of Minnesota, 1990.

John Keats
(1795–1821)

John Keats's date of birth is believed to be October 31, 1795. He was the oldest of five sons born to Thomas and Frances Jennings Keats. His parents met while Thomas was employed by his maternal grandfather, at a livery stable. The couple brought their infant son back to the Jennings homestead, and over the next few years, their small family grew by four.

Thomas Keats took over management of the stables, and by 1800 he was able to move his family to a home near London's Charles Square. The family's middle class position opened some, if not all, options for the boys' education. After initially considering Harrow, a prestigious public school, the Keatses decided to send their sons to the more progressive Clarke School. John Keats was enrolled in 1803, and his brothers joined him as each came of age. The Clarke family took an interest in the Keats children, and Keats became a special friend of the headmaster's son, Charles Cowdon Clarke, a student seven years Keats's senior.

After the death of his father, and the subsequent loss of the family business, the young Keats and his siblings were sent to live with their maternal grandparents in Middlesex. There they found stability and order. However, the death of his father apparently affected the young poet. In school, John Keats displayed a quick temper and showed little interest in pleasing his teachers.

Keats's maternal grandmother, Alice Jennings, was near seventy as Keats approached young adulthood. She assigned the financial and practical concerns of the Keats children to merchant and family acquaintance Richard Abbey. He proved to be quite controlling with the dispensation of the children's funds and took little emotional interest in them. Abbey removed the Keats boys from the Clarke School in 1810, apprenticing John to a surgeon and apothecary, his brothers to other trades. Keats spent five years studying medicine and pharmacology and in 1815 registered to train at Guy's Hospital. Though he worked diligently for his employers, Keats's interests and ambitions were of a decidedly different nature.

During his time as an apprentice, he maintained his friendship with Charles Cowden Clarke. Clarke provided Keats with a wealth of reading material, including radical political publications. Keats was drawn to poetry. Spenser was a favorite, and Keats's first attempts at writing his own poems, begun at the age of eighteen, were modeled on Spenser's works. Keats began to write sonnets as he moved to Southwark and took on the responsibilities of surgical practice at St. Thomas' and St. Guy's Hospital.

Keats's first published poem appeared in April of 1816. "O Solitude," a sonnet he'd written months earlier, was published in Leigh Hunt's *The Examiner.* Keats composed a series of verse letters while on a trip following his apothecary's licensing examination. Keats was increasingly drawn to writing. He wrote the first of his major poems, "On First Looking into Chapman's Homer," after a night sharing a translation of the epic with Clarke.

Throughout the early part of 1818, Keats made the rounds of London's busy social scene and attended lectures at the Surrey Institution. He learned that younger brother Tom had symptoms of consumption. John edited *Endymion* while caring for his brother. By May, he had also written *Isabella; or, The Pot of Basil,* followed by *Ode to Maria.* Keats's brother George planned a move to the United States after marrying; John Keats was troubled by the news. Keats traveled to Scotland. It was a sobering experience, as he witnessed scenes of poverty, tolerated raw weather, and was eventually advised by a physician to head home. He found that Tom was dying. John helped care for his brother despite his own illness, and was exposed to consumption through their close contact.

John Keats began to write his next major work, *Hyperion,* but put it aside after Tom died in December of 1818. Keats was producing a wealth of letters to his now distant brother, George; these and other letters Keats wrote to family and friends have provided a wealth of information about and insight into Keats's life and works.

That winter, Keats fell in love with eighteen-year-old Fanny Brawne. Keats resumed work on *Hyperion* and produced *Lamia,* the ode "To Autumn," and a collaborative play in verse, *Otho the Great.* Keats had to become involved with Richard Abbey again, in the matter of his sister, Fanny Keats; Abbey had removed Fanny Keats from school and attempted to keep her from contact with her brothers. John Keats intervened, restoring his sister to school and to family.

Keats was reunited with his longtime friend Charles Cowden Clarke, a visit that proved both enjoyable and depressing; by this time, Keats was aware that his health was deteriorating.

Keats began work on a series of four odes: "Ode to a Nightingale," "Ode to Melancholy," "Ode to Indolence," and "Ode to a Grecian Urn." The poems are more sober and contemplative than some of his earlier works and have an almost tactile quality. They are among those most frequently anthologized and are used widely in secondary schools.

Keats's works are among those most studied in English literature. Despite the brevity of his life and career, his impact on English Romanticism was significant, and his poems and letters have become part of the standard curriculum for high school and college students.

Website

John Keats home page: http://www.john-keats.com/index_ie.htm

Poetry

Poems. London: C. & J. Ollier, 1817.
Endymion: A Poetic Romance. London: Printed for Taylor & Hessey, 1818.
Lamia, Isabella, The Eve of St. Agnes, and Other Poems. London: Taylor & Hessey, 1820.
The Poetical Works of Coleridge, Shelley, and Keats. Paris: A. & W. Galignani, 1829; Philadelphia: J. Howe, 1831.
The Poetical Works of John Keats. London: William Smith, 1840.
The Poetical Works of John Keats. New York: Wiley & Putnam, 1846.
Life, Letters, and Literary Remains of John Keats. Ed. Richard Monkton Milnes, Lord Houghton. London: Moxon, 1848; Philadelphia: Putnam, 1848.
The Poems of John Keats. Ed. Jack Stillinger. Cambridge, MA: Belknap Press, 1978.

Letters

The Letters of John Keats 2 vols. Ed. Hyder Edward Rollins. Cambridge, MA: Harvard University Press, 1958.
Letters of John Keats: A New Selection. Ed. Robert Gittings. New York: Oxford University Press, 1978.

References and Suggested Reading

Hilton, Timothy. *Keats and His World*. New York: Viking, 1971.
Kissane, James. "John Keats." In Dictionary of Literary Biography, Volume 110: British Romance Prose Writers, 1789–1832, Second Series. Detroit: Gale Research, 1991, pp. 166–79.
Motion, Andrew. *Keats: A Biography*. New York: Farrar, Straus & Giroux, 1997.
Ward, Aileen. *John Keats: The Making of a Poet*. New York: Farrar, Straus & Giroux, 1963.

Jack Kerouac
(1922–1969)

Jack Kerouac. Courtesy of Photofest.

The name of Jack Kerouac, along with the titles of some of his most famous works such as *On the Road* and *Mexico City Blues*, is inextricably linked to a movement that he named the Beat Generation. It was a name Kerouac assigned to an attitude, to a generation coming of age in post–World War II America. Kerouac's life and writings reflected the spirit of a man on the move, in a quest for self-definition and a determination to challenge conformity. Although his books are emblematic of the two decades they reflect, they retain their popularity and relevance among young adult readers who embrace Kerouac for giving voice to a spirit of independence and nonconformity.

He was born in Lowell, Massachusetts, on March 12, 1922, and baptized Jean-Louis Lebris de Kerouac. He was the third child of strict Roman Catholic parents of French-Canadian descent. The family moved frequently within the confines of their small mill town. An early loss would remain with Kerouac throughout his life: his brother, Gerard, five years his elder, died in 1926 following a lengthy, painful bout with rheumatic fever. Kerouac witnessed both his brother's physical agonies and his mother's consuming grief. He would continue to revisit images and dreams of his brother, and he wrote the book *Visions of Gerard* as memoir. Kerouac developed fears of death and took to sleeping in his mother's bed, along with sister Madeline (known in the family as "Nin").

The family spoke French, and Kerouac did not learn English until he was seven years old, a first-grader at St. Joseph's Brothers School. He was imaginative, creating elaborate fantasies, playing baseball games, and becoming immersed in radio serials.

Kerouac was influenced by a wide range of interests, including Buddhism. He was among the first authors to introduce some of its concepts into contemporary American literature. Buddhist themes are reflected in such works as his 1955–1956 two-part book, *Tristessa,* and in *Maggie Cassidy* and *Desolation Angels.* His lament for his brother, *Visions of Gerard*, addressed grief from a Buddhist perspective. He wrote religious tracts and incorporated some Buddhist elements into *The Dharma Bums.* He found the rhythms of jazz and blues music appealing, and those forms would make their appearance in his poetry as well.

Kerouac began writing poetry in earnest in the mid-1950s, although many of his verse collections were not published until after his death. He wrote most of the poems for *San Francisco Blues* during and following a trip to that city in the fall of 1952. The poems center on the images of street people that Kerouac observed from his hotel room. The poems use rhythms of jazz and blues measures, and embody a narrative more reminiscent of songs than of conventional poems. He often performed his poems with musical accompaniment at clubs.

In the early 1960s, Kerouac became increasingly reclusive as his family responsibilities grew. His mother was living with his sister Nin in Florida, but following Nin's untimely death from a heart attack, she moved to Hyannis, Massachusetts, to live with Jack. By 1966, critics and academics were viewing Kerouac's work seriously, and he was developing an eclectic following among music and poetry aficionados. He had never doubted his own genius and, at times, had voiced discontent at the lack of recognition; still, he could not enjoy this renewed flurry of interest because of his poor health and troubling circumstances. Kerouac's mother had become debilitated by a stroke.

In 1966, Kerouac married for a third time. Stella Sampas was the sister of a childhood friend, a slightly older woman who had helped care for Kerouac's mother. He remained isolated from many of his old friends and wrote only when he was in dire financial need.

Kerouac took short trips to Lowell in his final years, and he became preoccupied with thoughts of death. In October 1969, he was rushed into surgery for an abdominal hemorrhage, but did not survive the operation.

Kerouac died at the age of forty-seven. His widow buried him in his beloved Lowell, Massachusetts.

Stella Sampas Kerouac maintained control over her husband's writings, allowing the publication of some of his poetry and books within a few years of his death, sealing other works until after her own demise. For readers interested in Kerouac's body of work, this meant that there was a rich succession of new material over several decades.

Poetry

Mexico City Blues: Two Hundred Forty-Two Choruses. New York: Grove Press, 1959.
Hugo Weber. New York: Portents, 1967.
Someday You'll Be Lying. Privately printed, 1968.
A Lost Haiku. Privately printed, 1969.
Scattered Poems. San Francisco: City Lights, 1971.
(With Albert Saijo and Lew Welch) *Trip Trap: Haiku Along the Road from San Francisco to New York, 1959.* San Francisco: Grey Fox, 1973.
Heaven and Other Poems. San Francisco: Grey Fox, 1977.
San Francisco Blues. New York: Beat Books, 1983.
Hymn: God Pray for Me. Dover, NH: Caliban, 1985.
American Haikus. Dover, NH: Caliban, 1986.
Pomes All Sizes. San Francisco: City Lights, 1992.
Old Angel Midnight. San Francisco: Grey Fox, 1993.
Book of Blues. New York: Penguin, 1995.
Book of Haikus. New York: Penguin, 2003.

References and Suggested Reading

Charters, Ann. *Kerouac: A Biography.* Foreword by Allen Ginsberg. New York: St. Martin's Press, 1973.
Jones, James T. *A Map of Mexico City Blues.* Edwardsville: Southern Illinois University Press, 1992.
Maher, Paul, Jr. *Kerouac: The Definitive Biography.* Foreword by David Amram. Lanham, MD: Taylor Trade Publishing, 2004.
Miles, Barry. *Jack Kerouac: King of the Beats.* New York: Henry Holt & Co., 1998.

Yusef Komunyakaa
(1947–)

A unique figure in American poetry, Komunyakaa is a former information specialist who grew up in Bogalusa, Louisiana, and received the Bronze Star for his service during the Vietnam War. He is the author of eleven volumes of poetry. Komunyakaa's work is celebrated for its short lines, simple language, and use of jazz rhythms and for being rooted in the poet's experiences.

He received master of arts degrees from the University of California, Irvine, and from Colorado State University. In fall 1997, he began teaching at Princeton University, where he is currently professor in the Council of Humanities and Creative Writing. Wesleyan has published six of his ten books, including the 1993 Pulitzer prize–winning *Neon Vernacular*, which also won the Kingsley-Tufts Poetry Award from the Claremont Graduate School. Komunyakaa's most recent collection is *Talking Dirty to the Gods*. His earlier collections include the 1998 *Thieves of Paradise*, which was nominated for the National Book Critics Circle Award. His numerous awards include the Thomas Forcade Award, the Los Angeles Times Book Prize in Poetry, and the William Faulkner Prize from the University of Rennes in France. In addition to his many publications and poetry collections, he is coeditor, with Sascha Feinstein, of two volumes of *The Jazz Poetry Anthology* from Indiana University Press.

Komunyakaa's poetry has been described as "razor-sharp pieces" that are insighful and informative. Although Komunyakaa's tone is sometimes acerbic, the poet plays sharp attention to structure. Komunyakaa's young readers will discover imaginative verse that practically dances on the page, becoming fluid and malleable, never stagnant, yet somehow fixed in spite of it all. Komunyakaa is adept at making his craftsmanship invisible; young readers will not notice the skilled master at work as he coaxes them into reading mythology, history, or the classics under the guise of reading a simple four-stanza poem. This American poet writes in free verse as well, and even though his subject matter is often complex, young readers will risk the challenge once introduced to imaginative verse that sings to them from the page. The poet writes at once about acts of desperation and acts of redemption, as in the poem "My Father's Love Letters."

His imaginative verse is often imagistic, and those images are created through his use of language and metaphor. Komunyakaa's language is so breathtakingly simple that readers leave the poem marveling at its simplicity. This American poet gives every reader the feeling that he or she could write a poem; he makes the process seem effortless, as natural as breathing. However, hidden within Komunyakaa's simplicity are life's sweetest and hardest stories: those of abandonment, of lost hope, of renewed strength, of wonder.

Komunyakaa's work poses questions as much as answers them. He writes about the human experience. In that regard, he shares themes common to poetry written by Gwendolyn Brooks and Walt Whitman. And although Komunyakaa began writing early and was encouraged in those early efforts, he did not begin writing seriously until he returned from Vietnam. After his tour was done, he enrolled in a creative writing class at the University of Colorado. He has been writing poetry consistently since that first class.

Websites

"Academy of American Poets." http://www.poets.org
"Poem Hunter." http://www.poemhunter.com

Poetry

The Jazz Poetry Anthology. Ed. Sascha Feinstein and Yusef Komunyakaa. Bloomington: Indiana University Press, 1991–1996.

Magic City. Middletown, CT: University Press of New England, 1992.

Neon vernacular: New and Selected Poems. Middletown, CT: University Press of New England, 1993.

Thieves of Paradise. Middletown, CT: University Press of New England, 1998.

Talking Dirty to the Gods: Poems. New York: Farrar, Straus & Giroux, 2000.

Blue Notes: Essays, Interviews, and Commentaries. Ed. Radiclani Clytus. Ann Arbor: University of Michigan Press, 2000.

References and Suggested Reading

Asali, Muna. "An Interview with Yusef Komunyakaa." *New England Review 16.1* (Winter 1994): pp. 141–47.

Aubert, Alvin. "Yusef Komunyakaa: The Unified Vision—Canonization and Humanity." *African American Review 27.1* (Spring 1993): pp. 119–23.

Baer, William. "Still Negotiating with the Images: An Interview with Yusef Komunyakaa." *Kenyon Review 20.3–4* (Summer–Fall 1998): pp. 5–29.

Fabre, Michael. "On Yusef Komunyakaa." *Southern Quarterly 34.2* (Winter 1996): pp. 5–8.

Gotera, Vicente F. "'Lines of Tempered Steel' An Interview with Yusef Komunyakaa." *Callaloo 13.2* (Spring 1990): pp. 215–29.

Johnson, Thomas C. "Interview with Yusef Komunyakaa." *Worcester Review 19.1–2* (1998): pp. 119–27.

Jones, Kirkland C. "Folk Idiom in the Literary Expression of Two African American Authors: Rita Dove and Yusef Komunyakaa." *Language and Literature in the African American Imagination*. Ed. Carol Blackshire-Belay. Westport, CT: Greenwood Press, 1992, pp. 149–65.

Salas, Angela M. "'Flashbacks through the Heart': Yusef Komunyakaa and the Poetry of Self-Assertion." In *The Furious Flowering of African American Poetry*. Ed. Joanne V. Gabbin. Charlottesville: University of Virginia Press, 1999, pp. 298–309.

Suarez, Ernest. "Yusef Komunyakaa." In *Southbound: Interviews with Southern Poets*. Columbia: University of Missouri Press, 1999, pp. 130–43.

Maxine Kumin
(1925-)

Perhaps best known for her poems about life in rural communities, Maxine Kumin lives on a horse farm in rural New Hampshire. As a child, she lived with her family in Germantown, Philadelphia, next door to the Convent of the Sisters of St. Joseph. The young Kumin attended the first few years of primary school under the careful tutelage of the nuns at the teaching order and she muses that her early years spent observing the religious services of her Jewish faith as well as those required of students at the Convent may well account for the juxtaposition of Christian and Jewish images in many of her poems.

The poet received both her bachelor of arts and her master of art degrees from Radcliffe, where she studied history and literature. Kumin did not express an interest in poetry during her years at Radcliffe. In fact, poetry did not become an important part of her life until some fourteen years after she graduated from college and enrolled in a poetry workshop offered by the Boston Center for Adult Education. There she met Anne Sexton, and the two women became fast friends. Encouraged by her experiences in the poetry workshop and by her classmate, Kumin began to write poetry. Not long afterward, her work began to receive critical and public acclaim. Her first collection of poems, *Halfway,* was published in 1961, four years after her attendance at that fateful workshop.

In describing her relationship with poetry, Kumin confesses to an "unreasonable and passionate commitment [to] language." Both her passion and her commitment are evinced in her surprisingly personal yet expertly crafted poetry. Kumin's poetry is at once a personal and universal retelling of events in the natural world as well as of things in that world that can be touched, tasted, and smelled. Kumin's poetry also reveals her observations regarding the bond between the human and animal worlds. One poem, "Credo,", describes the development of a trusting relationship between animal and man, with the human species owning the responsibility to nurture and sustain that trust. Kumin's concern for and love of animals is not exhausted in her poetry, for she does not simply celebrate the dignity and beauty of animals in verse; she has adopted and nursed many abused and abandoned animals. Kumin attributes the development of her own bond with less fortunate beings to the good fortune of growing up in suburban Philadelphia with "an enormous amount of freedom" and without the worry of "being abducted, sexually abused or whatever."

Although Kumin has studied and collaborated with Anne Sexton, her work is recognized as less stylistically distinctive than Sexton's, perhaps because Kumin favors traditional poetic forms over the free-verse form. In fact, because of her use of formal structure and the iambic line, Kumin is more likely to be compared to the poets Elizabeth Bishop and Robert Frost than to Sexton. Kumin's unadorned and conventional style blends whimsy and exactness to frame her observations about life, loss, and renewal.

Kumin has written more than twenty children's books, four of which she wrote with Sexton. She has served as Consultant in Poetry to the Library of Congress and as Poet Laureate of New Hampshire, and she has taught at several respected American universities, including Princeton, Columbia, Brandeis, MIT, Washington at St. Louis, and the University of Miami. Kumin has served on the staff of the Atlantic Center for the Arts, the Bread Loaf Writers' Conference, and the Sewanee Writers' Conference, and she has given readings or conducted writers' workshops throughout the United States.

Kumin has published poetry for more than thirty years. Her more recent collections, *Jack and Other New Poems, Bringing Together, The Long Marriage, Connecting the Dots* and *Looking for Luck,* were preceded by *Selected Poems 1960–1990, Nurture, The Long Approach, Our Ground Time Here Will Be Brief: New and Selected Poems, House, Bridge, Fountain, Gate*, and *Up Country: Poems of New England.* She received the 1992 Poets' Prize for *Looking for Luck,* and she received the Pulitzer Prize for *Up Country: Poems of New England* (1972), in which she recalls moments spent on her farm in New Hampshire, a place she describes as her "small corner of the earth." Kumin has received the Aiken Taylor Award for Modern Poetry, an American Academy of Arts and Letters Award, the Sarah Joseph Hale Award, the Levinson Prize, and a National Endowment for the Arts grant, as well as fellowships from the Academy of American Poets and from the National Council on the Arts. Her poetry collections for children range from gleeful stories of innocence to rhymed recitations of scientific discovery. True to her convictions regarding fairness and reciprocity, in 1999, after four years of service on the prestigious board of chancellors of the Academy of American

Poets, she resigned her position in protest over the board's reluctance to admit poets of color.

In May 2005, Maxine Kumin received The Harvard Arts Medal during that school's annual arts festival. The prestigious award was created in 1995 to honor distinguished Harvard or Radcliffe alumni (male or female) or faculty members who achieved excellence in the arts and who made special contributions through the arts to education or to the public good. Kumin's latest collection of poetry, *Mites to Mastodons*, is a book of poems about animals and is scheduled for release in September 2006.

Websites

University of Illinois at Urbana-Champaign, "Modern American Poetry on Line."
 http://www.english.uiuc.edu

Poetry

House, Bridge, Fountain, Gate. New York: Viking, 1975.
What Color Is Caesar? Illustrated by Evaline Ness. New York: McGraw-Hill, 1978.
The Retrieval System: Poems. New York: Viking, 1978.
Our Ground Time Here Will Be Brief. New York: Penguin, 1982.
The Microscope. Pictures by Arnold Lobel. New York: Harper & Row, 1984.
Looking for Luck: Poems. New York: Norton, 1992.

Fiction

Why Can't We Live Together Like Civilized Human Beings: Stories. New York: Viking, 1982.

References and Suggested Reading

The Atlantic Monthly Audible Anthology, with text and RealAudio versions of "Grace" (1961), "January 25th (1965), "Continuum: A Love Poem" (1980), and "The Nuns of Childhood: Two Views" (1992).
Davidson, Cathy N., and Linda Wagner Martin, eds. *Women's Writing in the United States.* New York: Oxford University Press, 1995.
Grosholz, Emily, ed. *Telling the Barn Swallow: Poets on the Poetry of Maxine Kumin.* Hanover, NH: University Press of New England, 1997.
Gould, Jean. "Anne Sexton—Maxine Kumin." *Modern American Women Poets* (1984): pp. 151–75.
Hamilton, Ian, ed. *The Oxford Companion to Twentieth-Century Poetry in English.* New York: Oxford University Press, 1994.
Howard, Ben. "A Secular Believer: The Agnostic Art of Maxine Kumin." *Shenandoah* 52.2 (Summer 2002): pp. 141–59.
Savage, Diana. "Maxine Kumin: The Poetry of a New England Landscape. An Interview." *Rambles* (October 1994).

Madeleine L'Engle
(1918-)

Although she had been a published author since 1945, it was with the release of *A Wrinkle in Time*—and its subsequent Newbery Award—that Madeleine L'Engle became a recognized writer of young people's literature. Since that first publication, L'Engle has produced poetry as well as novels, memoirs, and drama, and she has become an advocate for young readers and writers.

Madeleine L'Engle Camp was born in New York City on November 29, 1918, to journalist Charles Wadsworth Camp and pianist Madeleine Barnett Camp. Charles Camp was recovering from the effects of his service in World War I when his wife gave birth; by the time he returned home, months later, he had suffered intense damage to his lungs from exposure to toxins used in chemical warfare. This altered his career plans and ultimately forced his family into a series of moves.

Madeleine spent her first years raised by a nanny in the family's apartment on New York's Upper East Side. Both the nanny and Mrs. Camp read to Madeleine daily, and by five the child had learned every story in her collection. During her early years, she read as she ate dinner alone in her room, and by age ten she had tried her hand at her own story. The Camps had a lively social schedule, and Madeleine would often sneak out of her room to eavesdrop on her parents and their friends and to listen to the piano music at their parties. She developed a lifelong love of the piano.

Her sixth-grade teacher greatly influenced the young writer by encouraging her in her studies and by boosting the shy youngster's self-confidence. Madeleine's family abruptly relocated when the girl was thirteen. The family traveled to Europe seeking relief for Charles Camp's deteriorating health. Madeleine was sent away to a Swiss boarding school, a singularly miserable experience for her. It was a harsh environment, and the girls were not permitted to read or write on their own time. The conditions at the school made many of the girls ill. L'Engle would write about these experiences in *And Both Were Young* (1949).

Madeleine's parents took her back to America, and she was enrolled at the Ashley Hall Boarding School in Charleston, South Carolina, for the eighth grade, and she remained there through high school. Madeleine enjoyed her years at Ashley Hall, and published pieces in the literary journal, which she eventually edited. She took a position on the Student Council and won writing competitions. Madeleine's happiness was tempered by her father's death during her senior year.

After graduating with honors in 1941, L'Engle moved to New York. She planned to act in order to support herself, but continued to write as well, sending stories under her middle name, L'Engle, to avoid special consideration based on her father's fame as a journalist.

The 1950s were a difficult period in L'Engle's career. She had limited success getting work accepted for publication, other than one book and some poems, and was frustrated by numerous rejections. This was especially true when she and her agent sent the manuscript of *A Wrinkle in Time* to more than thirty publishers. L'Engle knew that this book was unusual— a blend of science fiction and fantasy grounded in deeply personal and moral themes. It was finally accepted by publishing magnate John Farrar himself and was released in 1962. *A Wrinkle in Time* was immediately popular, and it received the American Library Association's Newbery Medal in January 1963.

L'Engle worked on a cycle of poems in 1966, many on spiritual themes, some with annotations and distinct allusions, often from unusual perspectives. "The Stripper" is not about a striptease artist, but about Christ being stripped of his ability to perform miracles. "Intention for Mass: Watts, Vietnam, Johannesburg . . ."gives witness to L'Engle's faith that Christ's sacrifice is still justified in the hope of redeeming modern-day sinners and sinful social systems. Other poems explored L'Engle's interests in physics and astrophysics, which she had touched on in *A Wrinkle in Time.*

L'Engle's poetry collection *Lines Scribbled on an Envelope* (1969) contained an eclectic mix of poems. The title poem (subtitled "While Riding the 104 Broadway Bus") is a plea for guidance as the narrator catches slices of lives and chides herself for being unable to encompass all of the people she glimpses in her own prayers. There are poems written as a series of reflections from a hospital room, pieces about the nature of love, the ruminations of a dragon, and a poem about watching her daughter marry.

Young readers find in these poems echoes of their own questions about spirituality and, at times, about the nature of love.

The Irrational Season, published in 1977, poetically recounts the stages of life from infancy to old age and relates, in verse, the poignant story of a youngster who receives news of her father's imminent death.

L'Engle's honesty and her vulnerability render fresh poetic retellings of biblical and historical events. Her poetry, fiction, and nonfiction speak to young readers' interests in fantasy, science fiction, and religion. She uses powerful spiritual images to examine the many phases of spiritual love, including its frustrations. Although she publishes infrequently, L'Engle continues to write.

Website

Madeleine L'Engle home page: . http://www.madeleinelengle.cm/

Poetry

Lines Scribbled on an Envelope, and Other Poems. New York: Farrar, Straus & Giroux, 1969.
The Irrational Season. New York: Seabury Press, 1977.
The Weather of the Heart. Wheaton, IL: Harold Shaw, 1978.
Walking on Water: Reflections on Faith and Art. Wheaton, IL: Harold Shaw, 1980.
A Cry like a Bell. Wheaton, IL: Harold Shaw, 1987.
The Ordering of Love: The New and Collected Poems of Madeleine L'Engle. Colorado Springs, CO: The Shaw Press, 2005.

Fiction

The Sphinx at Dawn: Two Stories. Illustrated by Vivian Berger. New York: Harper, 1982.
A Severed Wasp. New York: Farrar, Straus & Giroux, 1982.
A House like a Lotus. New York: Farrar, Straus & Giroux, 1984.
Certain Women. New York: Farrar, Straus & Giroux, 1992.
A Live Coal in the Sea. New York: Farrar, Straus & Giroux, 1996.
Miracle on 10th Street and Other Christmas Writings. Wheaton, IL: Harold Shaw, 1998.
The Genesis Trilogy. Colorado Springs, CO: WaterBrook Press, 2001.

Time Fantasy Series

A Wrinkle in Time. New York: Farrar, Straus & Giroux, 1962.
A Wind in the Door. New York: Farrar, Straus & Giroux, 1973.
A Swiftly Tilting Planet. New York: Farrar, Straus & Giroux, 1978.
Many Waters. New York: Farrar, Straus & Giroux, 1986.
An Acceptable Time. New York: Farrar Straus & Giroux, 1996.

Crosswicks Journals (Autobiography and Memoir)

A Circle of Quiet. New York: Farrar, Straus & Giroux, 1972.
The Summer of the Great-Grandmother. New York: Farrar, Straus & Giroux, 1974.
The Irrational Season. New York: Seabury Press, 1977.
Two-Part Invention. New York: Farrar, Straus & Giroux, 1988.

References and Suggested Reading

Chase, Carol. *Madeleine L'Engle Herself: Reflections on a Writing Life.* Colorado Springs, CO: WaterBrook Press, 2001.
Gonzales, Doreen. *Madeleine L'Engle: Author of A Wrinkle in Time.* New York: Dillon Press, 1991.

John Lennon
(1940–1980)

John Lennon. Courtesy of Photofest.

It would be difficult to summarize John Lennon's career or his life without sliding into superlatives. His rise from the streets of working-class Liverpool to the unprecedented success and fame of the Beatles is only part of Lennon's story. Throughout his time as part of the musical and cultural revolutions of the 1960s, on through his mission as a peace activist, and during his years as a solo artist and househusband, Lennon embodied artistry, individualism, and a voice of change.

John Winston Lennon was born on October 9, 1940, as Liverpool was suffering an air raid during the Battle of Britain in World War II. Julia Stanley Lennon brought her infant son to her parents' home, where she raised him with intermittent support from her husband Alfred, a seaman who kept sporadic contact with the family. When Lennon was five, Julia Lennon lost custody of her son and he was turned over to the care of his maternal Aunt Mimi and Uncle George Smith, who provided a stable home for their young charge. Lennon felt the separation from his mother deeply; it would produce a longing he would explore and express artistically. Julia Lennon visited her son, but by this time she had begun a new family with her second husband.

Lennon's Aunt Mimi shared her own love of books with her nephew, and John became an enthusiastic reader and writer. At Dovedale Primary (lower elementary) School, he was constantly drawing, composing stories and poetry, and acting out familiar books with his friends. He memorized Lewis Carroll's "Jabberwocky," especially enjoying Carroll's wordplays, and the *Just William* series by Richmal Crompton. He carried a harmonica around with him. Lennon was extremely sensitive, always dealing with feelings of abandonment, and claimed to see things differently than other people, frequently describing some childhood hallucinatory experiences.

By the mid-1950s, Lennon was a teenager and American rock and roll reached England, both in film and on the radio. Lennon became hooked on the music of Elvis Presley, Little Richard, and fellow Englishman Lonnie Donegan, who popularized skiffle music, a blend of folk and blues played on simple instruments. John eagerly tried his hand at his mother's banjo, then his own guitar. He and a set of friends formed a band, the Quarry Men. They played at small local events.

Lennon's preoccupation with music caused stress at home. His aunt worried about his future, as Lennon failed his college entrance exams. Despite his poor results and school record, he was admitted to the Liverpool College of the Arts. The summer before he entered, he met Paul McCartney while playing a local gig. Lennon invited McCartney, two years his junior but more skilled at guitar, to join his group. The two began what would become one of the more successful songwriting partnerships in history.

In addition to writing songs, Lennon published books of his own writings. *In His Own Write* was released in March 1964. The slim volume contained Lennon's musings in the form of poems, drawings, and narratives. The images are sharp, often caustic.

Lennon's second book, *A Spaniard in the Works*, followed the same format as *In His Own Write*, giving fans a glimpse at Lennon's wry wit and unconventional view of the world. His songs were becoming more insightful, too. In part encouraged by Bob Dylan's advice about songwriting, Lennon explored more sophisticated themes in such tracks as "In My Life," which he considered his first literary musical piece, and "Nowhere Man." The album *Rubber Soul* marked a turning point in Lennon's writing, and his tracks and McCartney's were less collaborative than on early recordings. Lennon was using LSD and experimenting with unusual sounds and concepts by the time the group recorded the album *Revolver*.

An interview Lennon did with a *London Evening Standard* reporter in 1966 started a firestorm. Lennon commented that the Beatles were more popular than Jesus, and he predicted that Christianity would eventually end. Conservative radio stations banned Beatles music, extremists publicly smashed and burned their records, and the band was met with protests on its American tour.

During a hiatus from recording, Lennon took part in the feature film *How I Won the War.* He was spending more time away from the other Beatles. In late 1966, he met avant-garde artist Yoko Ono. Lennon divorced his first wife and married Ono; she would become a primary influence on Lennon's life and art.

On December 8, 1980, John Lennon was murdered outside his home, shot to death by a deranged man. News of his violent death sent shockwaves around the world. Ono requested a vigil instead of a memorial, and fans worldwide gathered at different sites, including Central Park, to remember Lennon on December 14. A patch of Central Park near the Lennons' Dakota home was dedicated to him; a mosaic with the word "Imagine" adorns the spot. His sons have gone on to pursue careers in music, and Yoko Ono continued her own career while taking on the task of keeping Lennon's memory alive, and releasing some posthumous works.

Lennon was a major force in popular culture. His writing reflects a pure energy and a rawness that seems to reach each new generation of music fans. His work ranged from the intensely personal to the broadly political, and he challenged audiences to seek their own truths while retaining global awareness. Lennon's brutal honesty resonates among young readers and music fans. In sharing his own quest for love and self-awareness, Lennon touched on universal loves, fears, questions, and fantasies.

Poetry and Other Writings

In His Own Write. Self-illustrated. New York: Simon & Schuster, 1964.
A Spaniard in the Works. Self-illustrated. New York: Simon & Schuster, 1965.
The Penguin John Lennon. New York: Penguin, 1966.
(With Jann Wenner) *Lennon Remembers.* San Francisco: Straight Arrow Books, 1971.
(With Yoko Ono) *Skywriting by Word of Mouth; and Other Writings.* New York: HarperCollins, 1986.
(Illustrator) *Real Love: The Drawings for Sean.* New York: Random House, 1999.

Songbooks

(With Paul McCartney) *Eine Kleine Beatlemusik.* London: Northern Songs Ltd., 1965.
(With McCartney and George Harrison) *The Golden Beatles.* London: Northern Songs Ltd., 1966.
(With McCartney) *The Music of Lennon and McCartney.* New York: Hansen, 1969.

References and Suggested Reading

Coleman, Ray. *Lennon.* New York: McGraw-Hill, 1985.
Partridge, Elizabeth. *John Lennon: All I Want Is the Truth.* New York: Viking/Penguin, 2005.

Myra Cohn Livingston
(1926–1996)

Myra Cohn Livingston was born on August 17, 1926, in Omaha, Nebraska, the daughter of Mayer Louis and Gertrude Marks Cohn. She frequently described her earliest years as idyllic; the Cohns lived in a close community, including extended family, and these early experiences would provide the subject matter for many of her early poems for children. Her mother read stories aloud, and encouraged the youngster to write. By the age of ten, Cohn was keeping a journal, a practice she continued throughout her life.

Cohn attended Sarah Lawrence College in the Bronxville section of Westchester County, New York, where she was advised by a teacher to submit some of the poems she had written for class to children's magazines. Three of the fledgling writer's poems were immediately accepted by *Story Parade*. One of those was "Whispers," a work that became the title piece for her first collection, published in 1958; it has been her most frequently anthologized poem.

After college, Cohn relocated to California from New York. She took jobs in public relations, wrote book reviews, and worked as secretary to singer Dinah Shore and to musician Jascha Heifetz. Cohn married CPA Richard Livingston in 1952. The couple moved to Dallas, where they lived for thirteen years, raising their three children.

In 1958, Livingston began working as a creative writing teacher in the Dallas Public School system and at the city's public library. Her first book, *Whispers and Other Poems*, was published the same year. These were poems she'd written during her college years. The book won an honor from the *New York Herald Tribune*. *Whispers* was followed quickly by *Wide Awake, and Other Poems* (1959) and a series of collections directed to young readers. Livingston's early work focused on the everyday images of her own and her children's childhood. Some of Livingston's collections consist of poems that can be read as a single extended piece.

The Livingston family moved to Los Angeles in 1964. Myra took a position of poet-in-residence for a school district in Beverly Hills. She worked with children in grades kindergarten through twelve and provided resources for professionals.

Livingston began her career as compiler in 1968, first editing a collection meant for adolescents, *A Tune Beyond Us: A Collection of Poetry.* In one of her most inventive anthologies, *Speak Roughly to Your Little Boy* (1971), Livingston placed famous poems alongside parodies of the originals to humorous effect. She edited collections of the poems of Lewis Carroll and Edward Lear. Livingston's interest in the works of other poets went beyond her professional responsibilities; she personally amassed a collection of ten thousand volumes.

In 1972, Livingston published *The Malibu, and Other Poems.* This collection included more poems directed toward middle- and secondary-school readers. Poems included in this collection addressed environmental concerns and explored teenager's increasingly complex emotions. Similar themes are echoed in *The Way Things Are*, which won a Golden Kite Honor from the Society of Children's Book Writers and Illustrators.

Livingston's 1974 book *No Way of Knowing: Dallas Poems* earned several prizes, including accolades from the *Horn Book* and a Texas Institute of Letters award, but it also sparked controversy. The poems are written in a language pattern that has been described as a Southern, working-class dialect, and Livingston's use of the local voice was perceived as inappropriate and thus offensive to some readers. Reviews were generally favorable, and the collection is considered one of her strongest. The poems are based on Livingston's time living in Texas, and center on themes that range from the mundane to the topical. Narrators tell of their hopes and their dreams, of such everyday experiences as fishing or dating, but there are also poems that address the racial tensions of the 1960s and the sense of disquiet that followed the John F. Kennedy assassination in Dallas. The book is dedicated to a friend of Livingston's from that city.

Livingston realized that not all of her readers had the good fortune of an uncomplicated childhood, and she wanted to reach children and youth whose lives posed challenges. She spent time as a member of the Poetry Therapy Institute's board of directors, which recognized the importance of art education in reaching young people in need. She also took an active stand in bringing ecological concerns to readers. In some of her later works, Livingston used seasons and other natural elements both as subjects in a series of works including *Sky Songs* (1984), *Earth Songs* (1986), and *Space*

Songs (1988) as well as in some animal anthologies, and as metaphors, most notably in her use of the seasons in *A Circle of Seasons* (1982).

Livingston's 1979 release *O Sliver of Liver: Together with Other Triolets, Cinquains, Haiku, Verses, and a Dash of Poems* used those traditional forms in pieces that varied from dark, reflective themes to other, more affirming and humorous poems, as in the gentle "Lights: Cambridge, Massachusetts." *Monkey Puzzle and Other Poems* (1984) gave middle and secondary readers rich verses about Livingston's awe for the natural world, but it also included cautionary notes about deforestation and the repercussions of human activity.

From 1975 through 1996, Livingston worked as a consultant for a publishing house and spent a fifteen-year tenure as a member of the Southern California chapter of RIF (Reading Is Fundamental). She wrote a series of professional books that reflected her convictions as a writer and as a teacher: a strong understanding of and respect for poetic forms and formal poetry, the need for poetry education and exploration, and the need to inspire the imaginations of children. Livingston believed in the value of structure in writing—a lesson she ascribed, in part, to her background in learning the rhythms and meter in the compositions she studied as a musician. As a writer, Livingston chose from among the forms to suit each subject she handled. Even works Livingston initially intended for very young readers are now being catalogued as appealing to a broad audience, and they are indexed in multiple ways in sources such as *Twentieth Century Children's Writers* (1978).

Livingston lived in a mountain villa in the Santa Monica area until her death from cancer in 1996.

Website

"Children's Literature Network." http://www.childrensliteraturenetwork.org

Poetry

Whispers, and Other Poems. Illustrated by Jacqueline Chwast. New York: Harcourt, 1958.
A Lolligag of Limericks. Illustrated by Joseph Low. New York: Atheneum, 1978.
O Sliver of Liver: Together with Other Triolets, Cinquains, Haiku, Verses, and a Dash of Poems. Illustrated by Iris Van Rynbach. New York: Atheneum, 1978.
No Way of Knowing: Dallas Poems. New York: Atheneum, 1979.
A Circle of Seasons. Illustrated by Leonard Everett Fisher. New York: Holiday House, 1982.
Sky Songs. Illustrated by Leonard Everett Fisher. New York: Holiday House, 1984.
Monkey Puzzle, and Other Poems. Illustrated by Antonio Frasconi. New York: Atheneum, 1984.

Worlds I Know and Other Poems. Illustrated by Tim Arnold. New York: Atheneum, 1984.

A Song I Sang to You: A Selection of Poems. Illustrated by Margot Tomes. New York: Harcourt, 1984.

Celebrations. Illustrated by Leonard Everett Fisher. New York: Holiday House, 1985.

Earth Songs. Illustrated by Leonard Everett Fisher. New York: Holiday House, 1986.

Higgledy-Piggledy: Verses and Pictures. Illustrated by Peter Sis. New York: Macmillan, 1986.

Sea Songs. Illustrated by Leonard Everett Fisher. New York: Holiday House, 1986.

Space Songs. Illustrated by Leonard Everett Fisher. New York: Holiday House, 1988.

There Was a Place and Other Poems. New York: Macmillan, 1988.

Up in the Air. Illustrated by Leonard Everett Fisher. New York: Holiday House, 1989.

Birthday Poems. Illustrated by Margot Tomes. New York: Holiday House, 1989.

Remembering, and Other Poems. New York: Macmillan, 1989.

My Head is Red and Other Riddle Rhymes. Illustrated by Tere Lo Prete. New York: Holiday House, 1990.

Let Freedom Ring: A Ballad of Martin Luther King, Jr. Illustrated by Samuel Byrd. New York: Holiday House, 1992.

Light and Shadow. Photographs by Barbara Rogasky. New York: Holiday House, 1992.

I Never Told and Other Poems. New York: McElderry, 1992.

Abraham Lincoln: A Man for All the People. Illustrated by Samuel Byrd. New York: Holiday House, 1994.

Call Down to the Moon: Poems of Music. New York: HarperCollins, 1994.

Keep on Singing: A Ballad of Marian Anderson. Illustrated by Samuel Byrd. New York: Holiday House, 1994.

Flights of Fancy and Other Poems. New York: McElderry, 1994.

B Is for Baby: An Alphabet of Verses. Photographs by Steel Stillman. New York: McElderry, 1996.

Festivals. Illustrated by Leonard Everett Fisher. New York: Holiday House, 1996.

Cricket Never Does: A Collection of Haiku and Tanka. New York: Margaret K. McElderry Books, 1997.

References and Suggested Reading

Fogelson, Marilee, consultant. *Lives and Works: Young Adult Authors, Vol. 5.* Danbury, CT: Grolier Educational, 1999.

Hopkins, Lee Bennett. *Pauses: Autobiographical Reflections of 101 Creators of Children's Books.* New York: HarperCollins, 1995.

McElmeel, Sharron. *100 Most Popular Children's Authors: Biographical Sketches and Bibliographies.* Englewood, CO: Libraries Unlimited, 1999.

Rochman, Hazel. "Myra Cohn Livingston." In *Dictionary of Literary Biography, Volume 61: American Writers for Children Since 1960: Poets, Illustrators, and Nonfiction Authors.* Detroit: Gale Research, 1987, pp. 153–65.

W. S. Merwin
(1927–)

William Stanley Merwin was born in New York City on September 30, 1927, the son of a minister and his wife. At the age of five, William showed an early interest in poetry, and he began composing verses as hymns for his father, who served at the First Presbyterian Church in Union City, New Jersey.

When Merwin was nine, the family moved to Scranton, Pennsylvania. The city was in a financial crisis, and the family was thrust into dire straits as the church trustees reneged on payment of the minister's salary. Merwin's father could scarcely object. One of his great fears was being exposed for not having the educational or ecclesiastical credentials to hold his position. He became distant from his son, limiting their interactions almost exclusively to disciplinary matters. The family was separated during World War II, when the reverend became an army chaplain. The strained relationship between Merwin and his father would inspire poetry, notably in the opening sections of *Opening the Hand*. Merwin also explored these father–son dynamics in his memoirs.

After an elementary public school education, supplemented by tutelage from his maternal aunt, Merwin won a scholarship to a boarding school in Wyoming. He was only fifteen when he took his college entrance examinations. He was interested in attending the U.S. Naval Academy in Annapolis and applied to schools he thought would help him gain entry when he came of age. Merwin was offered a full scholarship to Princeton University. Although he was not an outstanding student and claimed to have spent as much time at the school's stables as at his studies, Merwin began reading and writing in earnest. He was especially taken with the works of Spinoza, Shelley, Federico Garcia Lorca, William Arrowsmith, T. S. Eliot, and Ezra Pound. He met two poets who would become his mentors, John Berryman and R. P. Blackmur, the latter a critic as well as a working writer. Merwin has attributed the two with being, outside of his parents, the most influential forces in what he called his outlook, through their passion for language and their active involvement in his literary development—from editing his pieces to encouraging him to continue his education.

Merwin completed his bachelor's degree in English in 1947, then spent a year studying Romance languages in Princeton's Department of Modern Languages. He married girlfriend Dorothy Jeanne Ferry and began to travel. He would not complete his master's degree, choosing instead to live abroad for seven years. Merwin worked as a tutor, first in Portugal, in the employ of a princess, then on Majorca, teaching the son of renowned British poet Robert Graves. He took a job in London, translating scripts for the British Broadcasting Corporation. He would do extensive work on translations throughout his career, including prose, poetry, and dramas from the French, Spanish, and ancient Sanskrit. The influence of these languages on Merwin manifested in different ways; he would sometimes infuse foreign rhythms into his own poetry.

W. H. Auden chose Merwin's manuscript *A Mask for Janus* as the winner of the Yale Series of Younger Poets Award, and the book was published in 1952. The collection featured themes that would be echoed throughout Merwin's career: the exploration of self; a view of the collapse of civilization as well as its reemergence; and an awareness of things immaterial or absent, missing pieces, a sense of loss, an unanswered want. Another theme, Merwin's sensitivity to nature, became apparent early. His works would increasingly include calls for ecological awareness.

Merwin's second book, *The Dancing Bears*, was released in 1954 to strong critical notices, earning its author a *Kenyon Review* fellowship. In "On the Subject of Poetry," Merwin's narrator admits that he does not understand the world, and, as with much of Merwin's work, invites the reader to explore along with him. There is a recognition that words might not be enough to capture the world or human emotions, yet he as poet must speak of the world and man's place in it. Merwin retells a Norwegian folktale in the lengthy "East of the Sun and West of the Moon," a poem of more than five hundred lines. Elements of the mythic are present in many of Merwin's poems. He has stated a conviction that life itself, and poetry, or any real use of language, is mythic (Hix, *W. S. Merwin*, p. 23).

Green with Beasts (1956) included more lyrical poems, with less emphasis on the mythic. The opening poem, "Leviathan," which follows a whale through images of chaos and creation, has become his most frequently anthologized work. Animals feature prominently in the collection. In several poems, Merwin considers man's relationships in the balance of the natural world. He questions whether their lack of language hinders us from understanding animals, concluding that even human language is not sufficient to capture the soul, being more like the animals' own nonverbal manifestations than might first be apparent. Merwin's fourth poetry collection, *The Drunk in the Furnace* (1960), would complete what he later regarded as his first cycle.

By the mid- to late 1950s, Merwin was becoming increasingly concerned with threats to nature and with the peril of nuclear weaponry. He worked as a writer and editor for the magazine *The Nation.* As Merwin became more politically aware, his writing style changed. He began to write more free verse, departing from the more traditional forms found in his first four books. In *The Moving Target*, poems evoke images of the natural world, viewed as insights into the psyche and explorations of memory and grief. In his examinations of the future of mankind, Merwin develops tones of melancholy and rage.

One of the main sequences in *The Carrier of Ladders* (1970) acted as Merwin's own exploration of the country, particularly of issues that troubled him deeply: the plight of Native Americans, the exploitation of lands and resources, the abuse of presidential powers. Merwin won the Pulitzer Prize for this collection. He used the celebrity afforded by the award as a platform to voice his objection to policies in Southeast Asia.

Merwin's themes and his shifts in style resonate with teen and young adult readers. His work spans the deeply personal, the mythic, and the topical, sounding the voice of a crusader. Merwin offers unflinching looks at the world, taking on environmental causes and geopolitical issues with sincerity and fervor. His ability to match his style to his purpose, from the early lyrical works to the terse, succinct verse of his activist middle career, to the more conversational tone of his later collections allows young readers a microcosmic study of varied narration. His intolerance of human arrogance and his fears of its eventual, cataclysmic repercussions cause teen readers who seek their own answers to the complexities of man's place in the world to find a voice that, in richly textured rhythms and elegant language, invites them to find their own paths and their own voices.

Website

"Modern American Poetry." http://www.english.uiuc.edu

Poetry

A Mask for Janus. New Haven, CT: Yale University Press, 1952.
The Dancing Bears. New Haven, CT: Yale University Press, 1954.
Green with Beasts. New York: Knopf, 1956.

The Drunk in the Furnace. New York: Macmillan, 1960.

The Moving Target. New York: Atheneum, 1963.

The Lice. New York: Atheneum, 1967.

The Carrier of Ladders. New York: Atheneum, 1970.

Writings to an Unfinished Accompaniment. New York: Atheneum, 1973.

The First Four Books of Poems. New York: Atheneum, 1975.

The Compass Flower. New York: Atheneum, 1977.

Finding the Island. San Francisco: North Point Press, 1982.

Opening the Hand. New York: Atheneum, 1983.

The Rain in the Trees. New York: Knopf, 1988.

Selected Poems. New York: Atheneum, 1988.

The Second Four Books of Poems. Port Townsend, WA: Copper Canyon Press, 1993.

The Vixen. New York: Knopf, 1996.

Flower & Hand. New York: Knopf, 1997.

The Folding Cliffs: A Narrative. New York: Knopf, 1998.

The River Sound. New York: Knopf, 1999.

The Pupil. New York: Knopf, 2001.

Fiction

The Miner's Pale Children. New York, Atheneum, 1970.

Houses and Travelers. New York: Atheneum, 1977.

The Lost Upland. New York: Atheneum, 1992.

The Mays for Ventadorn. New York: National Geographic Directions, 2002.

The Ends of the Earth. Emeryville, CA: Shoemaker & Hoard, 2004.

Nonfiction and Memoir

Regions of Memory: Uncollected Prose. Urbana: University of Illinois Press, 1987.

Unframed Originals: Recollections. New York: Atheneum, 1982.

The Lost Upland: Stories of Southwest France. New York: Knopf, 1992.

Travels. New York: Knopf, 1993.

Summer Doorways: A Memoir. Emeryville, CA: Shoemaker & Hoard, 2005.

Anthology

Lament for the Makers: A Memorial Anthology. Washington, DC: Counterpoint, 1996.

References and Suggested Reading

Hix, H. L. *W. S. Merwin.* Columbia: University of South Carolina Press, 1997.

Kraus, Jim. "W. S. Merwin." In *American Writers,* Suppl. 3, Vol. 1. New York: Charles Scribner's Sons, 1991, pp. 339–60.

Nelson, Cary, and Ed Folsom, eds. *W. S. Merwin: Essays on the Poetry.* Urbana: University of Illinois Press, 1987.

Edna St. Vincent Millay
(1892–1950)

Millay was born on February 22, 1892, in Rockland, Maine, to Henry Tolman and Cora Buzelle Millay. Cora Millay mistakenly thought that she was having a son and was determined to name the child Vincent in honor of a hospital where her own brother was a patient. The family often called Edna "Vincent," and she used variations of the name throughout her writing career.

After Cora Millay divorced Henry in 1900, she trained as a nurse in order to support herself and her daughters. Beginning in 1903, the Millays lived in Camden, Maine, in relatively modest circumstances, surrounded by literature and music. Cora Millay began teaching Edna music, and a local teacher took Edna on as a student. Edna's early hopes to become a concert pianist were dashed when the teacher said that Edna's hands were too small, so Edna turned to writing. Edna and sisters Kathleen and Norma made up their own songs and short poems. While Edna was in her teens, six of her poems were published in *St. Nicholas*, a children's magazine; she won the top prize for her poem "Friends."

Millay attended Camden High School, where she wrote for the school newspaper, graduating high school in 1909. She traveled to Kingman, Maine, in 1912 to care for her father, who was in failing health. It was during this stay away from home that Cora wrote to her daughter about a literary contest for pieces to be included in the annual anthology *Lyric Year*. Millay submitted a lengthy poem titled "Renaissance" (subsequently changed to "Renascence") and "Interim," a monologue. "Renascence" came in at fourth place and attracted immediate critical attention. Described as a visionary poem, it embodied Millay's spiritual and emotional awakenings. Poets Witter Bynner and Arthur Davison Ficke began correspondences with Millay.

A YWCA program director, Caroline B. Dow, heard Millay perform music and poetry, and encouraged Millay to continue her education. Millay took a few courses at New York City's Barnard College in 1913, enjoying the strong literary community. She was awarded a scholarship to Vassar College. Millay matriculated in 1914, and was active in writing poetry and plays, acting in plays and pageants, even writing song lyrics.

Millay graduated in 1917, and set out with her sister Norma for New York to take full advantage of the city's literary and theatrical communities. She was determined to forge a career as an actress. She gave poetry readings and joined two Greenwich Village acting troupes, writing and directing. That same year, Mitchell Kennerley published Millay's first book, *Renascence, and Other Poems*, consisting of twenty-three poems. Millay included sonnets, monologues, and short lyrics. Some of the poems reflected Millay's views on female empowerment, in voices as diverse as a woman who confesses to feeling no control over her life in "Indifference," a man becoming resigned to his inability to truly understand his wife in "Witch-Wife," and the voice of a female pirate in "Bluebeard."

Vanity Fair began publishing Millay's poems in 1920. Following a set of romantic involvements, Millay was beginning to suffer from exhaustion and mental fatigue. The editor of *Vanity Fair* provided Millay a salaried trip to write in Europe. Millay left for France early in 1921, and wrote sketches for the magazine as well as a play for the occasion of Vassar's anniversary, *The Lamp and the Bell*.

Second April (1921), included love poems and free verse as well as sonnets, works rich in images of love and beauty, artistry, and loss. The book was released while Millay was in Europe, working on the novel *Hardigut*, which would never be finished. She was suffering bouts of ill health and traveled back to the United States by the beginning of 1923. *The Harp-Weaver, and Other Poems* came out that year. The poems were dedicated to Millay's mother. The book's final section is a major work, "Sonnets from an Ungrafted Tree." The melancholy saga of a woman nursing her previously-estranged husband becomes a lament for her own mother's failed marriage and for women who sublimate themselves to others' needs.

Millay married businessman Eugene Jan Boissevain in the summer of 1923, and he devoted himself to Millay's personal care and to her career. He consistently nurtured her; throughout the 1920s, he coordinated public readings for the generally shy Millay. The couple moved to a farm in Austerlitz, New York. Millay continued to have difficulties, especially with her vision, and with painful headaches.

In 1927, Millay was arrested for protesting the executions of Sacco and Vanzetti. Her experiences led to the *Outlook* article "Fear," and influenced several of the pieces in her next collection of poems, *The Buck in the Snow, and Other Poems.* In 1937, Millay wrote a full length libretto, *The King's Henchman* (music by Deems Taylor), for the Metropolitan Opera. It was successful both in book form and in performance.

Millay, stricken with increasing bouts of neurosis, suffered a breakdown in 1944. Her husband died of a stroke following lung surgery in 1949, and she began working on a volume of poetry titled *Mine the Harvest.* Millay completed the poems in 1950 but did not live to see the book published. She died at home of a heart attack on October 19, 1950. *Mine the Harvest* was released posthumously in 1954.

Millay's early work appeals to youthful audiences though its intensity and its themes of first love, searches for self, defining and breaking free of conventional roles, and an exuberance toward life. Her sonnets are considered models of the form, and her impact on contemporary literature is as an innovator as well as an artist who embraced traditional literary techniques.

Website

"Poet Seers." http://www.poetseers.org

Poetry

Renascence, and Other Poems. New York: M. Kennerley, 1917.
A Few Figs from Thistles: Poems and Four Sonnets. New York: M. Kennerley, 1920.
Second April. New York: M. Kennerley, 1921.
The Ballad of the Harp-Weaver. New York: F. Shay, 1922.
The Buck in Snow, and Other Poems. New York: Harper, 1928.
Fatal Interview. New York: Harper, 1931.
Wine from These Grapes. New York: Harper, 1934.
Conversation at Midnight. New York: Harper, 1937.
Huntsman, What Quarry? New York: Harper, 1939.
There Are No Islands, Any More: Lines Written in Passion and in Deep Concern for England, France, and My Own Country. New York: Harper, 1940.
Make Bright the Arrow: 1940 Notebook. New York: Harper, 1940.
The Murder of Lidice. New York: Harper, 1942.
Second April and the Buck in the Snow. New York: Harper, 1950.
Mine the Harvest. New York: Harper, 1954.
Selected Poems / The Centenary Edition. New York: Harper Perennial, 1992.

Fiction

(Under pseudonym Nancy Boyd) *Distressing Dialogues.* New York: Harper, 1924.

Letters

Letters of Edna St. Vincent Millay. New York: Harper, 1952.

References and Suggested Reading

Hart, Paula L. "Edna St. Vincent Millay." *Dictionary of Literary Biography, Vol. 45: American Poets, 1880–1945, First Series.* Detroit: Gale Group, 1986.

Showalter, Elaine, ed. *Modern American Women Writers.* New York: Charles S. Scribner's Sons, 1991.

N(avarre) Scott Momaday (1934–)

Navarre Scott Momaday grew up in an environment rich in creativity, ensconced in the culture of the Kiowa people. Building a career as a poet, essayist, critic, novelist, and author of memoirs, Momaday has become a focus of study among students and academics.

N. Scott Momaday was born at the Kiowa and Comanche Indian Hospital in Lawton, Oklahoma, on February 27, 1934, to Alfred Morris (also called Huan-toa) and Mayme Natachee Mommadaty. Though his birth was registered under the name of Novarro Scotte Mammedatty, his family adopted the current spelling of Momaday. Momaday's father was nearly full-blooded Kiowa. His mother was of only limited Native American ancestry and was also a descendant of early American pioneers, but she felt a deep connection to the Native American community. She named herself Little Moon as a child and chose to matriculate at a Native American School after high school.

Following Navarre's birth, the Momadays took their son to live for a year at the home of his grandmother as the young couple sought work. It was a spare existence, in a home without plumbing or electricity. Momaday's parents found work teaching with the help of the Bureau of Indian Affairs, and the family of three lived on a series of reservations across Arizona and New Mexico. This provided a mix of experiences among the Apaches, the Navajo, and the Pueblo, the Jemez Pueblo reservation recalled as a favorite among Momaday's early homes.

As a young child, Momaday was exposed to the arts in and around his home. In addition to their careers in education, his father was a painter, teaching art as his specialty in a two-teacher school; his mother was a writer. Momaday was heavily influenced by both parents' artistic inclinations. His mother shared with him a wealth of literature, encouraging his writing, and his father inspired Momaday's interest in painting and print-making. He developed a love of storytelling as both art form and as means of carrying on the oral tradition of his people. Momaday also had an ardent interest in sports, from his own passion for horseback riding (he received his own first horse at the age of twelve) and boxing.

In the 1950s Momaday enrolled at the University of New Mexico (UNM). He left UNM and enrolled at the University of Virginia for one year, and returned to UNM to complete his degree. He graduated from UNM in 1958 with a degree in political science. Momaday took a position teaching middle and high-school students at the Dulce School on the Jicarilla Reservation in New Mexico. In 1959, Momaday married Gay Mangold, a union that would produce three daughters, Cael, Jill, and Brit, but one that would eventually end in divorce.

During his year at the Dulce school, Momaday wrote poetry in his spare time and submitted several poems to Stanford University as his applied for a fellowship. He won the grant and took a leave of absence from his teaching job to earn his master's degree in Stanford's writing program. Once in California, though, under the mentorship of fellowship coordinator, poet, and critic Yvor Winters, Momaday decided to work toward his doctorate, and he spent the next twenty years in California. Winters helped Momaday develop his poetic style and forms. Momaday's first published work, dating from his time at Stanford, was not a collection of poetry but an academic work on the poems of Frederick Goddard Tuckerman, the subject of Momaday's dissertation. Momaday's study of Tuckerman reflected their shared interest in naturalism, and Momaday's poem "Before an Old Painting of the Crucifixion" is believed to be heavily influenced by his study of Tuckerman. His poem "The Bear," also a product of Momaday's time at Stanford, won the Academy of American Poets prize.

Momaday began teaching college, joining the faculty at the University of California in Santa Barbara. He developed a program in American Indian studies and published a set of Kiowa tales under the title *The Journey of Tai-Me* (1967), later included as part of his 1969 release *The Way to Rainy Mountain*. Momaday was granted a Guggenheim fellowship for 1966–67, and he balanced his time writing between poetry and work on his first novel, *House Made of Dawn*. This novel, published in 1968, was initially going to be a poetic work, but it developed as a set of short stories, then into a full-length work of fiction. This story of an Indian veteran returning to life in New Mexico after World War II brought Momaday instant fame and critical acclaim as Momaday received the Pulitzer Prize for fiction. His next book, *The Way to Rainy Mountain*, combined poems, memoirs, and myths chronicling the story of the Kiowa people. The book represented a collaboration with his father, whose artwork appears in it.

Momaday's work is celebrated and embraced by a wide audience. His poetry is taught in secondary school as emblematic of a distinctly American voice, and it is recognized for its blend of humanism and spirituality. Momaday views poets as the ones charged with enlightening, inspiring, and encouraging readers. Still active in his craft and as a spokesman for environmental concerns, Momaday has received honorary degrees from twelve universities. He currently resides in Tucson, Arizona.

Website

"Poet Seers." http://www.poetseers.org

Poetry

Angle of Geese and Other Poems. Boston: Godine, 1974.
The Colors of Night. San Francisco: Arion, 1976.
The Gourd Dancer. New York: Harper & Row, 1976.
In the Presence of the Sun: A Gathering of Shields. Santa Fe, NM: Rydal, 1992.
In the Bear's House. New York: St. Martin's Press, 1999.

Fiction

House Made of Dawn. New York: Harper & Row, 1968.
The Way to Rainy Mountain. Albuquerque: University of New Mexico Press, 1969.
The Ancient Child. New York: Doubleday, 1989.
Circle of Wonder: A Native American Christmas Story. Santa Fe, NM: Clear Light, 1993.

Nonfiction

The Journey of Tai-me. Santa Barbara, CA: Privately printed, 1967.
The Names: A Memoir. New York: Harper & Row, 1976.
The Man Made of Words: Essays, Stories, Passages. New York: St. Martin's Press, 1997.

Drama

The Indolent Boys (1994).
Children of the Sun (1997).

References and Suggested Reading

Barry, Paul C. "N. Scott Momaday." *Canku Ota: A Newsletter Celebrating Native America 9* (May 6, 2000).

Roember, Kenneth M. "N. Scott Momaday: Biographical, Literary, and Multicultural Context." *Modern American Poetry* (2005).

Schubnell, Matthias, ed. *Conversations with N. Scott Momaday.* Jackson: University Press of Mississippi, 1997.

Woodard, Charles L. *Ancestral Voice: Conversations with N. Scott Momaday.* Lincoln: University of Nebraska Press.

Marianne Moore
(1887–1972)

During her lifetime, Marianne Moore created a body of literature that earned her many of the field's most prestigious awards as well as more than a dozen honorary degrees, yet she is remembered just as much for her inimitable style. A well-known figure, easily recognized in her black cape and three-cornered hat, Moore publicly celebrated a wide range of interests.

Marianne Craig Moore was born in Kirkwood, Missouri, on November 15, 1887, the second child of John Milton Moore and Mary Warner Moore. John Milton Moore was not an active presence in the lives of his children. He suffered a breakdown following the failure of

Marianne Moore. Courtesy of Photofest.

a business venture before Marianne was born. Mary Warner Moore raised her children at the home of her father, the Reverend Doctor John Riddle Warner, a widower. After Warner's death, the young family moved to Pennsylvania, where Mary Moore taught English at the Metzger Institute for Girls in Carlisle, a school Marianne attended. Marianne and her mother had a close relationship, one that would continue until Mary Moore's death in 1947. The only time the two did not live together was during Marianne's college years.

At Bryn Mawr College, Marianne Moore took special interest in a class on seventeenth-century literature. When Moore was not permitted to major in English because of her deficiency in writing, she enrolled in science courses, with a minor concentration in biology. It is the exactness of a surgeon's scalpel, captured in poetic form and language, that greets readers of her imaginative verse. She also studied politics, history, and economics as an undergraduate student. Her studies influenced her writing. Moore's poetry about animals finds special favor with young readers. The poems show a sharp eye for detail and an educated understanding of wildlife.

Moore wrote both short stories and poetry in college, publishing eight of each in the literary magazine. She graduated in 1909. After taking a business course at a commercial college, Moore traveled to Europe in 1911, an experience that provided a good deal of inspiration. Upon her return from Europe, Moore wrote and submitted pieces to the Bryn Mawr alumnae journal while teaching business courses and coaching boys' sports at a Carlisle Indian school.

Several of Moore's poems were published in journals such as *The Egoist* and *Poetry* in 1915, including the politically motivated "To the Soul of Progress," in response to the advent of World War I and a climate of militarism. An early collection of sixty-four poems was rejected by publishers that same year. Moore sought assistance from fellow Bryn Mawr alumnus Hilda Doolittle (H.D.) in getting that volume published. Doolittle actually took over that project, and edited it along with staff from the Egoist Press; Moore was not given the opportunity to edit the collection. It was first released in England in 1921 and marked Moore's fledgling full-length publication.

A set of Moore's poems appeared in *The Dial* in 1920, including "England" and "Picking and Choosing." Her work was garnering recognition, especially "England," seen as a tribute to America juxtaposed with sharp, concisely worded glimpses at other countries. Moore became known as a modernist, and her free verse compositions read, at times, almost as streams of thought; their appeal to young readers lies in finding meanings in a series of visual cues. The poems convey a feeling of speed or urgency, compelling readers to see everything and to formulate judgments. Moore sprinkled quotes and allusions throughout her works, adding to the feeling of interaction between author and audience, and adding to their appeal to young adult readers. Moore's work on behalf of reading communities has not been limited to her prose or imaginative verse. She worked for the New York Public Library from 1921 through 1925, and she was editor of *Dial* magazine, which ceased publication in 1929.

By the mid-1920s, Moore was viewed as one of the luminaries in contemporary poetry, and she developed friendships with such figures as Elizabeth Bishop, who had spirited exchanges with Moore over Bishop's work, and with T. S. Eliot, Ezra Pound, William Carlos Williams, and Wallace Stevens.

Moore's work in the 1940s and 1950s was not as universally well received. Several pieces, such as "What Are Years?" and "In Distrust of Merits" (1940 and 1943, respectively) are still regarded as among her finest works, but her poetry in general was perceived as less consistent in quality than what she had previously produced. However, Moore's unique style has guaranteed her continuing appeal to new generations of readers. Moore died on February 5, 1972.

Website

"Modern American Poetry." http://www.english.uiuc.edu

Poetry

Poems. London: Egoist Press, 1921.
Marriage. New York: Manikan, 1923.
Observations. New York: Dial Press, 1924.
Selected Poems. New York: Macmillan, 1935.
The Pangolin and Other Verses. London: Brendin, 1936.
What Are Years? New York: Macmillan, 1941.
Nevertheless. New York: Macmillan, 1944.
Collected Poems. New York: Macmillan, 1951.
Like a Bulwark. New York: Viking, 1959.
O to Be a Dragon. New York: Viking, 1959.
Complete Poems. New York: Viking, 1967.

Nonfiction

Predilections. New York: Viking, 1955.

Reader

A Marianne Moore Reader. New York: Viking, 1961.

Translations and Adaptations

The Fables of La Fontaine. New York: Viking, 1954.
Perrault, Charles. *Puss in Boots, The Sleeping Beauty, and Cinderella.* New York: Macmillan, 1963.

References and Suggested Reading

Bromwich, David. "Emphatic Resonance in Marianne Moore's Poems." In *American Women Poets, 1650–1950.* Ed. Harold Blood. Philadelphia: Chelsea House, 2002.

Costello, Bonnie. "The Feminine Language of Marianne Moore." In *American Women Poets, 1650–1950.* Ed. Harold Blood. Philadelphia: Chelsea House, 2002.

Garrigue, Jean. "Marianne Moore." In *American Writers, Vol. 3.* New York: Charles Scribner's Sons, 1974.

Goodridge, Celeste. "Marianne Moore." *Modern American Writers.* Ed. Elaine Showalter. New York: Charles Scribner's Sons, 1991.

Lillian Morrison
(1917-)

It is unlikely that, when Lillian Morrison began her lengthy career at the New York Public Library, she envisioned that she would one day be shelving her own works of poetry there. Throughout her professional life, Morrison balanced time in the branch library system, followed by positions in the young adult services office, with creating literature for the very audience she greeted daily.

Lillian Morrison was born on October 27, 1917, in Jersey City, New Jersey. As a child, she was drawn to the rhythms and chants of city life and of playground games. Her love of poetry grew out of these simple beginnings. Following graduation from a local high school, Morrison entered Rutgers University's Douglass College. She earned a bachelor of science degree in 1938, then went on to earn a second degree at Columbia University in 1942. Morrison began her career as a librarian in 1942, and remained in the branch system of the New York Public Library for five years before adding the responsibilities of working with vocational high schools, from 1947 through 1952. Her next promotion was to the Office of Young Adult Services, where Morrison acted as Assistant Coordinator through 1969, followed by a tenure as Coordinator from 1969 through her retirement in 1982.

Morrison realized early in her dealings with the young readers who frequented her library branch, and later her office, that many of them could feel little, if any, connection with poetry. Children and young adults in the 1950s and 1960s had little grounding in the classics and in the conventions of poetry, which seemed to dull their interest rather than pique their curiosity. Morrison struggled to find poems that would have high appeal to the interests of contemporary audiences while introducing them to some of the more traditional forms. She began to compile riddles, traditional sayings, autograph verses, and rhymes. Her first book, *Yours Till Niagara Falls*, published in 1950, was a collection of autograph verses. Three years later, Morrison's *Black Within and Red Without: A Book of Riddles* was published, followed in 1955 by a series of adages and sayings in *A Diller, a Dollar: Rhymes and Sayings for the Ten O'Clock Scholar*.

Morrison was finding a following among readers who enjoyed the simplicity of the verses she selected, their humor, and her keen judgment in choosing poems that appealed even to reluctant readers. Morrison moved on to the less conventional with her next work, *Touch Blue*, which highlighted love charms, chants, and ancient wisdom in clear, unembellished language. More autograph verses followed in *Remember Me When This You See* (1961).

In 1965, Morrison's *Sprints and Distances* reads as a tribute to sports and sportsmanship, blending poetry by both modern and ancient writers. The poems embrace the spirit of athleticism, often as personal narratives, and reached out in a particular way to young men, many of whom rarely read poetry. Fresh and exciting, the use of the sports motif made an effective hook, especially among educators and visitors to urban libraries.

Morrison's first book of original poetry was *The Ghosts of Jersey City, and Other Poems*, a work for young adult and adult audiences, published in 1967. She resumed her focus on younger readers and in 1968 released *Miranda's Music*, which was coauthored by Jean Boudin. Morrison returned to the autograph verse format with the 1974 volume *Best Wishes, Amen* before returning to original poetry with *The Sidewalk Race, and Other Poems of Sports and Motion* (1977). This book addresses many sports interests, from the street favorite stickball to boxing, from jump rope to professional sports. With rhythms evocative of those she'd heard in her own childhood, Morrison found a separate style for each sport, all tactile, all sharply drawn.

Morrison's next collection, *Who Would Marry a Mineral?* (1978) is described as a series of poems about nature, people, and nonsense. *Overheard in a Bubble Chamber* celebrated discovery and ingenuity, with poems about math and the sciences alongside striking paintings. Morrison returned to anthologizing works along themes of sports and movement with her 1985 release *Break Dance Kids* and 1988's *Rhythm Road*. The original work *Whistling the Morning In: New Poems* (1992) celebrated the natural world.

Also in 1992, Morrison released the anthology *At the Crack of the Bat*, an energetic look at baseball and the personalities in the sport. The book was a quick audience favorite, and Morrison followed the success of *Crack of the Bat* with *Slam Dunk: Basketball Poems* in 1995. This collection featured poems from such teen and childhood favorites as Walter Dean Myers and Jack Prelutsky, and it highlighted such superstars as Michael Jordan, Shaquille O'Neal, and Magic Johnson.

Morrison's next book, the collection *I Scream, You Scream: A Feast of Food Rhymes* mixed chants, rhymes, autograph verses, teaching verse, jingles, and valentines about food. In 2001, Morrison published *More Spice Than Sugar*, a mix of poetry and women's history (an area of interest in Morrison's own life), in words from contemporary and classic authors. Three sections separate the poems by theme, such as "When I Am Me," "She's a Winner," and "Against the Odds," and as a whole celebrate the achievements of girls and women who refuse to surrender to stereotypes.

Morrison returned to sports as a theme for the 2001 collection *Way to Go! Poems of Sports and Motion*, and revisited autograph verse for *It Rained All Day That Night*. She also acted as editor of Crowell Publishers' *Poets* and *Poems of the World* series. She has written for a number of periodicals.

Lillian Morrison's commitment, both by her choice of a career as a librarian and her own literary contributions, to getting poetry into the hands of those who might least seek it on their own have singled her out for distinction among her peers. Morrison was the recipient of the 1987 Grolier Foundation Award for outstanding contribution to the stimulation of reading by young people. Morrison's dynamic approach to revitalizing collections for young adults was instrumental in providing the current model for young adult rooms in many systems. Morrison's own interest in poetry as language in motion—as a kinetic experience—has enriched the field of young adult literature, and her persistence in meeting audiences at their own levels only to elevate them, has been an inspiration for those who seek to make vital connections between books and readers. Morrison currently resides in New York City.

Websites

"Baseball Poetry." http://www.baseball-almanac.com/poetry/po_donn.shtml
"Boyds Mill Press." http://www.boydsmillpress.com/authors

Poetry

The Ghosts of Jersey City, and Other Poems. New York: Crowell, 1967.
(With Jean Boudin) *Miranda's Music.* Illustrated by Helen Webber. New York: Crowell, 1968.
Who Would Marry a Mineral? Riddles, Runes, and Love Tunes. Illustrated by Rita Floden Leydon. New York: Lothrop, 1978.

Overheard in a Bubble Chamber and Other Sciencepoems. Illustrated by Eyre de Lanux. New York: Lothrop, 1981.

Whistling the Morning In: New Poems by Lillian Morrison. Illustrated by Joel Cook. Honesdale, PA: Boyds Mills Press, 1992.

Way to Go: Sports Poems. Illustrated by Susan Spellman. Honesdale, PA: Boyds Mills Press, 2002.

Editor and Compiler

Black Within and Red Without: A Book of Riddles. Illustrated by Jo Spier. New York: Crowell, 1953.

A Diller, a Dollar: Rhymes and Sayings for the Ten O'Clock Scholar. Illustrated by Marjorie Bauernschmidt. New York: Crowell, 1955.

Touch Blue: Signs and Spells, Love Charms and Chants, Auguries and Old Beliefs, in Rhyme. Illustrated by Doris Lee. New York: Crowell, 1958.

Remember Me When This You See: A New Collection of Autograph Verse. Illustrated by Marjorie Bauernschmidt . New York: Crowell, 1961.

Best Wishes, Amen: A New Collection of Autograph Verses. Illustrated by Loretta Lustig. New York: Crowell, 1974.

The Break Dance Kids: Poems of Sport, Motion, and Locomotion. New York: Lothrop, Lee, and Shepard, 1985.

Rhythm Road: An Anthology of Poems to Move To. New York: Lothrop, 1988.

Sprints and Distances: Sports in Poetry and the Poetry in Sport. Illustrated by John Ross and Clare R. Ross. New York: HarperCollins Children's Book Group, 1990.

Yours Till Niagara Falls: A Book of Autograph Verses. Illustrated by Sylvie Wickstrom. New York: HarperCollins Children's Book Group, 1990.

At the Crack of the Bat. Illustrated by Steve Ciselawski. New York: Hyperion Books for Children, 1992.

Slam Dunk: Poems About Basketball. New York: Dorling Kindersley, 1995.

I Scream, You Scream: A Feast of Food Rhymes. Illustrated by Nancy Dunaway. New York: Ingram, 1997.

(With Anne Boyajian) *More Spice than Sugar: Poems about Feisty Females.* New York: Houghton Mifflin, 2001.

It Rained All Day That Night. Illustrated by Christy Hole. Little Rock, AR: August House, 2003.

References and Suggested Reading

Shannon, Mike. *Tales from the Dugout: The Greatest True Baseball Stories Ever Told.* Chicago: Contemporary Books, 1997.

Wyndham, Lee, and Arnold Madison. *Writing for Children and Teenagers.* Cincinnati, OH: Writer's Digest Books, 1989.

Zinsser, William. *Worlds of Children: The Art and Craft of Writing for Children.* New York: Mariner, 1998.

Walter Dean Myers
(1937-)

When Walter Dean Myers was a child growing up in Harlem, it seemed unlikely to those around him that he would build a career around words: words did not seem to come easily to young Walter. A bright child, he had a pronounced speech defect that made him nearly incomprehensible to many outside of his own family, and he found himself falling into trouble, both in school and outside of it. In the end, though, Myers became determined to express himself through writing—with a resolve to address audiences that resembled himself, speaking in voices that resonate with the sounds of urban youth.

Walter Milton Myers was born on August 12, 1937, in Martinsburg, West Virginia. His parents, Mary Green and George Myers, already had six children at home, four of their own and two born to George and his first wife, Florence Brown. When Mary Green Myers died giving birth to her sixth child, George Myers sent his oldest daughters to live with their mother and her new husband, Herbert Dean. The Deans offered to also raise young Walter. George Myers agreed, and Walter moved to Harlem, New York, where he quickly accepted this extended family as his own. Although never formally adopted, he later took their family name as his own middle name.

Myers entered school already able to read, but he was immediately singled out because of his speech problems. He escaped special education classes only because his teacher recognized that he was bright. Myers responded to the chronic teasing of his classmates by fighting; consequently, he was frequently in trouble, suspended at times, even threatened with expulsion. An emergency appendectomy and complications ended his fourth grade year abruptly. Myers's interest in school was energized by his fifth-grade teacher, Mrs. Conway, who introduced Walter to a wider range of literature than his usual fare of comic books. Myers began to write poetry and found that he was able to read his work without his characteristic impediment. He also wrote fiction, filling notebooks as he continued through his junior high-school years. Myers especially enjoyed the rhythms and the lilt of Dylan Thomas, at times sneaking into a tavern to hear the poet perform. He became a regular patron of the New York Public Library. He was also an enthusiastic athlete, reveling in street sports, even taking dance classes. As a youth, Myers loved Harlem and its people; his devotion to the neighborhood would figure prominently in almost all of his literary works.

Myers entered New York City's prestigious and competitive Stuyvesant High School. His teachers recognized his talents in the language arts area, and Walter excelled at reading and writing. His father bought Walter his first typewriter. His high-school experience was not an unqualified success, however, as Myers struggled with math and science, two of the more concentrated disciplines. He began to spend more time on the streets and frequently cut school. Myers joined a gang that hired out as fighters. A close call with the police forced him to assess his life. At sixteen, a chronic truant at high risk, he joined the army, though he had to wait until his seventeenth birthday for his actual enlistment.

A high point in Myers's three years of military service was time spent in the polar regions, an assignment that he later used as inspiration for a non-fiction work about Antarctica. Discharged at the age of twenty, Myers returned to civilian life in his parents' new neighborhood of Morristown, New Jersey. He chose to return to Manhattan, moving to the midtown area as he tried several jobs, including one at the post office. He married in 1960, and he and wife Joyce welcomed daughter Karen Elaine in 1961 and son Michael Dean in 1963. Myers took writing classes at the community college, despite his lack of so much as a high-school diploma. Soon, he was publishing poetry in literary magazines and in publications geared toward African American readers. Myers began to model himself after the artists and writers who populated lower Manhattan. He learned to play musical instruments, donned a beret, and spent long hours in Greenwich Village. The Myers family moved to Queens, New York. Myers supplemented his income as a New York State Department of Labor employee by writing articles and short stories.

In 1968, Myers tried his hand at writing the text for a picture book, entering it in a competition for African American writers. *Where Does the Day Go?* won first prize, and was published the following year. It was his first major work for young readers, and seeing the book in print encouraged him to learn more about writing as a career. He enrolled in Columbia University's writing program and obtained a job as editor of a publishing house, where he studied the more practical side of writing, including the selection of manuscripts for publication.

His second picture book, *The Dancers*, was published in 1971, the first of his works to bear the middle name Dean. His third picture book, *The Dragon Takes a Wife*, stirred controversy. What Myers intended as a contemporary retelling of a fairy tale, complete with urban setting and nonstandard dialogue, was attacked by some as perpetuating stereotypes of black characters. Myers felt he had just infused the voices that surrounded him into the story.

Myers completed a college degree in 1984, and began to teach writing at a middle school in New Jersey. It was the start of his mission to connect students with their own voices; Myers has since become a sought-after speaker at schools and conferences.

Myers's *Sweet Illusions* (1986) featured a series of pieces on teen pregnancy. He inserted blank pages following each narrative, inviting readers to reflect and comment on what they'd read. It became useful as a teaching tool, widely used in high-school health education and guidance programs.

Myers took a poetic approach to representing the people and culture of Harlem in the 2004 collection *Here in Harlem: Poems in Many Voices.* Myers adopts the personas of residents from all walks of life, from the Reverend George Ambrose, looking to take his stand and build a storefront church, to gossiping hairdresser Delia Pierce and street historian John Lee Graham. Nanny Eleanor Haydon comments on her employers' condescension as she offers an excuse for her lateness; she reveals to the reader that she'd been up late at the Cotton Club. The book is rich in the storied history of the neighborhood, with allusions to Langston Hughes selling books on street corners, Joe Louis shaking hands with children, Countee Cullen teaching, and the local pride and hope in accomplishments of legends W. E. B. Du Bois, Jackie Robinson, James Baldwin, Richard Wright, Adam Clayton Powell, Jr., and Zora Neale Hurston. Myers again used the rhythms and tones of contemporary urban language.

Among his many recognitions, Walter Dean Myers received the American Library Association's prestigious Margaret E. Edwards Lifetime Achievement Award in 1994. He has maintained a freshness of voice and a clarity of vision in reaching and connecting with audiences through many forms of writing.

Website

"Meet the Author" (Houghton Mifflin). http://www.eduplace.com/kids/hmr/mtai/wdmyers.html

Poetry

The Great Migration: An American Story. Paintings by Jacob Lawrence. New York: HarperCollins, 1993.

Brown Angels: An Album of Pictures and Verses. New York: HarperCollins, 1993.

Glorious Angels: A Celebration of Children. New York: HarperCollins, 1995.

Harlem: A Poem. Illustrated by Christopher Myers. New York: Scholastic, 1997.

Angel to Angel: A Mother's Gift of Love. New York: HarperCollins, 1998.

blues journey. Illustrated by Christopher Myers. New York: Holiday House, 2001.

Here in Harlem: Poems in Many Voices. New York: Holiday House, 2004.

Juvenile Fiction

Where Does the Day Go? Illustrated by Leo Carty. New York: Parents Magazine Press, 1969.

The Dragon Takes a Wife. Illustrated by Ann Grifalconi. Indianapolis: Bobbs-Merrill, 1972.

The Dancers. Illustrated by Ann Rockwell. New York: Parents Magazine Press, 1972.

Fly, Jimmy, Fly! Illustrated by Moneta Barnett. New York: Putnam, 1974.

The Story of the Three Kingdoms. Illustrated by Ashley Bryan. New York: HarperCollins, 1995.

How Mr. Monkey Saw the Whole World. Illustrated by Synthia Saint James. New York: Doubleday, 1996.

The Blues of Flats Brown. Illustrated by Nina Laden. New York: Holiday House, 2000.

Young Adult Fiction

The Mouse Rap. New York: HarperCollins, 1990.

Somewhere in the Darkness. New York: Scholastic, 1992.

The Righteous Revenge of Artemis Bonner. New York: HarperCollins, 1992.

Mop, Moondance, and the Nagasaki Knights. New York: Delacorte, 1992.

Darnell Rock Reporting. New York: Delacorte, 1992.

The Glory Field. New York: Scholastic, 1994.

Slam! New York: Scholastic, 1994.

Smiffy Blue, Ace Crime Detective: The Case of the Missing Ruby and Other Stories. New York: Scholastic, 1996.

The Journal of Joshua Loper: A Black Cowboy. New York: Scholastic, 1999.

The Journal of Scott Pendleton Collins: A World War II Soldier. New York: Scholastic, 1999.

Monster. Illustrated by Christopher Myers. New York: HarperCollins, 1999.

145th Street: Short Stories. New York: Delacorte, 2000.

The Journal of Biddy Owens, the Negro Leagues. New York: Scholastic, 2001.

Patrol. Illustrated by Ann Grifalconi. New York: HarperCollins, 2001.

Handbook for Boys. New York: HarperCollins, 2002.

Three Swords for Granada. Illustrated by John Spiers. New York: Holiday House, 2002.

The Dream Bearer. New York: HarperCollins, 2003.

Shooter. New York: HarperCollins, 2004.

Autobiography of My Dead Brother. Illustrated by Christopher Myers. New York: HarperTempest, 2005.

Young Adult Nonfiction

Malcolm X: By Any Means Necessary. New York: Scholastic, 1993.

Remember Us Well: An Album of Picture and Verse. New York: HarperCollins, 1993.

Toussaint L'Ouverture: The Fight for Haiti's Freedom. New York: Simon & Schuster, 1996.

One More River to Cross: An African-American Photograph Album. New York: Harcourt, 1996.

Amistad: A Long Road to Freedom. New York: Dutton, 1998.

At Her Majesty's Request: An African Princess in Victorian England. New York: Scholastic, 1999.

Malcolm X: A Fire Burning Brightly. Illustrated by Leonard Jenkins. New York: HarperCollins, 2000.

Bad Boy: A Memoir. New York: HarperCollins, 2001.

The Greatest: Muhammad Ali. New York: Scholastic, 20021.

A Time to Love: Tales from the Old Testament. Illustrated by Christopher Myers. New York: Scholastic, 2002.

Antarctica: Journeys to the South Pole. New York: Scholastic, 2004.

References And Suggested Reading

Jordan, Denise M. *Walter Dean Myers: Writer for Real Teens.* Berkeley Heights, NJ: Enslow, 1999.

(Frederick) Ogden Nash
(1902–1971)

(Frederick) Ogden Nash. Courtesy of Photofest.

Nash reigns as a master of wordplay and humorous verse, with a legacy of lines and quotes that are instantly recognizable. His style is imitated by poets, lyricists, and advertising professionals. Young readers find particular amusement in his wit.

Frederick Ogden Nash was born on August 19, 1902, in suburban Rye, New York. His parents, Edmund Strudwich and Mattie Chenault Nash, hailed from Southern families, with ancestors who included a state governor, and a relative for whom Nashville was named. The Nashes were a large family; Ogden grew up with sisters Shirley, Gwendolyn, and Eleanor and brothers Edmund Witherell and Aubrey. The family spent part of each year in Savannah, Georgia, and part at their large home in Ramaqua, New York. The Nashes were fixtures in local society columns. Nash used many of the images gleaned from this upbringing as fodder for his humorous writings, often poking fun at the attitudes of the upper classes.

As young children, Ogden and younger brother Aubrey spent more time with their nurse, Jane Hamilton, than with their mother. Ogden had a reputation as a prankster and showed an early interest in poetry. When his sister Gwen, with whom he was particularly close, married, ten-year-old

Ogden recited an original poem at her wedding, and he wrote additional verses following the births of each of her children.

In Savannah, Ogden had a tutor; when in Rye, he attended a day school. In 1912, he was enrolled at the Shaw School in Groton, Connecticut, which was meant to be a preparatory school for students planning entry to the Groton School. Nash attended for only one year. Mattie Nash was concerned about Ogden's vision problems and began teaching him at home.

In 1917, Ogden Nash wrote a patriotic poem, which was published on the cover of the local *Rye Chronicle.* His father found a job, and Ogden was admitted to St. George's School in Newport, Rhode Island, where he was active in sports, civics, the newspaper and literary magazine, and the yearbook. He graduated three years later, receiving the school's Binney Prize for scholastic achievement.

After high school, Nash spent a year at Harvard University. He tried teaching, but then relocated to New York City to take a job as a bond salesman. His tenure there was brief, though, and by his own description less than successful. He left to take a job with the firm of Barron Collier, writing streetcar advertisements.

By 1925, Nash had moved on to working for the advertising department at the Doubleday publishing house. At the same time, he wrote a children's book, *The Cricket of Carador*, with the help of his friend Joseph Alger. Nash tried his hand at more serious poetry; however, he abandoned it, at least temporarily, for the wordplays and puns that would become his signature style.

While he continued to work at Doubleday, Nash began writing more verse, humorous pieces featuring word plays, irony, and his own slightly skewed view of the world. From these earliest efforts, Nash invented and twisted words to invent rhymes, fracture rhythms, and build amusing compounds and spellings. He published his first book of humorous verse, *Hard Lines*, in 1931. The book was an immediate success, going through seven printings in its first year. Encouraged by sales and by having two poems accepted by the *New Yorker*, Nash quit his job to join the staff of that magazine. This only lasted a few months, though, as Nash turned to full time writing. *Free Wheeling* was released the same year. 1931 also marked his marriage to Frances Rider Leonard.

Nash's next books of verse were *Happy Days* in 1933 and *The Primrose Path* in 1935. Some of the books that followed quickly in the 1930s were humorous reflections on family life, as in the 1936 collection *The Bad Parents' Garden of Verse*, inspired by life with his two baby girls. These themes continued through *I'm a Stranger Here Myself* (1938), *The Face is Familiar* (1940), *Good Intentions* (1942), and *Many Long Years Ago* (1945).

Nash was less successful in his attempts to write screenplays, but a musical he wrote with S. J. Perelman (music by Kurt Weill), *One Touch of Venus*, was a major Broadway hit. He wrote for television and radio, notably for several children's specials, for Bing Crosby, and for Rudy Vallee. Occasionally he made guest appearances and he recorded many of his own poems.

During the 1950s, Nash produced a mixed bag of writings for both children and adult audiences. Some of his humor for older readers poked fun at aging and at Nash's own hypochondriac tendencies. He did advertising work, wrote greetings for Hallmark cards, and took on a lecture schedule.

In March 1971, Nash was hospitalized with an intestinal condition that necessitated surgery. Despite two operations, blood transfusions, and rounds of dialysis, Nash died on May 19, 1971, at Johns Hopkins Hospital in Baltimore.

Nash's art and humor form a body of work unparalleled in originality. His work appears in collections, including books compiled for young readers, and several of his titles remain in print, from the *Custard* books to *Parents Keep Out!*, *A Boy Is a Boy*, and *Carnival of the Animals*. Elementary-school educators use his picture books and rhymes, and middle-school teachers work with his limericks and puns, which are often included in basal texts. Young adult and teen readers often find his more sophisticated word plays appealing, and he maintains a following among audiences of many ages.

Website

"Harry Ransom Humanities Research Center at the University of Texas at Austin." http://www.hrc.utexas.edu/research/fa/nash.bio.html
"A Tribute to the Poet, Ogden Nash." http://www.aenet.org/poems/ognash2.htm

Poetry

Parents Keep Out: Elderly Poems for Youngerly Readers. Boston: Little, Brown, 1951.
The Private Dining Room and Other New Verses. Boston: Little, Brown, 1953.
The Pocket Book of Ogden Nash. New York: Pocket Books, 1954.
You Can't Get There from Here. Boston: Little, Brown, 1957.
The Boy Who Laughed at Santa Claus. London: Cooper & Beatty, 1957.
The Christmas That Almost Wasn't. Boston: Little, Brown, 1957.
Verses from 1929 On. Boston: Little, Brown, 1957.
Collected Verse from 1929 On. London: Dent, 1961.
Custard the Dragon. Boston: Little, Brown, 1959.
Beastly Poetry. Hallmark Editions, 1960.

(Frederick) Ogden Nash

A Boy Is a Boy: The Fun of Being a Boy. New York: Watts, 1960.

Scrooge Rides Again. New York: Hart, 1960.

Custard the Dragon and the Wicked Knight. Boston: Little, Brown, 1961.

The New Nutcracker Suite, and Other Innocent Verses. Boston: Little, Brown, 1962.

Girls Are Silly. New York: Watts, 1962.

Everyone but Thee and Me. Boston: Little, Brown, 1962.

A Boy and His Room. New York: Watts, 1963.

The Adventures of Isabel. Boston: Little, Brown, 1963.

The Untold Adventures of Santa Claus. Boston: Little, Brown, 1964.

An Ogden Nash Bonanza. Boston: Little, Brown, 1964.

Marriage Lines: Notes of a Student Husband. Boston: Little, Brown, 1967.

The Animal Garden. New York: Evans, 1965.

The Mysterious Ouphe. Spadea Press, 1965.

Santa Go Home: A Case History for Parents. Boston: Little, Brown, 1967.

The Cruise of the Aardvark. New York: Evans, 1967.

There's Always Another Windmill. Boston: Little, Brown, 1968.

Funniest Verse of Ogden Nash: Light Lyrics by One of America's Favorite Humorists. Hallmark Editions, 1968.

(With Edward Lear) *The Scroobius Pip.* New York: Harper, 1968.

Bed Riddance: A Posy for the Indisposed. Boston: Little, Brown, 1972.

The Old Dog Barks Backwards. Boston: Little, Brown, 1972.

I Wouldn't Have Missed It: Selected Poems of Ogden Nash. Boston: Little Brown, 1972.

Custard and Company. Boston: Little, Brown, 1980.

A Penny Saved Is Impossible. Boston: Little, Brown, 1981.

Ogden Nash's Zoo. Steward, Tabori, 1986.

Candy Is Dandy: The Best of Ogden Nash. Deutsch, 1994.

Selected Poetry of Ogden Nash: 650 Rhymes, Verses, Lyrics, and Poems. Black Dog Leventhal, 1995.

Under Water With Ogden Nash. Illustrated by Katie Lee. Boston: Little, Brown, 1997.

Letters

Loving Letters from Ogden Nash: A Family Album. Boston: Little, Brown, 1990.

References and Suggested Reading

Parker, Douglas M. *Ogden Nash: The Life and Works of America's Laureate of Light Verse.* Chicago: Ivan R. Dee, 2005.

Marilyn Nelson
(1946-)

Marilyn Rae Nelson was born on April 26, 1946, in Cleveland, Ohio. Her father, Melvin M. Nelson, was an officer in the Air Force, a member of the last class graduated from Tuskegee Institute. His job as a pilot was a point of pride in Marilyn's young life but also the reason for numerous moves to military bases around the country. Marilyn Nelson showed an early interest in books and in poetry. During the family's time in Maine, it was a sixth-grade teacher named Dorothy Gray who recognized Nelson's talents and encouraged her to keep writing.

In 1968, Nelson earned her bachelor's degree in English from the University of California at Davis. Nelson also trained at a Lutheran seminary and worked in a campus ministry position at an Oregon college from 1969 through 1970. Nelson earned her master's degree from the University of Pennsylvania in 1970, and in the fall of that year, she married fellow graduate student Erdmann F. Waniek. Nelson used her married name in several of her early writings, but the couple divorced within several years, and she subsequently stopped using his name professionally.

Nelson taught at Lane Community College and at Reed College in Oregon for several semesters, then spent a year on the faculty of the Norre Nissum Seminarium in Denmark. When Nelson and her husband returned to the United States in 1973, she took a position at St. Olaf College in Minnesota, where she worked until 1978.

Nelson was also writing. She'd written poetry and participated in workshops during her undergraduate years, but as a graduate student she focused on academics. She became active in writing articles and papers about black identity in literature while in her graduate program. Nelson's contention that sociopolitical issues were an inextricable subtext to any

African American works would color her own writing, including her choices of topics for children and young adults.

Nelson relocated to Connecticut in 1978, where she took a post at the University of Connecticut at Storrs, a position she held until 2002. She also published her first poetry collection. *For the Body* featured forty-eight poems, most in free verse, which explored themes of human connections—of families, of life and death, and of identity, often through metaphor.

Nelson married fellow professor Roger Wilkenfield in 1979. She published a chapbook of translations, a series of children's poems by Danish poet Halfdan Rasmussen, called *Hundreds of Hens and Other Poems* (1982). Nelson collaborated with Pamela Espeland on the project; they would team up again to cowrite the original collection *The Cat Walked through the Casserole and Other Poems for Children.* These poems ranged in tone from humorous, as in the title poem, to more poignant pieces, expressing longing in works about adoption and isolation.

Nelson claimed that she hoped her 1985 book *Mama's Promises* would be read as a book of feminist theology. Each poem explores dimensions of the mother figure, inspired by Nelson's own experiences, at times as tangible as the voice of a little girl lost at a store, an episode that inspired "The Lost Daughter." Nelson also considered her mother's life and the roles of women across time. There are biblical references, and the work has a more formalized stanza structure than her earliest poems.

Nelson's father's career and the legacy of the storied Tuskegee Airmen inspired some of the pieces in the 1990 collection *The Homeplace.* Stories from Nelson's family history provide a vehicle for the author's social commentary about the travails and the achievements of her maternal ancestors. The book was nominated for the National Book Award. Her 1994 collection, *Magnificat* featured poems along overtly spiritual themes, taking as its title the prayer of Mary, and included proverbs and sayings.

Nelson employed a series of forty-four poems to write a biography of iconic African American scientist and innovator George Washington Carver. Nelson's book *Carver: A Life in Poems* (2001) interspersed archival photos and a timeline with poems in the words of many people in Carver's life. The poems illuminate Carver's diverse gifts and interests—far beyond his most familiar accomplishments and including his hobbies, such as crocheting, and his passion for the nascent field of aeronautics. His life is placed in historical context; racial issues and Carver's responses to challenges are explored. The book was nominated for the National Book Award for Young People's Literature, and it won the Boston Globe-Horn Award, a Bank Street College Award, a Coretta Scott King Award, and a Newbery Honor.

In the 2004 book *Fortune's Bones: The Manumission Requiem*, Nelson worked with the staff of the Mattatuck Museum in Connecticut, composing a series of poems in the form of a requiem. It was a tribute to a slave named Fortune whose skeleton is the subject of both study and sociological debate. These were the remains of a man who had lived most of his life as the slave of a doctor and whose manumission came only with his death. The doctor, who was a bonesetter, dismembered Fortune's body, cleaning and labeling the bones for reconstruction. The skeleton remained in the family for years and then was placed on exhibit in Europe. It is now part of a display in Connecticut. Nelson blends a deep spirituality, including Buddhist teaching and the touches of the exuberance of a New Orleans funeral, with a determination to celebrate the humanity of a man who lived a life in bondage and who remained anonymous for many years while his bones remained in plain sight.

Nelson continues to write and to teach. She has completed translations as well as work that explores the many identities of American citizenship.

Websites

"Marilyn Nelson's Labyrinth." http://web.uconn.edu/mnelson/index.html
"Academy of American Poets." http://www.poets.org

Poetry

For the Body. Baton Rouge: Louisiana State University Press, 1978.
Mama's Promises. Baton Rouge: Louisiana State University Press, 1985.
The Homeplace. Baton Rouge: Louisiana State University Press, 1990.
Partial Truth. Willington, CT: Kutenai Press, 1992.
Magnificat. Baton Rouge: Louisiana State University Press, 1994.
The Fields of Praise: New and Selected Poems. Baton Rouge: Louisiana State University Press, 1997.
Triolets for Triolet. Willimantic, CT: Curbstone Press, 2001.
She-Devil Circus. West Chester, PA: Aralia Press, 2001.
The Cachoeira Tales, and Other Poems. Baton Rouge: Louisiana State University Press, 2005.

Children's and Young Adult Poetry

(With Pamela Espeland) *The Cat Walked through the Casserole and Other Poems for Children.* Minneapolis, MN: Carolrhoda, 1984.
Carver: A Life in Poems. Asheville, NC: Front Street, 2001.
Fortune's Bones: The Manumission Requiem. Asheville, NC: Front Street, 2004.
A Wreath for Emmett Till. Illustrated by Philippe Lardy. Boston: Houghton Mifflin, 2005.

As Editor

Rumors of Troy. Boston: Pearson Custom Publishing, 2001.

References and Suggested Reading

Griffith, Paul A. "Marilyn Nelson." In *Dictionary of Literary Biography, Vol. 282: New Formalist Poets.* Detroit: Gale Group, 2003, pp. 233–40.

Pettis, Joyce. *African-American Poets: Lives, Works, and Sources.* Westport, CT: Greenwood Press, 2002.

Naomi Shihab Nye
(1952–)

Naomi Shihab Nye's poems are grounded in the images of everyday life; her words lend grace and lyricism to the ordinary. Her messages of peace, tolerance, and the celebration of life resound through her body of work.

Nye was born Naomi Shihab on March 12, 1952, in St. Louis, Missouri, to a Palestinian father and a mother of German-Swiss ancestry. She first began writing poetry at the age of six, submitting her work to children's magazines. Naomi was a voracious reader throughout her childhood, and her favorite authors included Margaret Wise Brown, E. B. White, Carl Sandburg, Louisa May Alcott, and Langston Hughes.

When Nye was twelve years old, her family left their Missouri farm to live for a year in her father's home town of Jerusalem. She attended school there, and for the first time was immersed in the culture of her paternal family, forging a deep love for the richness of Middle Eastern culture and for the nature of an extended family.

Upon their return to the United States, the Shihabs settled in San Antonio, TX. Nye has made that city her home since then. After earning her bachelor's degree in English from Trinity University in 1974, Nye embarked on a career as a freelance writer, editor, and speaker, often serving as writer-in-residence at schools around the country.

She married lawyer and photographer Michael Nye in 1978, and they reside in Texas with their son, Madison Cloudfeather. She has traveled to the Middle East and Asia as a representative of the United States Information Agency, advocating understanding through the arts.

Nye's first collections, the chapbooks *Tattooed Feet* (1977) and *Eye-to-Eye* (1978), explored identity and journeys, themes that are constants in her work. Her first commercially published collection, *Different Ways to Pray*

(1980), established Nye's voice, espousing universal themes through what Nye refers to in the introduction as "the gleam of the particulars." She embraces the differences among the communities to which she feels the closest connections—Arab Americans, Palestinians, and the voices of her own neighborhood, which bustled with Mexican immigrants, Native people, and Midwesterners. Her writing is deeply personal, reflecting what she sees as her mission. She carefully metes out words, resulting in a puree of the obvious and the subtle. For example, Nye's *Hugging the Jukebox* (1982) relates stories of travel, real and imagined, street scenes, advice, and admonitions as in "Rebellion Against the North Side," that entreats readers to eschew status symbols. The voice captures the tone of youthful urgency.

In the 1986 collection *Yellow Glove*, Nye again approaches subjects consisting of everyday objects and the briefest slices of life. The images and issues come through a sharp, mature voice. Nye tackles the madness of violence in "No One Thinks of Tegucigalpa," "Lunch in Nablus City Park," and "Blood." The latter invites us to meet the little girl who first discovers that she is Arab, then moves forward to a time of confusing images, headlines from Palestine "clotting in my blood," asking a father overwhelmed by the stories from his homeland, "What does an Arab do now?" The speaker asks, "Who calls anyone civilized?" Selections focusing on scenes as diverse as a visit to Mother Theresa's orphanage, the simple act of a bowl breaking, and recollections of a French film all center on a quiet sadness, albeit one that clings to hope. Cultures mix, clash, and blend, seeking to be embraced. Nye empowers the reader to continue to seek answers to the questions posed by all of the shrinking, expanding, and morphing stories—even through the mundane, the monotonous, and the inexplicable. That call to be part of the story, to become the teller, recurs throughout Nye's work.

Nye has also written books of fiction for young people. *Sitti's Secret* (1994) tells of a little girl finding ways to bridge a language divide so that she can communicate with her Palestinian grandmother. The following year, Nye published *Habibi*, a semiautobiographical young adult novel in which an Arab American girl relocates to Jerusalem and is confronted with complex cultural mores as well as violence and its aftermath. *Benito's Dream Bottle*, a picture book inspired by Nye's young son, and *Lullaby Raft*, also a picture book, were published in 1995 and 1997, respectively.

In her 2002 collection *19 Varieties of Gazelles*, Nye's messages of tolerance and her pleas for peace take on a renewed urgency. Addressing the terrorist attacks of September 11, 2001, she entreats readers to avoid the temptation to stereotype people of Middle Eastern descent. Nye claims "Perhaps Arab Americans must say, twice as clearly as anyone else, that we deplore the unbelievable." The poems reflect Nye's sadness and sympathy, but never lose sight of a sense of hope. The book was a finalist for the National Book Award for Young People's Literature.

Nye's love of the younger audience is centered on its collective ability to be open-minded, to listen as she helps them navigate around life's rough edges. She retains a strong conviction that the arts are central to self-exploration. Nye's literature and her work in anthologies carry out a mission to promote cross-cultural understanding and a climate of humanism over nationalism. The words are clear, crisp, and dynamic; the messages of hope are unflagging, the spirit indomitable.

Website

"Texas Kaos." http://www.soapblox.net/texaskos
"Contemporary Poets Speak Out." http://www.geocities.com/
    poetryafterseptember112001/contemppoets.html

Poetry

Different Ways to Pray. Portland, OR: Breitenbush, 1980.
On the Edge of Sky. Privately published, 1981.
Hugging the Jukebox. New York: Dutton, 1982.
Yellow Glove. Portland, OR: Breitenbush, 1986.
Invisible. Denton, TX: Tribolite, 1987.
Mint. Brockport, NY: State Street Press, 1991.
Red Suitcase. Rochester, NY: BOA Editions, 1994.
Words Under the Words: Selected Poems. Portland, OR: Far Corner Books, 1995.
Fuel. Rochester, NY: BOA Editions, 1998.
Mint Snowball. Anhinga Press, 2001.
19 Varieties of Gazelle: Poems of the Middle East. New York: HarperCollins, 2002.

Anthologies

This Same Sky: A Collection of Poems from Around the World. New York: Four Winds, 1992.
The Tree Is Older Than You Are. New York: Simon & Schuster, 1995.
(With Paul Janeczko) *I Feel a Little Jumpy Around You: A Book of Her Poems and His Poems Collected in Paris.* New York: Simon & Schuster, 1996.
The Space Between Our Footsteps: Poems and Paintings from the Middle East. New York: Econoclad Books, 1998.
What Have You Lost? Photographs by Michael Nye. New York: Greenwillow Books, 1999.
Salting the Ocean: 100 Poems by Young Poets. New York: Greenwillow Books, 2000.
Come With Me: Poems for a Journey. New York: Greenwillow Books, 2000.

Fiction

Sitti's Secret. New York: Macmillan, 1994.
Benito's Dream Bottle. New York: Simon & Schuster, 1995.
Lullaby Raft. New York: Simon & Schuster, 1997.
Baby Radar. (picture book) New York: Greenwillow Books, 2003.

Essays

Never in a Hurry. Columbia: University of South Carolina Press, 1996.

References and Suggested Reading

Jayyusi, Salma Khadra. *Anthology of Modern Palestinian Literature.* New York: Columbia University Press, 1992.

Malek, Kamal Abdel, and David C. Jacobson, eds. *Israeli and Palestinian Identities in History and Literature* New York: St. Martin's Press, 1999.

Joyce Carol Oates
(1938–)

Joyce Carol Oates was born on June 16, 1938, the first child of Carolina Bush Oates and Frederic James Oates. Her parents' own family histories were characterized by poverty and violence. Oates's paternal grandmother was a victim of domestic violence, and her maternal grandfather was beaten to death in a tavern fight. Oates's childhood, while appearing secure and stable, was characterized by the legacy of violence and poverty she inherited.

Frederic Oates and Carolina Bush married in 1937. They settled on a farm outside Lockport, in upstate New York, alongside Niagara and Erie counties. It was an area hard hit by the Depression, and Oates's parents worked hard to provide Joyce and her siblings, Frederic Jr. and Lynn Ann, with the necessities. The Oateses had had limited education opportunities themselves, and they encouraged their three children to pursue schooling.

Before Joyce Carol Oates could write, she drew whole stories. She attended a one-room schoolhouse, and throughout elementary school she wrote, designed, and bound 200-page books. Oates transferred to North Park Junior High after sixth grade, then went on to Williamsville Central High School. Oates was a voracious reader, even of comic books, and when she was fourteen her grandmother gave her an especially treasured gift—a typewriter. At fifteen, she sent out a manuscript of a novel about a junkie who is rehabilitated while helping a horse; it was soundly rejected.

Because Oates was no particularly close with her brother or with her much younger, autistic sister, she gravitated more toward friends. While at Williamsville Central, Joyce wrote for the school newspaper and was awarded a full scholarship to Syracuse University; afterward she won a summer school fellowship for two terms at Harvard University. Oates distinguished herself as a top student at both schools, majoring in English with a minor in philosophy, and graduated as valedictorian of her class in 1960. As a junior, she won first prize in a short story competition sponsored by *Mademoiselle* magazine and had another story published in *Epoch*.

Oates went on to do her graduate work in English at the University of Wisconsin, earning her master's degree in one year. It was in Wisconsin that she met Raymond Smith, whom she married on January 23, 1961, after a brief courtship. They moved to Beaumont, Texas, because of a teaching job Smith had accepted. Oates went to Rice University to register for their doctorate program in English, but while in the University library she found her short story cited in the anthology *Best American Short Stories* and decided to dedicate herself to full-time writing. Vanguard Press accepted her short story "By the North Gates" for publication. Oates became concerned that the images of Lockport combined with a good deal of violence and sexual content would not be received well by family, by the academics with whom she worked and published, or by critics.

During the late 1960s, Oates published her first poetry collections, *Women in Love and Other Poems* (1968) and *Anonymous Sins* (1969). Oates was nominated for the National Book Award in 1968 and 1969 for *Expensive People* and for *Earthly Delights;* she won the prestigious award in 1970 for *them,* a fictional work that pays homage to Oates's skill in crafting a story.

Oates taught at the University of Windsor in Canada from 1968 through 1978. She continued to immerse herself in teaching and writing and produced an impressive collection of works in an array of genres, including nonfiction and literary criticism. Oates and her husband started a small literary magazine, *The Ontario Review.* The Smiths moved from Ontario for Joyce to teach at Princeton in the university's writing program. Oates adopted the pen name Rosemond Smith as she wrote a series of mysteries.

Oates has published seven volumes of poetry that explore some of the same themes as her prose, but in the tightest of verse. Her poem "Edward Hopper's Nighthawks, 1942," won an award as Best American Poetry in 1991.

Young readers find Oates's stark views of the interpersonal dynamics of families, friends, and lovers gripping and charged with raw energy. Her short story "Where Are You Going, Where Have You Been?" is used throughout high school and college literature and writing programs. Oates has become a formidable voice in young adult fiction, with several popular and well-received novels addressed specifically to that readership. Other novels have been finding young audiences, especially as her adult fiction often features teen protagonists and leads, as in the acclaimed *We Were the Mulvaneys*, which was also adapted for the screen. Her poetry explores the sensual and the sexual, the workaday and the exotic, and she speaks with a sense of isolation recognizable to many teens.

Oates has contended with physical frailty, including struggles with anorexia nervosa, tachycardia (rapid heartbeat), exhaustion, depression, and insomnia. Despite her undisputed critical and commercial successes, Oates has never seemed to dispel fears of failure. She has won nearly every award in her fields, including the PEN/Malamud Award for lifetime achievement and the Fairfax Award for Lifetime Achievement in Literary Arts. Oates currently holds the title of Distinguished Professor of Humanities at Princeton, while continuing to produce a prodigious number of works each year.

Website

"A Celestial Timepiece: A Joyce Carol Oates Homepage." http://www.usfca.edu/~southerr/jco.bio.html

Poetry

Women in Love and Other Poems. New York: Albondacani Press, 1968.
Anonymous Sins and Other Poems. Baton Rouge: Louisiana State University Press, 1969.
Love and Its Derangements. Baton Rouge: Louisiana State University Press, 1970.
Angel Fire. Baton Rouge: Louisiana State University Press, 1973.
Dreaming America. Aloe Editions, 1973.
Love and Its Derangements and Other Poems. New York: Fawcett, 1974.
The Fabulous Beasts. Illustrated by A. G. Smith, Jr. Baton Rouge: Louisiana State University Press, 1975.
Season of Peril. Santa Barbara, CA: Black Sparrow Press, 1977.
Women Whose Lives Are Food, Men Whose Lives Are Money: Poems. Baton Rouge: Louisiana State University Press, 1978.
The Stepfather. Northridge, CA: Lord John Press, 1978.
Celestial Timepiece. Dallas, TX: Pressworks, 1981.
Invisible Women: New and Selected Poems, 1970–1972. New York: Ontario Review Press, 1982.
The Luxury of Sin. Northridge, CA: Lord John Press, 1983.
The Time Traveler. New York: Dutton, 1989.

Fiction

Because It Is Bitter, and Because It Is My Heart. New York: Dutton, 1990.
I Lock the Door upon Myself. New York: Ecco Press, 1990.
The Rise of Life on Earth. New York: New Directions, 1991.
Black Water. New York: Dutton, 1992.
Foxfire: Confessions of a Girl Gang. New York: Dutton, 1993.
What I Lived For. New York: Dutton, 1994.
Zombie. New York: Dutton, 1995.

Tenderness. New York: Ontario Review Press, 1996.
We Were the Mulvaneys. New York: Dutton, 1996.
First Love: A Gothic Tale. New York: Ecco Press, 1996.
Man Crazy. New York: Dutton, 1997.
Come Meet Muffin! Illustrated by Mark Graham. New York: Ecco Press, 1998.
My Heart Laid Bare. New York: Dutton, 1998.
Broke Heart Blues: A Novel. New York: Dutton, 1999.
Blonde. New York: HarperCollins, 2000.
Middle Age: A Romance. New York: Ecco Press, 2001.
Beasts. New York: Carroll & Graf, 2002.
I'll Take You There. New York: Ecco Press, 2002.
The Tattooed Girl. New York: Ecco Press, 2003.
Rape: A Love Story. New York: Carroll & Graf, 2003.
The Falls. New York: Ecco Press, 2004.

Short Stories

Raven's Wing. New York: Dutton, 1986.
The Assignation. New York: Ecco Press, 1988.
Where Is Here? New York: Ecco Press, 1988.
Heat: And Other Stories. New York: Plume, 1992.
Where Are You Going, Where Have You Been? Selected Early Stories. New York: Ontario Review Press, 1993.
Haunted: Tales of the Grotesque. New York: Dutton, 1994.
Will You Always Love Me? And Other Stories. New York: Dutton, 1995.
The Collector of Hearts: New Tales of the Grotesque. New York: Dutton, 1999.
Faithless: Tales of Transgression. New York: Ecco Press, 2001.

References and Suggested Reading

Johnson, Greg. *Invisible Writer: A Biography of Joyce Carol Oates.* New York: Penguin Putnam, 1998.

Lydia Omolola Okutoro
(1974-)

Although Lydia Omolola Okutoro was born in Lagos, Nigeria, when she was nine years old she relocated to New York City, where she lived with an American family for approximately six years before leaving for high school. Okutoro has recalled that she did not see her mother for twelve years after she relocated to the United States, and she was often shy around strangers once she left her American family to attend St. Paul's School in Concord, New Hampshire. However, despite her shyness, Okutoro's efforts to showcase the voices of young people began while she was a senior in high school; it was there that she created a literary journal.

Okutoro graduated from Mount Holyoke College in 1998, and after graduation, she moved to Baltimore where she taught English to middle-school students and where she developed public art programs to increase participation in poetry writing among young people. Okutoro recalls that although she discovered her writer's voice at Mount Holyoke, in the years following graduation she was unable to find time to write. However, within a few years of her completion of undergraduate study, Okutoro won the Woolley Fellowship from Mount Holyoke, which funded her enrollment in the University of Arizona's prestigious Master of Fine Arts program. Currently, Okutoro teaches writing in the public school systems of Baltimore and New York. Okutoro is a recent name in poetry; however, her work is recommended by the PBS Teaching Source for teachers in primary and secondary schools.

A poet and educator, Okutoro developed poetry workshops to create outlets for young writers and to offer teaching opportunities about the experiences of children from the African diaspora. Her poetry celebrates the world's diversity; much of her verse captures the voices of young people who represent the many tribes in world culture. Her first book, *Quiet Storm:*

Voices of Young Black Poets, grew out of her personal experiences as an immigrant, a poet, and an educator. Okutoro was invited to her former high school to conduct a poetry workshop for the children there, many of whom, like her, had relocated to the United States. Okutoro was so impressed with the work that the students produced in that poetry workshop that she edited it and produced an anthology that is currently a staple in many classrooms.

Quiet Storm is a celebration of the African diaspora through the eyes of its youth; the writers included in this collection originate from the United States, the Caribbean islands, and several African countries. The entries are quirky and poignant, serious and humorous recitations of selfhood through the eyes of young people. The children's poetry captures their worlds in verse; themes range from complaints about one's hard-to-manage curly hair to surprisingly mature contemplations on issues seemingly beyond the years of most, if not all, of the youthful contributors who range in age from thirteen to twenty-one. The text includes biographical notes on the young poets.

Okutoro's poetry has appeared in *Essence Magazine*. Her verse is described as possessed of a singular voice, incredible passion. and insight into the human condition. She currently lives in New York City. where she is at work on a memoir titled *My Name is Omolola: An African Girl in America*. It is a story about an immigrant's experience from the perspective of a young girl.

Websites

"Mount Holyoke College, News and Events." http://www.mtholyoke.edu/offices/comm/news/okutoro.shtml

"College Street Journal." http://www.mtholyoke.edu/offices/comm/csj/970509/lydia.html

Poetry

Quiet Storm: Voices of Young Black Poets, 1st ed. Jump at the Sun Publication, 1999.

References and Suggested Reading

Christ, Carol P. *Diving Deep and Surfacing: Women Writers on Spiritual Quest.* Boston: Beacon Press, 1980.

Cook, William W. "The Black Arts Poets." In *The Columbia History of American Poetry.* Ed. Jay Parini and Brett C. Millier. New York: Columbia University Press, 1993, pp. 674–706.

Davis, Thadious M., and Trudier Harris, eds. *Dictionary of Literary Biography, Vol. 38: Afro-American Writers after 1955: Dramatists and Prose Writers.* Detroit: Gale, 1985.

Dorothy Parker
(1893–1967)

Dorothy Parker. Courtesy of Photofest.

This American poet, short story writer, and critic was a legendary figure in the New York literary scene during the early 1950s and 1960s. She was one of the most successful and influential writers of the twentieth century, and it is just as likely that Parker was one of the more melancholy poets of any century, for she became famous for her sadly witty poems, many about her own relationships. Despite her apparent sadness and recurring bouts of depression; however, Parker's solemn musings are frequently humorous, often sarcastic critiques that evoke smiles, chuckles and critical consideration from her readers.

Parker was educated in private schools in New Jersey and in New York City, and at the age of eighteen she moved into a New York City boarding house, where she played the piano for a dance school to pay her bills. Throughout her life, Parker attempted to recreate the feeling of family that she did not have as a child. Between her marriages and divorces, she alternated between boarding houses and a hotel in New York City, enmeshing herself into the community of life in those public places.

In addition to her job as a piano player, Parker worked as a writer for *Vanity Fair*. In fact, she was New York's only female drama critic at the time. Her connections at *Vanity Fair* and her reputation as a writer facilitated her founding of a renowned intellectual literary circle, the famous Algonquin Round Table. Parker was the only female member of this group, which included writers Robert Benchley, Robert Sherwood, James Thurber, George Kaufman, and many others who met at the Algonquin Hotel in New York City.

However, despite her popularity and reputation, Parker's sarcastic wit cost *Vanity Fair* subscribers. The magazine fired her because her reviews garnered unfavorable public criticism and put the magazine in the position of having to choose between keeping its subscribers and allowing Parker's pen full rein. Soon after leaving *Vanity Fair*, Parker was hired by *Ainslee Magazine.* The editors there encouraged her often caustic observations on urban life. Many biographers note the beginning of her literary career as evolving from her time at *Ainslee.* During her employment there, she wrote and published her first short story, "Such a Pretty Little Picture." In the first issue of *The New Yorker,* published in early 1925, Parker contributed drama reviews and poetry. By February of 1926, Parker left the United States for Paris; however, her articles and poetry continued to appear in *The New Yorker* and in *Life.*

In France, Parker became friends with Ernest Hemingway. Biographers find the relationship surprising, given Hemingway's supposedly chauvinistic persona and Parker's caustic one; however, it may be that the two writers shared a finely tuned, acerbic quality that made them likely, rather than unlikely, companions. In November 1926, Parker returned to the United States amid the commercial success of her first book of poetry, *Enough Rope,* which contains the poem "Resume," often cited by biographers as one of the poet's many contemplations on suicide. Despite Parker's attention to the topic of suicide and her several attempts to take her own life, she escapes being described as a confessional poet such as Sylvia Plath and Elizabeth Bishop. Instead, Parker was often described by her editors and biographers as possessing "the quickest tongue imaginable . . . and the keenest sense of mockery." *Enough Rope* was a bestseller. This collection of poems was followed by *Sunset Guns* in 1928 and *Death and Taxes* in 1931. Parker's poems were sardonic, dry, elegant commentaries on departing or departed love, or on the shallowness of life. "Comment" is one such poem. In the poem, Parker considers the polar extremes of life and love, offering that if "life is a glorious cycle of song," then she was "Marie of Roumania," a European queen who was an extraordinary and independent woman.

Parker's career also included work as a book reviewer for *The New Yorker;* she wrote under the pseudonym of "The Constant Reader." In 1929, she won the prestigious O. Henry award for the best short story of the year, and in that same year, she began writing for Hollywood. Parker wrote many screenplays, several of which were written collaboratively with her second husband, Alan Campbell. Parker continued to write prose and short stories, and she was widely published. However, in the 1950s, Parker was called before the House Committee on Un-American Activities after testimony was presented against her based on her stand against Fascism and Nazism. During the McCarthy era, a period of heightened vigilance with regard to American patriotism, Parker was declared a Communist. Not unlike many artists who had come under scrutiny by the Federal Bureau of Investigation (FBI), she was placed on the Hollywood blacklist and, for a time, she was effectively prevented from working in the industry.

Parker's life was the subject of a 1987 film, *Dorothy and Alan at Norma Place,* and the 1994 film *Mrs. Parker and the Vicious Circle.* Parker's image appeared on a twenty-nine–cent United States commemorative postage stamp in the Literary Arts series issued August 22, 1992. She was found dead of a heart attack in her room at Hotel Volney in New York City on June 6, 1967. She bequeathed her entire literary estate to the National Association for the Advancement of Colored People (NAACP).

Websites

Parker's plays: http://www.english.uiuc.edu/maps/poets/m_r/parker/plays.htm
"The Dorothy Parker Society." http://www.dorothyparkernyc.com

Poetry

Enough Rope.–New York: Boni & Liveright, 1926.
Sunset Gun. New York: Boni & Liveright, 1928.
Death and Taxes. New York: Viking, 1931.
Not So Deep as a Well. New York: Viking, 1936.
Collected Poetry of Dorothy Parker. New York: Modern Library, 1944.

Fiction

Laments for the Living. New York: Viking, 1930.
Here Lies. New York: Viking, 1939.
Collected Stories. New York: Modern Library, 1942.
Selected Short Stories. Editions for the Armed Services, 1944.

Criticism and Other Writings

(With Franklin Pierce Adams) *Men I'm Not Married To.* New York: Doubleday, 1922.
Constant Reader. New York: Viking, 1970.
A Month of Saturdays. New York: Macmillan, 1971.

Drama

(With Elmer Rice) *Close Harmony, or the Lady Next Door: A Play in Three Acts*. New York: Samuel French, 1929.

(With Arnaud D'Usseau) *The Ladies of the Corridor: A Play*. New York: Viking, 1954

(With Ross Evans) *The Coast of Illyria*. Iowa City: University of Iowa Press, 1990.

References and Suggested Reading

Capron, Marion. *Writers at Work*. New York:Viking, 1957.

Cowley, Malcolm. *And I Worked in the Writer's Trade: Chapters of Literary History, 1918–1978*. New York: Viking, 1978.

Drennan, Robert E. *The Algonquin Wits*. Sacramento, CA: Citadel Press, 1975.

Frewin, Leslie. *The Late Mrs. Dorothy Parker*. New York: Macmillan, 1986.

Hellman, Lillian. *An Unfinished Woman*. Boston: Little, Brown, 1970.

Keats, John. *You Might as Well Live*. New York: Simon & Schuster, 1970.

Meade, Marion. *Dorothy Parker: What Fresh Hell Is This?* New York: Random House/Penguin, 1987/1989.

Edgar Allan Poe
(1809–1849)

Edgar Allan Poe. Courtesy of Photofest.

Edgar Allan Poe created works of fiction and poetry that have never waned in their popularity among young readers, who often have a special affinity for the macabre. The intrigues and tragedies of Poe's short life add to his appeal among teen and young adult readers.

Poe's early life was marked by loss. He was born on January 19, 1809, the son of Eliza Arnold Poe, a talented stage actress, and her second husband, David Poe, an aspiring actor. As the Poes pursued their theatrical careers, they left Edgar and his siblings with members of their extended family in Baltimore. The children were shuttled among friends and family. David Poe, who descended into alcoholism, abandoned the family within a short time following Edgar's birth. Eliza Poe died of tuberculosis in 1811, leaving behind three young children; it is believed that David Poe also succumbed to tuberculosis that same year. Young Edgar Poe would feel the impact of his mother's loss especially during his later years, often revisiting images of lost beauty in his works.

Edgar was taken in by family friends John and Frances Allan. Although the couple did not formally adopt Edgar, they raised him as their own, adding their family name to Edgar's. The Allans provided Poe with educational and travel opportunities at a boarding school in London. He was seen as bright, but he felt stifled by the school's rigid curriculum.

After a time in England, the Allans returned to America, settling in Virginia and enrolling the teenaged Edgar in a school in Richmond. Poe displayed a competitive nature in sports and a strong interest in reading. He composed poetry, including a set of poems to and about young ladies in Richmond.

Poe turned to the mother of a schoolmate for the maternal attention that the frail Frances Allan could not readily provide. When Mrs. Jane Stanard died a year into their friendship, Edgar was deeply affected by this new loss. He became moody and rebellious, initiating what would become a series of tensions with guardian John Allan.

Allan did agree to pay Poe's expenses at the University of Virginia but withdrew his support after one year. Poe had begun drinking quite heavily and had accrued a substantial number of gambling debts. Poe was furious at Allan's refusal to continue indulging him and took off on his own, fleeing his creditors with tales of enlisting to fight in the war for independence in Greece. He was actually in Boston. In 1827, he was able to find a printer willing to publish a series of his early writings: *Tamerlane and Other Poems.* The title piece took the voice of a Mongol conqueror, one who finds his triumphs bittersweet as he returns to find his childhood sweetheart dead—an early example of Poe's preoccupation with themes of loss.

By the time *Tamerlane* was published, Poe was serving in the U. S. Army. He enlisted under the name Edgar A. Perry and sought to be discharged after only two years, because he had applied for admission to West Point Military Academy. It was during the interval between the two terms of service that he published *Al Aaraaf, Tamerlane, and Minor Poems.* Although "Al Aaraaf" was the lengthiest and most ambitious of the new pieces, the short poem "Sonnet to Science" has been recognized as one of Poe's best. It focuses on Poe's conviction that clinical and rational concerns cloud the worlds of art and literature. He would revisit this theme later, as in the introduction to a later volume, simply entitled *Poems by Edgar A. Poe* (1831). Poe held that poetry should be motivated by the desire to bring pleasure to the reader, not to moralize or to pontificate.

Poe entered West Point in 1830. He quickly decided to quit but, under the Academy's rules, was unable to resign. Poe consciously neglected his duties and was insubordinate, setting the stage for a court martial and dismissal.

In 1845, Poe's most famous poem appeared in *The Evening Mirror.* "The Raven," described by Poe as the "bird of ill omen," speaks the single word "nevermore" at the close of each stanza; the bereaved scholar in the poem assigns importance to the bird's echoed refrain as the man laments his lost love. The poem was an immediate hit, and its success allowed Poe to launch a public speaking tour. Despite his critical acclaim, however, Poe's finances remained strained. He moved with his wife to less expensive housing in the Fordham section of the Bronx. Poe and his wife lived in abject poverty, relying on the intervention of friends to meet basic needs. Perhaps understandably, Poe's rate of productivity declined; he complained that he was unable to work because of the noise of bells ringing in the streets. However, he did publish short pieces about New York as well as "The Cask of Amontillado" in *Godey's Lady's Book* during this period.

In "The Bells," a poem that captures the sights and sounds of Poe's poverty-stricken years, the poet chronicles stages of life using the images and sounds of bells; sleigh bells, wedding bells, fire alarm bells, and funeral bells represent innocence, loss, joy, and despair in the poem. Poe claimed to have spent more than a year working on this poem, and it is one of his more memorable and readily recognized poems. "The Bells," along with "The Raven" and "Annabel Lee," a ballad that focuses on themes of grief and the power of love to transcend the confines of mortality, have remained among those most commonly selected for use in oratories and recitations.

In 1847, when Poet was thirty-eight, his wife died of tuberculosis. Virginia was twenty-four at the time of her death. Poe was also ill by this time, and he lapsed into a deep depression after his wife's death. He composed "Ulalume: A Ballad" as a mourning piece; its final image is that of the poet visiting the grave of his beloved. Poe continued to lecture, and he began to explore science and its relationship to poetry. Poe rallied to lecture on "The Poetic Principle," acknowledged as an excellent series of talks.

In 1849, following his wife's death, a destitute Poe died in Baltimore of unknown causes. He was found semi-conscious on a sidewalk on October 3, 1949, and although he was hospitalized, the poet languished for four days before succumbing. Poe's appeal to young readers has remained consistent. Teens and young adults embrace his tales of terror and psychodrama as well as his poems of longing and melancholy.

Websites

"Edgar Allan Poe Society of Baltimore." http://www.lfchosting.com/eapoe/
"Literature Network." http://www.online-literature.com/poe/

Poetry

Tamerlane and Other Poems: By a Bostonian. Calvin F. S. Thomas, 1827.
Al Aaraaf, Tamerlane, and Minor Poems. Hatch & Dunning, 1829.
Poems, By Edgar A. Poe. Elam Bliss, 1831.
The Raven and Other Poems. Wiley and Putnam, 1845.
Eureka: A Prose Poem. Putnam, 1848.

Stories

Tales of the Grotesque and Arabesque, 2 vols. Lea and Blanchard, 1840.
Prose Romances: The Murders in the Rue Morgue and The Man That Was Used Up. Wiley and Putnam, 1845.

Other Writings

The Narrative of Arthur Gordon Pym, of Nantucket. Harper & Bros., 1838.
The Conchologist's First Book; or, a System of Testaceous Malacology. Haswell, Barrington, & Haswell, 1839.
The Literati. J. S. Redfield, 1850.
Politan: An Unfinished Tragedy. George Banta, 1923.

Collections

The Poetical Works of Edgar Allan Poe. London: W. J. Widdleton, 1870.
The Life and Poems of Edgar Allan Poe. London: W. J. Widdleton, 1877.
The Works of Edgar Allan Poe, 10 vols. Ed. Edmund C. Stedman and George E. Woodbury. Stone and Kimball, 1894–95.
Selections from the Critical Writings of Edgar Allan Poe. Ed. F. C. Prescott. New York: Henry Holt, 1909.
The Complete Tales and Poems of Edgar Allan Poe. New York: Modern Library, 1938.
Poe: Complete Poems. Ed. Richard Wilbur. Dell, 1959.

References and Suggested Reading

Binns, Tristan Boyer. *Edgar Allan Poe: Master of Suspense.* New York: F. Watts, 2005.
Hutchisson, James M. *Edgar Allan Poe.* Jackson: University of Mississippi Press, 2005.
Kent, Zachary. *Edgar Allan Poe: Tragic Poet and Master of Mystery.* Berkeley Heights, NJ: Enslow, 2001.
Meltzer, Milton. *Edgar Allan Poe: A Biography.* Brookfield, CT: Twenty-first Century Books, 2003.
Meyers, Jeffrey. *Edgar Allan Poe: His Life and Legacy.* New York: Scribner's, 1992.

Ishmael Reed
(1938–)

This American poet was born in Chattanooga, Tennessee; however, he grew up in a working-class neighborhood in Buffalo, New York, where he attended public schools and the University of Buffalo. Financial problems prevented Reed from graduating; however, rather than returning to Tennessee, he remained in New York and went on to co-host a local radio program that was canceled after he conducted an interview with Malcolm X.

Predominant themes in Reed's work are identity, race, and gender, and they reflect the poet's earnest, lifelong efforts to resist being named or categorized by anyone other than himself. Reed is committed to ridiculing mainstream values and mores in his poetry. Indeed, nothing is above reproach for this writer, who often relies on humor, satire, and ridicule to expose human foibles. The poet has satirized himself in "The Reactionary Poet," a poem that appears in his third collection of poetry, *Secretary to the Spirits*. In this regard, Reed hails from that school of poets who acknowledge social and political influences on their imaginative verse but who are reluctant to make comparisons between the author and his work. Reed is an inventive writer who finds much to protest; however, his imaginative verse never becomes a rant of self-indulgence.

Reed's commitment to a craft of poetry demands that readers relinquish any ideas they may possess regarding black or white literary traditions. He encourages readers to understand that there are, always have been, and always will be several literary traditions, and that these traditions are sometimes in accord and sometimes conflict. Reed's poetry cannot be aligned with any single literary tradition. He is, to be sure, an African American writer. He employs strategies seen in the work of classical writers in his efforts to create imaginative verse that both celebrates and explodes conventional forms and genres. Reed encourages readers to re-imagine Western canons as inclusive rather than as exclusive and thus to expand the scope of what it means to be a writer of imaginative verse.

This iconoclastic writer has been nominated for the Pulitzer Prize, and he was a finalist for the National Book Award twice: once in poetry and once in fiction. However, although he has earned numerous critical accolades, commercial success has eluded him. Among his honors and awards are the Richard and Hinda Rosenthal Foundation Award, a Guggenheim Foundation Award, the Lewis Michaux Award, an American Civil Liberties Union Award, and fellowships from the National Endowment for the Arts, the American Civil Liberties Union, and the California Arts Council. Reed is a prolific and inventive writer who has remained true to his ideals regarding art and its creation.

Since 1955, Reed has published poetry, nonfiction essays, and plays. He has also created productions for television, edited four anthologies, and formed a publishing company. Reed served as editor of a Newark, New Jersey, weekly, and he helped to establish the *East Village Other*, one of the first and best-known of the early underground or counterculture newspapers. Despite his reluctance to be characterized as representative of a school of black poets, Reed was also a member of the Umbra Writers Workshop, one of the organizations that fostered the creation of the Black Arts Movement. Reed cofounded the Before Columbus Foundation, a multiethnic organization dedicated to supporting the production of texts that promote a pan-cultural view of the United States. He also cofounded Yardbird Publishing Company and *Quilt* magazine (a literary magazine, not to be confused with the popular magazine about quilting). Reed has taught at the University of California at Berkeley, and he has held visiting appointments at Yale, Harvard, Dartmouth, Washington University in St. Louis, and the State University of New York (SUNY) in Buffalo. In fact, Reed has been a consistent and dedicated advocate of innovative and neglected writing by writers of all races and both genders. Characterized as a combative and antiestablishment writer, Reed is comfortable in the company of writers who make problematic any notions of literary agency based on race, gender, politics, or other arbitrary markers.

Website

"The Circle Association." http://www.math.buffalo.edu/~sww/reed/
reed_ishmael_bio.html

Poetry

Catechism of D Neoamerican Hoodoo Church. London: P. Breman, 1970.
Conjure: Selected Poems, 1963–1970. Amherst: University of Massachusetts
    Press, 1972.
Chattanooga: Poems. New York: Random House, 1973.
New and Collected Poems. New York: Atheneum, 1988.

Fiction

Mumbo Jumbo. Garden City, NY: Doubleday, 1972.
The Last Days of Louisiana Red. New York: Random House, 1974.
Yellow Back Radio Broke-Down. Chatham, NJ: Chatham Bookseller, 1975.
The Free-Lance Pallbearers. Chatham, NJ: The Chatham Bookseller, 1975.
Flight to Canada. New York: Random House, 1976.
The Terrible Twos. New York: St. Martin's/Marek, 1982.
Japanese by Spring. New York: Penguin Books, 1996.

Nonfictions

Shrovetide in Old New Orleans. Garden City, NY: Doubleday, 1978.
Reckless Eyeballing. New York: St. Martin's/Marek, 1986.
Writin' Is Fightin': Thirty-seven Years of Boxing on Paper. New York: Atheneum, 1988.
Airing Dirty Laundry. Reading, MA: Addison-Wesley, 1993.
MultiAmerica: Essays on Cultural Wars and Cultural Peace. New York: Viking, 1997.

References and Suggested Reading

Bibby, Michael. *Hearts and Minds: Bodies, Poetry, and Resistance in the Vietnam Era.* New
    Brunswick, NJ: Rutgers University Press. 1996.
Boyer, Jay. *Ishmael Reed.* Boise, ID: Boise State University Press, 1993.
Brutus, Dennis, Lee Sustar, and Aisha Karim., eds. *Poetry and Protest.* Chicago:
    Haymarket Books. 2006.
Cooke, Michael G. *Afro-American Literature in the Twentieth Century: The Achievement of
    Intimacy.* New Haven, CT: Yale University Press. 1984.
Dick, Bruce, and Amritjit Singh, eds. *Conversations with Ishmael Reed.* Jackson:
    University Press of Mississippi, 1995.
Dick, Bruce, and Amritjit Singh, eds. *The Critical Response to Ishmael Reed.* Westport, CT:
    Greenwood Press, 1999.
Gillian, Maria Mazziotti, and Jennifer Gillian, eds. *Unsettling America: An Anthology of
    Contemporary Multicultural Poetry.* New York: Penguin. 1994.
Kenseth, Arnold. *Poems of Protest, Old and New: A Selection of Poetry.* London:
    Macmillan, 1968.
Kramer, Aaron. *On Freedom's Side: An Anthology of American Poems of Protest.* New York:
    Macmillan, 1972.
Lee, Don L. *We Walk the Way of the New World.* Chicago: Broadside Press. 1970.

Ishmael Reed

Martin, Reginald. *Ishmael Reed and the New Black Aesthetic Critics*. New York: Macmillan, 1986.

McGee, Patrick. *Ishmael Reed and the Ends of Race*. New York: St. Martin's Press, 1997.

Reid, Margaret Ann. *Black Protest Poetry: Polemics from the Harlem Renaissance and the Sixties*. Studies in African and African-American Culture, Vol. 8. New York: Lang, 2002.

Adrienne Rich
(1929-)

An American writer of considerable influence and achievement, Adrienne Rich has written imaginative verse that is symbolic of the varied voices of contemporary women. Her work is often anthologized, and it appears on syllabi in feminist studies and American literature as well as in creative writing courses. Rich's poetry addresses topics of sexuality, race, language, power, and women's culture. That her work speaks to the experiences of women and girls perhaps accounts for Rich's increasing popularity over the past several decades.

Born in Baltimore, Maryland, Rich is the elder of two daughters of Arnold Rich, a college professor, and Helen Jones Rich, a pianist. Her parents, particularly her father, encouraged her early attempts to compose verse. In "Sources," an autobiographical poem published in 1983 when Rich was fifty-four years old, the speaker recounts that childhood encouragement and recalls the religious and cultural history of her family's Jewish and Protestant backgrounds to paint a portrait of her life as a young girl and, as the title of the poem suggests, to pay homage to the early influences on and sources of her poetic genius.

Rich attended Radcliffe College (at Harvard University). Soon after graduation, she won the prestigious Yale Younger Poets Prize for her first collection of poetry, *A Change of World.* W. H. Auden, a well-respected poet as well as a model for the young Rich, praised the collection for its apt demonstration of the young poet's mastery of technique and for its emotional restraint. Within two years after receiving the Yale Prize, Rich married and relocated to Cambridge, Massachusetts. During the next five years, from 1953 until 1958, she bore three sons and, from outward appearances, settled into the roles of mother and wife. However, those years of marriage and family were particularly difficult for Rich. Her journal entries during this period reveal the poet's inner turmoil and confusion, both directly connected to her own unraveling sense of her place in society and in her family. Rich struggled during this period of her life with the prescribed roles of women as well as with the restrictions that were placed on art because of gender. In an effort to record the particulars of a woman writer's experiences in the midst of other important and sometimes conflicting roles, Rich published a collection of poetry titled *Snapshots of a Daughter-in-Law.*

In 1966, against the backdrop of the Vietnam conflict and civil unrest in the cities, Rich relocated with her family to New York. There, she taught in a remedial English program for working-poor students of color and immigrants who were first-generation college students. In addition to her volunteer activities, Rich became involved in movements for social justice. Much of her poetry during this period is grounded in language that reveals her attempts to analyze the human condition, particularly for those individuals who are outside or alien to a culture or to society's mores because of race, gender, class, or sexual orientation. For example, in one poem from this period, "The Roofwalker," the narrator laments that "A life I didn't choose/chose me," and in another work from the same period, titled "Prospective Immigrants Please Note." Rich rhetorically aligns her years spent closeted (i.e., living as a heterosexual woman) to the immigrant's experience of being closed off from mainstream society to suggest that true freedom is found when one eschews the familiar, or comfortable, to risk the unfamiliar. However, even when she explores personal topics, Rich constructs imaginative verse in the tradition of formalist poets who favored a studied attention to structure as a way to create meaning. In this way, Rich is well situated in the company of poets whose similar attention to structure greatly informs their craftsmanship.

Rich has taught at Swarthmore, Columbia, Brandeis, Rutgers, Cornell, San Jose State, and Stanford universities. She is active in movements for gay and lesbian rights, and she has received the National Gay Task Force's Fund for Human Dignity Award. Rich received the National Book Award in 1974 for her collection of poetry, *Diving into the Wreck.* And in addition to being the first recipient of the Ruth Lilly Poetry Prize, she has received two Guggenheim Fellowships, as well as the Brandeis Creative Arts Medal, the Commonwealth Award, the William Whitehead Award for Lifetime Achievement, and the National Poetry Association Award for Distinguished Service to the Art of Poetry.

Website

"PAL: Perspectives in American Literature—A Research and Reference Guide" (California State University, Department of English). http://www.csustan.edu/english

Poetry

A Change of World. New Haven, CT: Yale University Press, 1951.

The Diamond Cutters and Other Poems. New York: Harper, 1955.

Necessities of Life. New York: Norton, 1966.

Snapshots of a Daughter-in-Law: Poems, 1954–1962. New York: Harper, 1963; rev. ed.
   Norton, 1967.

Leaflets: Poems, 1965–1968 New York: Norton, 1969.

The Will to Change: Poems, 1968–1970. New York: Norton, 1971.

Diving into the Wreck: Poems, 1971–1972. New York: Norton, 1973.

Poems: Selected and New, 1950–1974. New York: Norton, 1974.

Twenty-one Love Poems. San Francisco: Effie's Press, 1977.

The Dream of a Common Language: Poems, 1974–1977. New York: Norton, 1978.

A Wild Patience Has Taken Me This Far: Poems, 1978–1981. New York: Norton, 1981.

Sources. Woodside, CA: Heyeck Press, 1983.

The Fact of a Doorframe: Poems Selected and New, 1950–1984. New York: Norton, 1984.

Your Native Land, Your Life, New York: Norton, 1986.

Time's Power: Poems, 1985–1988. New York: Norton, 1988.

An Atlas of the Difficult World: Poems, 1988–1991. New York: Norton, 1991.

Collected Early Poems, 1950–1970. New York: Norton, 1993.

Dark Fields of the Republic, 1991–1995. New York: Norton, 1995.

Prose

On Lies, Secrets and Silence: Selected Prose, 1966–1978. New York: Norton, 1979.

Of Woman Born: Motherhood as Experience and Institution. New York: Norton, 1976; rev.
   ed., 1986.

Blood, Bread and Poetry: Selected Prose, 1979–1986. New York: Norton, 1986.

What Is Found There: Notebooks on Poetry and Politics. New York: Norton, 1993.

References and Suggested Reading

Bronner, Stephen Eric, and Douglas MacKay Kellner. *Passion and Rebellion: The
   Expressionist Heritage.* New York: Routledge, 1988.

Gelpi, Barbara Charlesworth, ed. *Adrienne Rich's Poetry and Prose: Poems, Prose, Reviews
   and Criticism.* New York: Norton, 1993.

Holman, C. Hugh. *A Handbook to Literature.* Indianapolis: Bobbs-Merrill. 1992.

Keyes, Claire. *The Aesthetics of Power: The Poetry of Adrienne Rich.* Athens: University of
   Georgia Press, 1986.

Martin, Wendy. *An American Triptych – Anne Bradstreet, Emily Dickinson, Adrienne Rich.*
   Chapel Hill: University of North Carolina Press, 1984.

The Oxford Companion to Women's Writing in the United States. New York: Oxford
   University Press, 1995.

Stein, Kevin. *Private Poets, Worldly Acts.* Athens: Ohio University Press, 1996.

Templeton, Alice. *The Dream and the Dialogue: Adrienne Rich's Feminist Poetics.* Knoxville:
   University of Tennessee Press, 1994.

Cynthia Rylant
(1954-)

Throughout an award-winning career featuring works in a variety of genres for children and young adults, Cynthia Rylant has become one of the most recognized voices in her field. Rylant was born in Hopewell, Virginia. on June 6, 1954, the daughter of June Rune, an army sergeant, and Leatral Rylant Smith. Rylant's early life was marked by turbulence and a series of transitions as her parents' unhappy marriage failed. Rylant's parents separated when she was four years old, and the youngster was sent to live with her maternal grandparents in West Virginia while her mother attended nursing school. Rylant's childhood among her maternal family members in the mountains of West Virginia provided inspiration for her fiction and nonfiction works. Her love of West Virginia and the Appalachian people is reflected in her poetry and fiction. In general, a strong sense of family permeates Rylant's writing, and specific episodes from her childhood are revisited in picture books such as *Silver Packages* and *When I Was Young in the Mountains*, the latter a Caldecott Honor Book.

Rylant was reunited with her mother at approximately eight years of age. They moved into an apartment in Beaver, West Virginia, and Cynthia enrolled in the third grade. Her third-grade teacher, Miss Evans, captivated the inquisitive, shy young girl. The teacher turned the year into an epic adventure for her students, making them the lead characters in weekly installments of original stories. In 1985, Rylant wrote an article entitled "Thank You, Miss Evans" as a tribute to her beloved teacher.

Rylant's happiness was tempered by loss; even though her father had renewed correspondence with his daughter, the two were never reunited. When Rylant was thirteen, her mother died. Rylant later claimed that this loss would prove enough to make her a writer, allowing her to draw on her own pain. Throughout her adolescence, Rylant was acutely aware of her family's modest means and of the limits of life in a small town. Despite her family's financial difficulties and her existence in a somewhat isolated community, Cynthia Rylant grew into an active, curious, and gregarious teenager who was passionate about the Beatles, and about Paul McCartney in particular. Rylant titled her autobiography *But I'll Be Back Again*, a quote from a Beatles song, and used their song lyrics to mark transitions among sections or chapters.

Throughout her childhood and adolescence, Rylant's experience of the world outside of her small town was limited. She was awed by the New Orleans Symphony Orchestra, which played a concert at her junior high school, an experience Rylant claimed to be her first exposure to any real sort of culture. Much of her early reading consisted of comic books, and Rylant had never visited a library or an art museum until her college years.

Rylant left Beaver for Morris Harvey College, since renamed the University of Charleston, and reveled in her studies and in campus life. She majored in English, and earned her bachelor's degree in 1975. She earned her master's degree from Huntington, West Virginia's Marshall University in 1976 and taught English there for one academic year. In 1978, Rylant entered the children's room at a public library—for the first time—and determined that she would make writing a career. Rylant then attended Kent State University, earning a second master's degree, this time in Library Science. Rylant's first book, *When I Was Young in the Mountains*, was published that year to critical acclaim for Diane Goode's artwork and for its simple, lyrical style.

In 1983, Rylant took a position as a librarian in Akron, Ohio. She lectured at the University of Akron throughout that academic year but would soon turn to full-time writing. Twice divorced by 1984 and raising son Nathaniel, Rylant began producing picture books and poetry. In the deeply personal *Waiting to Waltz*, Rylant produced thirty-three poems that describe movements and icons in the era of her youth, the turbulent 1960s. The book received numerous honors from the American Library Association and the National Council of Social Studies and was named *School Library Journal*'s Best Book of the Year.

In 1985, Rylant began publishing novels for intermediate and young adult readers. Her first novel, *A Blue-Eyed Daisy*, was followed quickly by a series of short stories, *Every Living Thing* (1985). *A Fine White Dust*, published in 1986, tells the story of a young boy's experiences when a charismatic preacher comes through his town. The book earned a Newbery Honor. Her 1989 novel, *A Kindness*, was also recognized by the American Library Association as one of the best books of its year.

Rylant continued to work on her series in fiction for younger readers, and in 1994 she returned to poetry with a collection titled *Something*

Permanent, a slim volume of poems written as companion pieces to Depression-era photographs by Walker Evans. The collection contains verse and photographs that depict a clear sense of life and of the physical setting in small towns across America throughout the 1930s.

A prolific writer, Rylant has written nearly one hundred books. Her works of poetry and fiction form a body of work characterized by sensitivity and clarity of voice.

Poetry

Waiting to Waltz . . . A Childhood. Illustrated by Stephen Gammell. New York: Bradbury, 1984.

Soda Jerk. Illustrated by Peter Catalanotto. New York: Orchard Books, 1990.

Something Permanent. Photographs by Walker Evans. San Diego, CA: Harcourt, 1994.

God Went to Beauty School. New York: HarperCollins, 2003.

Boris. New York: Harcourt, 2005.

Children's Books

When I Was Young in the Mountains. Illustrated by Diane Good. New York: Dutton, 1982.

An Angel for Solomon Singer. Illustrated by Peter Catalanotto. New York: Orchard Books, 1992.

Best Wishes. Photographs by Carlo Ontal. Katonah. New York: R. C. Owen, 1992.

The Dreamer. Illustrated by Barry Moser. New York: Blue Sky Press, 1993.

Dog Heaven. New York: Blue Sky Press, 1995.

The Van Gogh Café. San Diego, CA: Harcourt, 1995.

Gooseberry Park. Illustrated by Arthur Howard. San Diego, CA: Harcourt, 1995.

The Whales. New York: Blue Sky Press, 1996.

The Old Woman Who Named Things. Illustrated by Kathryn Brown. San Diego, CA: Harcourt, 1996.

The Bookshop Dog. New York: Blue Sky Press, 1996.

Cat Heaven. New York: Blue Sky Press, 1997.

Silver Packages: An Appalachian Christmas Story. Illustrated by Chris K. Soentpiet. New York: Orchard Books, 1997.

An Everyday Book. New York: Simon & Schuster, 1997.

Scarecrow. Illustrated by Lauren Stringer. San Diego, CA: Harcourt, 1997.

Bear Day. Illustrated by Jennifer Selby. San Diego, CA: Harcourt, 1998.

The Bird House. Illustrated by Barry Moser. New York: Blue Sky Press, 1998.

Fiction

A Kindness. New York: Orchard Books, 1992.

A Couple of Kooks, and Other Stories About Love. New York: Orchard Books, 1990.

Missing May. New York: Orchard Books, 1992.

I Had Seen Castles. San Diego, CA: Harcourt, 1993.
The Islander. New York: DK Ink, 1998.

Nonfiction

Appalachia: The Voices of Sleeping Birds. Illustrated by Barry Moser. San Diego, CA: Harcourt, 1991.
Margaret, Frank, and Andy: Three Writers' Stories. San Diego, CA: Harcourt, 1996.
Bless Us All: A Child's Yearbook of Blessings. New York: Simon & Schuster, 1998.
Give Me Grace: A Child's Daybook of Prayers. New York: Simon & Schuster, 1999.

References and Suggested Reading

Ballard, Sandra. *Listen Here: Women Writing in Appalachia.* Lexington: University Press of Kentucky, 2004.
Clark, Jim. *Mountain Memories: An Appalachian Sense of Place.* Morgantown, WV: Vandalia Press, 2003.
Gray, Richard. *A Companion to the Literature and Culture of the American South.* Malden, MA: Blackwell, 2004.
Smith, Barbara. *Wild Sweet Notes: Fifty Years of West Virginia Poetry, 1950–1999.* Huntington, WV: Publishers Place, 2000.

Sonia Sanchez
(1934–)

Sonia Sanchez (née Wilsonia Benita Driver) was born in Birmingham, Alabama during Franklin D. Roosevelt's second term as president of the United States and as the literary movements identified as the Jazz Age and the Harlem Renaissance were ending. Her first year of life was punctuated by her mother's death, after which Driver lived with her paternal grandmother, her father, and her stepmother. The girl's grandmother encouraged her love of reading and writing. By age four, the blossoming poet had learned to read, and by age six, she had begun to write poetry. After her grandmother's death in 1943, when the youngster was nine years old, she moved to Harlem with her sister to live with their father and stepmother.

Driver attended public schools in New York. In 1955, as the United States began its police action in Vietnam, she earned a bachelor's degree in political science from Hunter College. The young Driver also completed graduate work at New York University; she studied poetry with Louise Bogan and founded a writers' workshop in Greenwich Village. The workshops were attended by Amiri Baraka (née LeRoi Jones), Haki R. Madhubuti (née Don Lee), and Larry Neal, three of the most influential artists of the Black Arts Movement, a cultural and literary movement characterized by its accomplishments in founding theatres, creating literary magazines, and setting up small presses.

Although Driver began to write poetry at an early age, the poet Sonia Sanchez was not "born" until her marriage to Alberto Sanchez. Like many of her contemporaries, Sanchez adopted a pseudonym to represent her poet self. Indeed, many poets both past and present have used nom de plumes rather than their given names in connection with their published works. No doubt they do so for a variety of reasons, including the desire to separate the persona from the person. However, in Sanchez's case the opposite appears to be true: the persona created in her poetry often reflects events in the private world of the person who created the poetry.

As she wrote about the ills of segregation, Sonia Sanchez supported the Congress of Racial Equality (CORE) in its efforts to protest racially segregated interstate bus facilities. She listened to the words of el-Hajj Malik el-Shabazz (Malcolm X) and used his teachings to guide her work as a college professor. Sanchez began teaching in the San Francisco area in 1965; she developed black studies courses at what is now San Francisco State University, where she was an instructor at the time of the assassinations of Martin Luther King, Jr., and Robert F. Kennedy. She was the first Presidential Fellow at Temple University, where she began teaching in 1977, and she held the Laura Carnell Chair in English there until her retirement in 1999. In addition, Sanchez has lectured at colleges and universities in the United States and has read her poetry in Africa, Cuba, England, some Caribbean nations, Australia, Nicaragua, the People's Republic of China, Norway, and Canada. She has taught at the University of Pittsburgh, Rutgers University, The Manhattan Community College of City University of New York (CUNY), The City College of CUNY, Amherst College, and the University of Pennsylvania. Sanchez is currently a member of the faculty at Temple University and teaches Black American Literature and Creative Writing.

A tireless activist, Sanchez worked in California to bring black studies programs into the school curriculum. She is a member of MADRE, an international women's and human rights organization that provides health care services, education, and assistance with economic development and reproductive rights. Sanchez also supports MOMS in Alabama, an organization begun by a stay-at-home mother in California who wanted to network with other stay-at-home mothers. The organization was started in 1983 and has grown to more than 10,000 chapters in the United States, with over 100,000 members. In addition to her work with organizations that support mothers and families, Sanchez is a member of the National Black United Front. And despite her support of stay-at-home moms, Sanchez left the Nation of Islam because some of her views conflicted with that organization's position on women's roles.

Although Sanchez had been writing most of her life, her first book of poetry, *Home Coming*, was published in 1969, when she was thirty-five years old. A second book, *We a BaddDDD People*, followed in 1970. In both texts, Sanchez reflects the example set by Malcolm X in his fiery speeches. She uses both dialect and profanity to wage linguistic war against America's educational system, against its racism, and against its general mistreatment of poor people. Indeed, Sanchez is an unapologetic writer whose poems often depict the struggles between black people and white people, between men and women, and between cultures. Her innovative use of language, her brilliant recitation of history, and her mastery of haiku, tanka, and villanelle forms often combine in her work to create newer poetic forms.

Sanchez's poems describe a world mired in hardship, violence, and oppression; however, because she is determined to leave the world a better place than she found it, within her poetry readers also discover passion, fortitude, and tenderness. Her own unwavering commitment to voicing the concerns of those whose voices are often silenced has garnered her many awards. Among the awards she has received for her activism as well as for her poetry are the Community Service Award from the National Black Caucus of State Legislators, the Lucretia Mott Award, the Outstanding Arts Award from the Pennsylvania Coalition of 100 Black Women, the Peace and Freedom Award from the Women International League for Peace and Freedom, the Pennsylvania Governor's Award for Excellence in the Humanities, a National Endowment for the Arts Award, and a Pen Fellowship in the Arts.

Sanchez's 1984 collection, *Homegirls & Handgrenades*, won an American Book Award from the Before Columbus Foundation. In addition, her books for younger readers and writers include the 1973 collection of poetry, *It's a New Day: Poems for Young Brothas and Sistuhs*, as well as several collections of short stories, including *A Sound Investment and Other Stories* (1979) and *The Adventures of Fat Head, Small Head, and Square Head* (1971).

Sanchez is the author of more than a dozen books of poetry; her 1995 *Does your House have Lions?* was nominated for both the NAACP Image Award and the National Book Critics Circle Award. The poems included in this collection are written in rhyme royal, a stanza of seven lines of iambic pentameter, rhyming *ababbcc*. The form, invented by Chaucer, was popularized by King James I of Scotland, an early poet who used the form. Sanchez reinvents the form in her text by combining verses spoken by different characters with different speech patterns and tones. In this important text, Sanchez explored her brother's death from AIDS through the voices of her family members as she fearlessly confronted the silence surrounding gay sexuality in many black American families.

Sanchez has also worked with musicians to produce spoken word recordings. Her most recent recording, *Full Moon of Sonia*, was released in April 2001. *Full Moon of Sonia* provides an offering of musical and poetic styles that includes echoes of rhythm and blues, jazz, Afro-Cuban, gospel, and hip-hop. The release of the spoken word recording marks a new plateau in Sanchez's industrious, four decades career. The spoken-word compact disc celebrates Sanchez's life and work and underscores her contribution both to poetry and to performance in the modern era.

Websites

"Academy of American Poets." http://www.poets.org
"PAL: Perspectives in American Literature—A Research and Reference Guide" (California State University, Department of English). http://www.csustan.edu/english/reuben/pal/chap10/sanchez.html
"MOMS." http://www.momsclub.org/history.html

Poetry

Homecoming. Chicago: Broadside Press, 1968.
A Blues Book for Blue Black Magical Women. Chicago: Broadside Press, 1973.
Under a Soprano Sky. New Jersey: Africa World Press, 1987.
Wounded in the House of a Friend. Boston: Beacon, 1997.
Homegirls and Handgrenades. New York: Thunder's Mouth Press, 1997.
Does your House have Lions? Boston: Beacon, 1998.
Shake Loose My Skin: New and Collected Poems. Boston: Beacon, 2000.

Recording

Alexander, Kwame. Executive Producer. *Jazz Poetry Kafe* (poetry/jazz/spoken word). Contributors include Sonia Sanchez, Haki Madhubuti, Fertile Ground, and Tony Medina. Audio CD (1999).

References and Suggested Reading

Bloom, Harold, ed. *Black American Women Fiction Writers.* New York: Chelsea House, 1995.
Bontemps, Arna. *American Negro Poetry: An Anthology.* New York: Hill and Wang (reissue), 1995.
DeLancey, Frenzella E. "Refusing to Be Boxed In: Sonia Sanchez's Transformation of the Haiku Form." In *Language and Literature in the African American Imagination.* Ed. Carol A. Blackshire-Belay. Westport, CT: Greenwood Press, 1992.
Joyce, Joyce Ann. *Ijala: Sonia Sanchez and the African Poetic Tradition.* Chicago: Third World Press, 1996.
Miles, Johnnie H. *Almanac of African American Heritage.* New York: Jossey-Bass, 2001.
Reich, David. "As Poets, as Activists. An Interview with Sonia Sanchez." In *Black American Women Fiction Writers.* New York: Chelsea House, 1995.

Carl August Sandburg
(1878-1967)

Carl August Sandburg. Courtesy of Photofest.

Carl Sandburg was born in a three-room cottage in Galesburg, Illinois. The house has been maintained by the Illinois Historic Preservation Agency, and it reflects typical living conditions of a late nineteenth-century working-class family such as the Sandburgs. Many of the furnishings in the cottage once indeed belonged to the young Sandburg and his family.

Sandburg was the son of Swedish immigrants, August and Clara Anderson Sandburg. His father was a blacksmith's helper for a railroad; he purchased the family cottage in 1873, five years before his son was born. The young Sandburg was the second of seven children born into the family. After his son's birth, the elder Sandburg sold the cottage and purchased a larger house that would better accommodate his growing family.

The young Sandburg quit school when he was thirteen years old, and for the next ten years, he performed various jobs. He delivered milk, harvested ice, laid bricks, threshed wheat in Kansas, and shined shoes before taking up a life as a hobo. Sandburg's experiences working and traveling informed both his political views and his poetry, which, more often than not, reflected those views. During this period of experimentation, the young Sandburg began to write poems about labor issues, a subject to which he would frequently return in the years and poems to come.

Sandburg learned a number of folk songs during his travels, and he was often asked to perform those songs at colleges, universities, and other institutions where he was invited to speak. As a guest on college campuses, Sandburg observed for himself the sharp disparity between the rich and the poor, an experience that served to whet his passion on behalf of the working class and that served as well to increase his poetic critiques of the middle and upper classes. Sandburg's poetry gives voice to many of young readers' personal observations and criticisms regarding government policies on immigration and other issues.

Sandburg volunteered for service in the Spanish-American War, and although he was ordered to Puerto Rico, he did not see battle. Upon his discharge, he entered Lombard College, supporting himself as a fireman during his course of study. The next few years were instrumental in shaping further his literary interests and his political views. While a student at Lombard, Sandburg joined the Poor Writers' Club, founded by a Lombard professor who encouraged the young poet in his acerbic commentary on labor and other domestic issues. Although Sandburg appeared to enjoy the exchange of ideas in which he participated at Lombard, and although he continued to hone his writing skills, he left Lombard in his senior year. His first book of poetry, *In Reckless Ecstasy*, was printed on his former professor's basement press in 1904. Two subsequent volumes of poetry, *Incidentals*, and *The Plaint of a Rose* were printed on the basement press in 1907 and 1908.

Sandburg's concerns regarding the unfair treatment of American workers, including the lack of medical benefits and fair wages, led him to work as an organizer for the Wisconsin Social Democratic Party. In this position, he put his considerable literary talent to work writing political pamphlets and literature. Soon afterward; however, Sandburg returned to Illinois and took up journalism. For several years, he was a reporter for the *Chicago Daily News*. He covered mostly labor issues and thus was virtually unknown to the literary world in 1914, when several of his poems appeared in a nationally circulated magazine. Two years later, his book, *Chicago Poems*, was published. Sandburg published another volume of poems, *Cornhuskers*, in 1918, and in 1922 he published *Rootabaga Stories,* a collection of children's stories.

Sandburg won the Pulitzer Prize in 1940 for *Abraham Lincoln: The War Years*, the second installment of a biography in two parts. In 1945, he relocated to North Carolina, where he continued to produce poetry and fiction and to collect folk songs and books as well as raise prize-winning goats. He won a second Pulitzer Prize in 1951 for his collection, *Complete Poems*, which contained poetry from the various periods of his career. Sandburg died in 1967 at his North Carolina home, and, as he had requested, his ashes were returned to his Galesburg birthplace and interred beneath a red granite boulder he recalled fondly as Remembrance Rock. Ten years later, the ashes of his wife were interred there as well.

Website

"Carl Sandburg Historic Site." http://www.sandburg.org/

Poetry

Chicago Poems. New York: Holt, 1916.
Smoke and Steel. New York. Harcourt, 1920.
Selected Poems. New York: Harcourt, 1926.
Good Morning, America. New York: Crosby Gaige, 1928.
Bronze Wood. College Board, MD: Grabhorn Press, 1941.
Poems of the Midwest. Nashville, TN: World Publishing, 1946.
The Complete Poems. New York: Harcourt, 1950.
Harvest Poems. New York: Harcourt, 1960.
Six New Poems and a Parable. University of Kentucky Press, 1961.
Honey and Salt. New York: Harcourt, 1963.
A Sandburg Treasury. New York: Harcourt, 1970.
Breathing Tokens. New York: Harcourt, 1978.
Billy Sunday and Other Poems. New York: Harcourt, 1993.

References and Suggested Reading

Allen, Gay Wilson. *Carl Sandburg.* Minneapolis: University of Minnesota Press, 1972.
Crowder, Richard. *Carl Sandburg.* Chicago, IL: Twayne, 1964.
Durnell, Hazel B. *The America of Carl Sandburg.* Cary, NC: Cherokee, 1997.
Golden, Harry. *Carl Sandburg.* Nashville, TN: World Publishing, 1961.
Hacker, Jeffrey H. *Carl Sandburg.* Danbury, CT: Franklin Watts, 1984.
Meltzer, Milton. *Carl Sandburg, A Biography.* Breckenridge, CO: Twenty-first Century Books, 1999.
Niven, Penelope. *Carl Sandburg: A Biography.* Urbana: University of Illinois Press, 1994.
Niven, Penelope, and Katie Davis. *Carl Sandburg: Adventures of a Poet.* New York: Harcourt, 2003.
Perry, Lilla S. *My Friend Carl Sandburg: The Biography of a Friendship.* Lanham, MD: Scarecrow Press, 1981.
Reader, Dennis J., and John E. Hallwas, eds. *The Vision of This Land: Studies of Vachel Lindsay, Edgar Lee Masters and Carl Sandburg.* Western Illinois University Press, 1976.
Sutton, William Alfred. *Carl Sandburg Remembered.* Lanham, MD: Scarecrow Press, 1979.
Yannella, Phillip R. *The Other Carl Sandburg.* Jackson: Mississippi University Press, 1996.

Anne Gray Harvey Sexton
(1928–1974)

This American poet is perhaps most often remembered as a slightly off-kilter, depressed individual who wrote verse on controversial topics such as suicide, abortion, insanity, and menstruation. However, Sexton also wrote poetry on religion, myth, gender, and parenthood as well as on sexual themes, so to read her poetry as a private tour through the poet's evolving madness is to risk not hearing the voice of the other Anne Sexton—the one who marveled at the most seemingly minute event and who was then compelled to capture the moment of its occurrence in language set in tightly constrained meter, aided by deftly drawn imagery.

Although Sexton's exactness with language and form often renders her poetry difficult to decipher, her poetry is appropriate for young readers who wish to be rewarded in their search for authentic, challenging verse. Because Sexton caringly textures each poem, her work is rich not only in detail and specificity, but also in cultural significance. In fact, much of Sexton's poetry is spoken from a child's perspective. For example, her poem "The Double Image" is written in the voice of a girl who is examining the many relationships that exist between her mother and herself. Sexton's work is not only accessible to young readers, but also appropriate for use in literature or language arts courses.

Sexton was born in Norton, Massachusetts, and she lived most of her life in and around Boston. She attended junior college for one year and then married at age nineteen. Sexton also briefly considered becoming a model, and she enrolled in a modeling course to pursue that career. However, despite her quick intellect, and despite her early interest in literature, Sexton never received a college degree. In fact, she did not begin to pursue her craft until she was encouraged to do so by a doctor who had treated her for depression. She began attending poetry workshops where she met the poets Maxine

Kumin and Sylvia Plath. Plath's influence on Sexton's poetry is apparent in Sexton's excruciatingly detailed narratives about personal subjects in which the poet becomes a disinterested observer of the experiences she describes. Sexton expands Plath's confessional poetry model and steps back from her work to examine intimate moments in her own life and environment through the clear, cool eye of a surgeon. Still, despite Plath's obvious influence on Sexton's craft, it was with Maxine Kumin that Sexton developed a relationship that led to their collaborating to produce four children's books.

Although Sexton never studied with the poets Emily Dickinson, John Donne, or George Herbert, there can be no doubt that the themes readers discover in Sexton's poetry are present as well in poetry written by all three of those poets. For like Dickinson, Sexton wrote in unconventional ways about personal subjects, including religion and mortality. And like Donne's and Herbert's, Sexton's poetry often reflects her own processes of religious questioning.

Sexton's imaginative verse has gained wide acceptance among a diverse audience. Her vividly imagistic poetry captures simple as well as complex moments in her readers' lives in language that appeals to people from various backgrounds. Because of the variety of her work and the scope of the subjects on which she is able to speak both articulately and authoritatively, Sexton has enjoyed increasing popularity and acceptance among new readers while maintaining the scores of readers already familiar with her work.

Sexton published several books of poetry during her life. Perhaps the most well known are her first and last publications, *To Bedlam and Part Way Back*, published in 1960 when she was thirty-two years of age, and *Words for Dr. Y*, published posthumously in 1978. In addition, Sexton won the Pulitzer Prize in poetry in 1967 for her collection *Live or Die*. Writing poetry gave Sexton a foundation from which to stabilize her existence, and poetry helped her to order her life; however, despite a successful writing career, she lost her battle with mental illness and committed suicide in 1974 at age forty-six.

Website

"Academy of American Poets." http://www.poets.org

Poetry

All My Pretty Ones. New York: Houghton Mifflin, 1962. *Live or Die*. New York: Houghton Mifflin, 1966. *Love Poems*. New York: Houghton Mifflin, 1969. *Transformations*. New York: Mariner, 1971.

The Book of Folly. New York: Houghton Mifflin, (1973).

The Death Notebooks. New York: Mariner, 1974. *45 Mercy Street.* New York: Houghton Mifflin, 1976.

The Awful Rowing Toward God. New York: Chatto and Windus, 1977.

The Complete Poems. New York: Mariner, 1981.

Selected Poems. New York: Houghton Mifflin, 1988.

Children's Books (With Maxine Kumin)

Eggs of Things. New York: Putnam, 1963.

More Eggs of Things. New York: Putnam, 1964.

Joey and the Birthday Present. New York: McGraw-Hill, 1971.

The Wizard's Tears. New York: McGraw-Hill, 1975.

References and Suggested Reading

Bixler, Frances. *Original Essays on Anne Sexton.* Conway: University of Central Arkansas Press, 1988.

Colburn, Steven E. *Anne Sexton: Telling the Tale.* Ann Arbor: University of Michigan Press, 1988.

Hall, Barnard, and Caroline King. *Anne Sexton.* Boston: Twayne, 1989.

Martin, Linda Wagner. *Critical Essays on Anne Sexton.* Boston: G. K. Hall, 1989.

McClatchy, J. D. *Anne Sexton: The Poet and Her Critics.* Bloomington: Indiana University Press, 1978.

Middlebrook, Diane Wood. *Anne Sexton: A Biography.* Boston: Houghton Mifflin, 1991.

Sexton, Linda Grey. *Searching for Mercy Street: My Journey Back to My Mother.* Boston: Little, Brown, 1994.

Sexton, Linda Grey, and Lois Aimes. *Anne Sexton: A Self-Portrait in Letters.* Boston: Houghton Mifflin, 1979.

Wagner-Martin, Linda, ed. *Critical Essays on Anne Sexton.* Boston: G. K. Hall, 1989.

Tupac Amaru Shakur
(1971–1996)

Tupac Amaru Shakur. Courtesy of Photofest.

This American poet may be better known as the rap artist who died violently at the young age of twenty-five than as a writer of imaginative verse. However, young readers must attempt to separate Shakur's public image from his work if they are to learn to appreciate the simple beauty of the poetry this young writer wrote during his short life. For in language often mournful as well as celebratory, Shakur recorded events in his private adolescent and adult worlds that provoke readers to think critically about their own similar experiences.

Shakur's ability with language comes as no surprise to those who know the whole story of his life. Born in New York, Shakur enrolled in the famous Harlem *127th Street Ensemble* when he was twelve years old. As a member of this acting troupe, he played the character Travis in the play *A Raisin in the Sun*. In 1984, when Shakur was fifteen, his family relocated to Baltimore. Once there, Shakur enrolled at the Baltimore School for the Arts, where he became friends with Jada Pinkett. In Baltimore, Shakur studied ballet, poetry, jazz, and acting. He performed in Shakespearean plays and landed the role of the Mouse King in *The Nutcracker.* However, Shakur did not remain in Baltimore. In 1988, when he was approximately seventeen years of age, his family relocated to Marin City, California. Shakur continued to explore his creative interests, and in 1990 he became a backup dancer for the rap group Digital Underground. In 1991, when he was approximately twenty years old, he combined all of his prior studies and creative pursuits into a single art form: rap.

Rap artists, in synthesizing the art forms of poetry, dance, performance, and the traditional African call and response trope, created a new art form without benefit of a single model. Unfortunately, these primarily self-taught originators used the forms to express content of which audiences initially disapproved. And although Shakur often faced a disapproving audience in his music, which has been criticized for its images of violence, in his poetry readers sense the poet's desire for an ordered universe and his need to be a part of that order.

Shakur also used his poetry to address criticism of his rap songs. In "For Mrs. Hawkins," Shakur offers reasons for his perceived militancy in music, and calls himself a "Panther" with "the blood of Malcolm" coursing through his veins. In other poetry, Shakur contemplates the usefulness of a love that lasts forever but isn't available in a loved one's immediate present. Yet other poetry, for example, "The Fear in the Heart of a Man," is a revealing narration that strips away the narrator's bravado to reveal his vulnerability. Both "Life through My Eyes" and "Sometimes I Cry" are private glimpses into this poet's soul that are in direct contrast to those images seen in his other work.

Before his untimely death, Shakur had begun to look about for ways to give back to his community. Having run an earlier project called "The Underground Railroad," he had begun to develop community projects aimed at getting young people involved in the creative arts. His mother, Afeni Shakur, supported his efforts, and after his death, she opened *The Tupac Amaru Shakur Center for the Arts*, which is located in Stone Mountain, Georgia. In November 2005, U.S. Representative Cynthia McKinney of Georgia introduced House Resolution (H.R.) 4210, called "The Tupac Amaru Shakur Records Collection Act," to create a collection of papers related to the life and death of Shakur.

Website

Tupac Shakur's home page: http://www.2paclegacy.com/

Poetry

The Rose That Grew from Concrete. New York: Simon & Schuster, 1999.
Inside a Thug's Heart. New York: Dafina Books, 2004.

References and Suggested Reading

Bastfield, Darrin Keith. *Back in the Day: My Life and Times with Tupac Shakur.* New York: DeCapo Press, 2003.
Bynoe, Yvonne. *Encyclopedia of Rap and Hip-Hop Culture.* Westport, CT: Greenwood Press, 2005.
Dyson, Michael Eric. *Holler If You Hear Me: Searching for Tupac Shakur.* Jackson, TN: Basic Civitas Books, 2002.
Guy, Jasmine. *Afeni Shakur: Evolution of a Revolutionary.* New York: Atria, 2004.
Hoye, Jacob. *Tupac: Resurrection.* New York: Atria Books, 2003.
Keyes, Cheryl L. *Rap Music and Street Consciousness.* Urbana: University of Illinois Press, 2004.
Kitwana, Bakari. *The Rap on Gangsta Rap.* Chicago: Third World Press, 1994.
Lommel, Cookie. *The History of Rap Music.* New York: Chelsea House, 2001.

Ntozake Shange
(1948-)

Ntozake Shange (pronounced En-toe-zah-kay Shang-gay)is an American poet, playwright, dancer, actor, director and lecturer. Born Paulette Williams, she changed her name in 1971. The name she chose for herself expresses Shange's sense of her own identity. The name comes from the Zulu language and describes a woman of considerable strength and internal fortitude. Shange's celebration of the inherent stately nature of women is a recurring theme in her work. She has stated that one of her goals is to write books that could be presented as gifts to young girls.

Shange is the first poet to combine the genres of poetry and drama to create a new genre of poetry called the choreopoem. Her first such attempt is titled *for colored girls who have considered suicide when the rainbow is enuf*, and the choreographed poem tells the story of several women, each in her own voice. Like much of Shange's work, it focuses on the condition of women of color in the United States with regard to education, health care, and relationships.

Shange grew up in a rich intellectual environment. Her parents' friends included the musicians Dizzy Gilliespie, Chuck Berry, and Miles Davis, as well as the actor Paul Robeson and the writer W. E. B. DuBois. As a child, Shange often listened in on the conversations that took place among the adults in her home. It was during these conversations that she discovered her own love of language; encouraged by her parents, she began not only to attend poetry readings but also to critique and analyze the poetry that she heard.

Although Shange was born in New Jersey, in 1956 her family relocated to Missouri. Shange was approximately eight years old; however, she recalls being acutely aware of the limits placed on blacks and women during this period. In Missouri, she was sent several miles away from home to attend a school that catered to the needs of children with special abilities. For the first time in her life, she attended a nonsegregated school, where she recalls experiencing overt racism and constant harassment. This early experience was the impetus for much of her writing in which she attempts to abate, as she describes it, the "sense of anger and vacancy" that she felt as a young child thrust into an unfriendly and unfamiliar environment.

At age eighteen, Shange enrolled in Barnard College in New York. Her young adult years were punctuated by several significant events, including marriage and separation, as well as several suicide attempts. Despite the rocky beginnings of her young adult years; however, Shange graduated with honors in 1970 with a bachelor of arts in American Studies. Soon afterward, she moved from New York to California, where she attended graduate school at the University of Southern California (USC). At USC, Shange taught writing and once again began to attend poetry readings.

In 1972, she earned a master of arts in American Studies; she also taught courses in the humanities and in women studies. By this time, Shange was not only writing poetry but she had also begun to perform her poetry, setting it to music and incorporating dance. In addition to teaching, writing, and performing her poetry, Shange joined a dance company. She began developing the work that would become the world's first choreopoem while a graduate student in California.

Shange returned to New York in an effort to find a larger audience for her choreopoem. She began performing *for colored girls who have considered suicide when the rainbow is enuf* in Soho lofts and in bars on New York's lower east side. A producer saw one of the performances and with his help, Shange's choreopoem was staged at an off-Broadway theater. The choreopoem was staged at yet another off-Broadway theater before moving to Broadway in 1976. Shange has received Tony nominations, and she has won an Obie Award and an Outer Circle Award for her innovative poetry, *for colored girls who have considered suicide when the rainbow is enuf* has also been translated into Japanese.

However, despite the wide appeal of Shange's well-known work, *for colored girls who have considered suicide when the rainbow is enuf* caused controversy for its radical use of language and its equally radical creation of space for women of color to voice their discontent about relationships with men. In the work, Shange attempted to discover and to communicate to all who would listen the exact causes of the black woman's pain and alienation, an effort she observes that has been "denied and defiled."

Shange continues to produce poetry and plays, and she continues to combine the forms and perform her poetry on the stage. *Nappy Edges*, a collection of poetry, was published in 1978; it features fifty poems that celebrate women in all their splendor. In 1979, Shange published a trilogy titled *Three Pieces* that contained the choreopoems "Spell 37," "A Photograph: Lovers in Motion," and "Boogie Woogie Landscapes." *Three Pieces* won the Los Angeles Times Book Prize for Poetry. In addition, Shange has also won a Pushcart Prize for her poetry.

Shange's work creates a space for women to enter and take control of their lives. She has created similar spaces for women in the classes she has taught at California State College, the City College of New York (CUNY), the University of Houston, and at Rice, Yale, Howard and New York universities. In addition to poetry, Shange has published children's books, including two collections of prose, *Daddy Says*, and *Float Like a Butterfly: Muhammad Ali*. Other books of poetry by Shange include *I Live in Music, Ridin' the Moon in Texas: Word Paintings, From Okra to Greens: Poems, A Daughter's Geography*, and *Natural Disasters and Other Festive Occasions*. Currently, Shange is a faculty member in the Department of Drama at the University of Houston. Two research centers located in New York, The Schomburg Center for Research in Black Culture and the New York Public Library for the Performing Arts, house Shange's collections. The poet continues to lecture at various colleges and literary conferences across the country.

Website

"Women of Color; Women of Words." http://www.scils.rutgers.edu/~cybers/shange2.html
"Academy of American Poets." http://www.poets.org

Poetry

I Live in Music. New York: Welcome Books, 1994.
If I Can Cook/You Know God Can. New York: Beacon, 1999.
The Sweet Breath of Life: A Poetic Narrative of the African American Family. New York: Atria, 2004.
How I Come by This Cryin' Song. New York: St. Martin's Press, 2006.

Nonfiction

Black Book. Photographs by Robert Mapplethorpe. New York: St. Martin's Press, 1986.

Fiction

Sassafras, Cypress and Indigo: A Novel. New York: St. Martin's Press, 1982.
Betsey Brown. New York: Picador, 1995.
Whitewash. New York: Walker, 1997.

References and Suggested Reading

Betsko, Kathleen, and Rachel Koenig, eds. *Interviews with Contemporary Women Playwrights*. London: Beech Tree Books, 1987.

Christ, Carol P. *Diving Deep and Surfacing: Women Writers on Spiritual Quest*. Boston: Beacon Press, 1980.

Gates, Henry Louis, ed. *Bearing Witness: Selections from African-American Autobiography in the Twentieth Century*. New York: Pantheon Books, 1991.

Glikin, Ronda. *Black American Women in Literature: A Bibliography, 1976 through 1987*. Jefferson, NC: McFarland, 1989.

Lester, Neal A. *Ntozake Shange: A Critical Study of the Plays*. New York: Garland, 1995.

Smith, Valerie, et al., eds. *African American Writers*. New York: Charles Scribner's Sons, 1991.

Squier, Susan Merrill, ed. *Women Writers and the City: Essays in Feminist Literary Criticism*. Knoxville: University of Tennessee Press, 1984.

Leslie Marmon Silko
(1948-)

A writer of poetry and prose, Silko, in her imaginative verse, attempts to identify and explore the many nuances of her own identity, as well as others'. Silko, who is neither fully Native American nor wholly white, uses her writing to put into words her own efforts to merge the two halves of her identity into a complete whole. In her work she attempts to recover the old stories of her culture and merge them with modern reality, not only to strengthen her own cultural awareness but also to reflect her diverse heritage. Silko's writing reflects, overall, her efforts to merge all the parts of herself; thus, she resists being categorized as representative of all Native American culture or of all Native American people.

Highly regarded for her 1974 poetry collection, *Laguna Woman*, Leslie Marmon Silko became the first Native American woman to publish a novel (*Ceremony*, 1977) that draws upon Native American myths and combines poetry, family history, fiction, and photographs. Her correspondence with the poet James Wright was edited after Wright's death by his widow and published under the title, *The Delicacy and Strength of Lace.* Silko's novel *Almanac of the Death* has been translated into German.

Born on the Laguna Reservation in New Mexico, where her family had lived for generations, Silko was born as well into a culture in which each person was expected to make a contribution to his or her community. She has remarked that the oral tradition of storytelling that she observed in her community relied both on the memories of older members and on the participation by younger members. Silko's poetry represents her attempt to participate in her community as a keeper of its stories. She relates those stories through poetry and prose. *Laguna Woman* draws heavily upon her ancestry, her childhood, and her family's traditions.

Leslie Marmon Silko

A former professor of English, Silko has won prizes, fellowships, and grants for her writing. She has received awards from the National Endowment for the Arts (NEA) for her imaginative verse and from *The Boston Globe* for her fiction. Silko was the youngest writer to be included in *The Norton Anthology of Women's Literature.* Silko is an extremely private person and a prolific writer who has expressed amazement at being called the first Native American woman writer of imaginative verse. Her poems and stories relate narratives of belonging and of individuality, and they lead young readers to a personal discovery of what it means to be a member of a community.

Website

"Voices from the Gaps: Women Writers of Color." http://voices.cla.umn.edu/vg

Poetry

Laguna Woman Poems. New York: Greenfield Review Press, 1974.
Storyteller. Toronto: Arcade, 1989.

Nonfiction

Conversations with Leslie Marmon Silko. Jackson: University Press of Mississippi, 2000.

Fiction

Almanac of the Dead. New York: Penguin, 1992.
Yellow Woman and a Beauty of the Spirit: Essays on Native American Life Today. New York: Simon & Schuster, 1997.
Garden in the Dunes. New York: Simon & Schuster, 2000.

References and Suggested Reading

Allen, Paula Gunn, ed. *The Serpent's Tongue: Prose, Poetry and Art of the New Mexican Pueblos.* New York: Dutton Juvenile, 1977.
Castro, Michael. *Interpreting the Indian: Twentieth-Century Poets and the Native American.* Reprint edition. Norman: University of Oklahoma Press, 1991.
Lincoln, Kenneth. *Sing with the Heart of a Bear: Fusions of Native and American Poetry 1890–1999.* Berkeley: University of California Press, 1999.
Niatum, Duane. *Harper's Anthology of Twentieth Century Native American Poetry.* San Francisco: Harper, 1988.
Rader, Dean, and Janice Gould, eds. *Speak to Me Words: Essays on Contemporary American Indian Poetry.* Tucson: University of Arizona Press, 2003.

Rosen, Kenneth. *Voices of the Rainbow: Contemporary Poetry by Native Americans*. Reprint edition. Toronto: Arcade, 1993.

Schorcht, Blanca. *Storied Voices in Native American Texts: Harry Robinson, Thomas King, James Welch and Leslie Marmon Silko (Indigenous Peoples and Politics)* New Jersey: Routledge, 2003.

Wilson, Norma. *The Nature of Native American Poetry*. Albuquerque: University of New Mexico Press, 2000.

Wright, Anne. *The Delicacy and Strength of Lace: Letters between Leslie Marmon Silko and James Wright*. St. Paul, MN: Greywolf Press, 1985.

Gary Soto
(1952–)

Gary Soto's work is often labeled as Chicano literature, but he has cultivated a career that transcends categorization. He writes in several genres, and his works explore the remarkable and the commonplace while embracing images from his own upbringing and experiences in the Mexican-American community of Fresno, California.

Soto was born in Fresno on April 12, 1952, to Manuel and Angie Trevino Soto. Soto's grandparents emigrated from Mexico, and they worked in the fields and factories of California. Manuel Soto was killed in a work-related accident when Gary was only five years old, an event that caused the youngster to become withdrawn. Soto spent much of his time at the local playground, and he worked as a farm laborer, even as a child. Self-described as a lackluster student, and citing a low GPA from Roosevelt High School, Soto claims it was during his teen years that he began reading in earnest, immersing himself in the works of contemporary masters including John Steinbeck, Jules Verne, Thornton Wilder, Robert Frost, and Earnest Hemingway.

After graduating from high school, Soto entered Fresno City College. He initially planned to matriculate in geography, based on nothing more concrete than an interest in maps. It was in college, though, that he was drawn to poetry, becoming especially intrigued by the work of Edward Field, W. S. Merwin, Charles Simic, James Wright, and Pablo Neruda. Soto has cited novelist Gabriel Garcia Marquez as an early, important influence on his development as a writer. At age twenty, he decided to make writing his career. He enrolled in writing classes and studied with the poet Philip Levine, who helped him refine both the mechanics and the craft of his writing. Soto graduated magna cum laude in 1974, receiving his bachelor of arts degree in English from California State University at Fresno, then enrolling in the master's program in creative writing at the University of California, Irvine. On May 24, 1975, he married Carolyn Oda. Soto completed his Master's in Fine Arts in creative writing in 1976, while working at the University of California, Berkeley. He has maintained associate professor status in the English and Chicano studies departments there, and in the early 1990s he served as senior lecturer in the English department. He has subsequently held titles in creative writing and in English departments at several other universities.

Soto gained almost immediate recognition for his writing, winning the Academy of American Poets Prize and the Discovery-Nation Award in 1975, followed quickly by honors from the University of California at Irvine's Chicano Literary Prize and *Poetry* magazine's Bess Hokin Prize. In 1977, Soto's poetry collection, *The Elements of San Joaquin*, was released. The collection consisted of a series, divided into three sections, chronicling life in Fresno. The tripartite organizational structure of the text recalls the heroic epic form, which poets from Homer to the modern day have used to record man's triumphs and misfortunes. Gritty and realistic, the poems are at once evocative and unsentimental. Stories of life and death, violence, and the dreams and struggles of workers are told in spare, unflinching verse. Soto shows great sensitivity to a wide array of everyday people in the city, a theme that would time and again play a major role in many of his works.

In his second book, *The Tale of Sunlight*, Soto expanded his use of imagery and storytelling techniques. He included a tribute to his hero, Gabriel Garcia Marquez, in a poem from the collection titled "How an Uncle Becomes Gray." The book was a critical success. Soto was concurrently producing poetry that appeared in periodicals and journals such as *Antaeus, Partisan Review, Paris Review, Poetry, The Nation*, and *The New Yorker*. Many of these were compiled and issued in the 1980 chapbook *Father Is a Pillow Tied to a Broom*. Soto's 1981 book, *Where Sparrows Work Hard*, revisited the Mexican-American and Latino communities with which he felt his deepest connections, exploring poverty and the lives of working-class people.

In *Black Hair* (1985), Soto focused on childhood and loss. One of the poems from this volume, "Oranges," is a particularly poignant look at a boy's first walk with a girl; it remains one of Soto's most anthologized pieces, a standard in middle- and secondary-school texts. Soto captures the boy's shy eagerness as he hopes to please his companion, only to find himself short of the money he needs to pay for a treat the girl places on a deli counter. The poems engage the reader's sympathy for the boy's dilemma and capture a sense of relief as the owner, with a silent look of complicity, accepts an orange as partial payment. Soto's work is emotional without being maudlin.

Throughout the 1980s, Soto did not limit himself to poetry; he also wrote a three-part autobiography: *Living Up the Street, Small Faces*, and *Lesser Evils*. Recounting episodes both joyous and painful, it includes his own experiences with bias against Mexican-Americans. Soto tackled broad themes and was inspired by his exploration of his Catholic roots. He began to gain readership among teens.

It was in 1990 that Soto began writing books specifically targeted to a younger audience. His first juvenile entry, *Baseball in April, and Other Stories* features short stories about characters and themes reminiscent of those profiled in his adult fiction and poetry, including the insecurities of growing up Chicano in a poor neighborhood, seeking acceptance and opportunity. *Taking Sides* (1991) and *Pacific Crossing* (1992) took character Lincoln Mendoza into a broader world, out of his urban neighborhood, first to the suburbs, then to Japan. He added to his fiction for younger readers with *Pool Party* (1993), which was adapted for video. Soto began producing short films, including *The Bike* (1991) and *Novio Boy* (1994). *Local News* (1993) is a short story collection targeted to teens. In *Jesse* (1995), a seventeen-year-old leaves home to join a brother at college. Soto considers this book a favorite among his own backlist. Soto has also writing several picture books, beginning in 1992 with *Too Many Tamales*, followed by a series of books about Chato the cat.

In addition to his collections of imaginative verse and prose, Soto's concerns for local social issues, such as farm workers' rights, led to his work on nonfiction books, notably biographies of César Chavez, the American farm worker and labor leader who founded the National Farm Workers Association, and Jessie de la Cruz, a Mexican American woman who toiled as a farm worker for nearly fifty years.

Soto published poetry for younger readers in *A Fire in My Hands: A Book of Poems* (1990) and *Neighborhood Odes* (1992), in which he provides a background anecdote for each poem and offers glimpses of himself at different stages of his life. Soto even divulges to young readers how he became a poet, describing how he would immerse himself in words, developing a special affinity for Spanish and Latin-American poetry. He followed these with *Ferne and Me*, and *Worlds Apart*, published in 2002 and 2005, respectively. His poetry is particularly engaging to young audiences, with simple, clear images and a sense of immediacy in the voices of its young narrators.

Soto's own childhood memories have always pervaded his writing. His thematic and lyrical approaches to the universal emotions and longings of growing up, make his work authentic. Soto makes a special effort in his writing and in his personal appearances to encourage young people to tap into their own creativity. He balances a career in public speaking with his impressive literary output.

Website

"The Life and Works of Gary Soto." http://project1.caryacademy.org/echoes/ poet_Gary_Soto/DefaultSoto.htm

Official Gary Soto website: www.garysoto.com

"Academy of American Poets." http://www.poets.org

Poetry

The Level at Which the Sky Begins. Irvine: University of California, 1976.

The Element of San Joaquin. Pittsburgh: University of Pittsburgh Press, 1977.

The Tale of Sunlight. Pittsburgh: University of Pittsburgh Press, 1978.

Father Is a Pillow Tied to a Broom. Pittsburgh: Slow Loris, 1980.

Where Sparrows Work Hard. Pittsburgh: University of Pittsburgh Press, 1981.

Black Hair. Pittsburgh: University of Pittsburgh Press, 1985.

Who Will Know Us? San Francisco: Chronicle Press, 1990.

A Fire in My Hands. New York: Scholastic, 1990.

Home Course in Religion. San Francisco: Chronicle Books, 1991.

Neighborhood Odes. San Diego, CA: Harcourt, 1992.

Canto Familiar/Familiar Song. San Diego, CA: Harcourt, 1995.

New and Selected Poems. San Francisco: Chronicle Poems, 1995.

The Sparrows Move South: Early Poems. Berkeley, CA: Bancroft Library Press, 1995.

Junior College: Poems. San Francisco: Chronicle Books, 1997.

Buried Onions. San Diego, CA: Harcourt, 1997.

Shadow of the Plum: Poems. San Diego, CA: Cedar Hill, 2002.

Fernie and Me. New York: Putnam, 2002.

One Kind of Faith. San Francisco: Chronicle Books, 2003.

Worlds Apart: Traveling with Fernie and Me: Poems. New York: G. P. Putnam's Sons, 2005.

Fiction

Local News. San Diego, CA: Harcourt, 1993.

Petty Crimes. San Diego, CA: Harcourt, 1998.

A Natural Man. San Francisco: Chronicle Books, 1999.

Nickel and Dime. Albuquerque: University of New Mexico Press, 2000.

Poetry Lover. Albuquerque: University of New Mexico Press, 2001.

Help Wanted: Stories. New York: Harcourt, 2005.

Amnesia in a Republican Country. Albuquerque: University of New Mexico Press, 2005.

Nonfiction

Living Up the Street: Narrative Recollections. San Francisco: Strawberry Hill, 1985.
Small Faces. Houston, TX: Arte Publico, 1986.
Lesser Evils: Ten Quartet. Houston, TX: Arte Publico, 1988.
A Summer Life. (Autobiography) Hanover, NH: University Press of New England, 1990.
Jessie de la Cruz: Profile of a United Farm Worker. New York: Persea, 2000.
Cesar Chavez: A Hero for Everyone. New York: Simon & Schuster, 2003.
The Effects of Knut Hamsun on a Fresno Boy: Recollections and Short Essays. New York: Persea, 2000.

Picture Books

Too Many Tamales. New York: Putnam, 1992.
Chato's Kitchen. New York: Putnam, 1995.
Chato and the Party Animals. Illustrated by Susan Guevara. New York: Putnam, 1999.
If the Shoe Fits. Illustrated by Terry Widener. New York: Putnam, 2002.
Chato Goes Cruisin'. Illustrated by Susan Guevara. New York: Putnam, 2005.

References and Suggested Reading

Hipple, Ted, ed. *Writers for Young Adults.* New York: Charles Scribner's Sons, 1997.
Martinez, Julio A., and Francisco A. Lomell. *Chicano Literature: A Reference Guide.* Westport, CT: Greenwood Press, 1985.
Pérez-Torres, Rafael. *Movements in Chicano Literature: Against Myths, Against Margins.* New York: Cambridge University Press, 1995.
Sellers, Jeff M., Gary Soto, and Annika Maria Nelson. *Folk Wisdom of Mexico/Proverbios y dichos Mexicanos.* Bilingual edition. San Francisco: Chronicle Books, 2004.
Stavans, Ilan, and Harold Augenbraum, eds. *Lengua Fresca: Latinos Writing on the Edge.* New York: Mariner, 2006.

Annis Boudinot Stockton
(1736(?)–1801)

Annis Boudinot Stockton was of Huguenot (French Protestant) descent; members of her family immigrated to the American colonies soon after France revoked a law that had granted rights to non-Catholics within its borders. With the revocation of the Edict of Nantes, Protestants in France lost important civil rights, including the right to work for the state and the right to follow a religion other than Catholicism, as well as the right to air grievances and the right of protection from the Inquisition when traveling abroad.

Annis Boudinot was born in Darby, Pennsylvania, the eldest daughter and second of ten children born to Catherine and Elias Boudinot III. Her parents, who had been visiting a family-owned plantation, returned to Pennsylvania when their daughter's birth drew near. The Boudinots later settled in Princeton, New Jersey, in 1755, and it was there that young Annis was exposed to the intellectual and social circles that would remain a part of her adult life.

Born into a well-to-do family, Annis Boudinot was given ample opportunity to expand her mind through education. As a result of her early and frequent exposure to the literary arts, she soon developed a passion for writing poetry, an unusual pastime for a woman in her era. It was also in Princeton that Boudinot became acquainted with the man whom she would eventually marry; she met her future husband, Richard Stockton, through her brother, who studied law in his office.

The Stocktons lost most of their property as well as their personal belongings during the Revolutionary War. After Washington's retreat, Stockton fled her home with her children and relocated to Monmouth County; however, her husband was captured by loyalists and imprisoned. Because he had signed the Declaration of Independence, he was treated poorly by the loyalists and gained his release only by signing an oath that he would no longer participate in activities aimed to weaken Britain's control over the colonies. Despite her husband's withdrawal from public life, loyalists ransacked the Stockton home and burned their library. Most of the family papers, including Stockton's poetry, were lost in the fire.

Perhaps, given her family's history of questioning established rules governing religious practice and the role of the government in church matters, it is not surprising that after her marriage, Annis Boudinot Stockton became a patron saint of colonial patriots. She secured and secreted a number of records of the American Whig Society, an organization that supported religious freedom, from her husband's office prior to their home's plunder by Tories, who went in search of the documents as part of their efforts to quell Whig activity and to identify participants in the society. After the Revolutionary War, Stockton became the only woman to become a member of the Whig Society. She was elected to membership in this male stronghold in recognition of her efforts to protect the Society's records.

Recurring themes in Stockton's poetry are her zeal and her passion for independence of thought and action. She was well known by soldiers in the American Revolution for her patriotic verse written to encourage patriots in their efforts. Stockton wrote several poems to general, and later President, George Washington. One such poem, "Welcome, Mighty Chief, Once More!" was sung by young women of Trenton as President Washington passed through Princeton on his way to his first inauguration.

Stockton was widowed in February 1781; however, she continued to live at the estate she had shared with her husband, and she continued to host George and Martha Washington at her home. Included among Princeton's library holdings is an open file of manuscripts that attests to the many friendships Stockton formed with American patriots. Included among these manuscripts are wills, deeds, and correspondence between Stockton family members to such persons as Benjamin Rush, who published the first American textbook on chemistry; Aaron Ogden, who served in the American Revolutionary War; Phineas Bond, a Philadelphia doctor; and Garret D. Wall, a military officer from New Jersey. Several of Stockton's poems are included in the Princeton holdings, as is an 1829 deed of manumission for a slave who belonged to her estate. The New Jersey Historical Society maintains a listing of the contents of a copybook owned by Stockton. The book contains drafts and finished pieces of many of her poems and observations. For example, in addition to ballads, pastorals, elegies, and odes, the copybook contains Stockton's notes regarding a dance class, regarding the destruction of trees by icicles, and describing her own bouts of sleeplessness.

Although it appears that Stockton wrote frequently, she reluctantly offered her poetry for public view because she did not wish to appear impudent. In our country's early history, only men were expected to know how to write. Although the public schools taught reading to both genders, only men were taught writing. The ability to write was connected to male professions; men who worked on the loading docks, in the government offices, or as plantation owners had to be able to sign for the receipt of goods, including slaves. Women who wrote public pieces were often criticized for doing so, or the authenticity of their work was called into question.

Keenly aware of these restrictions placed on writers, Stockton, in a letter to George Washington, asked to be forgiven for her habit of writing about public figures. General Washington encouraged her to continue writing. Stockton was one of several early American women writers who composed verse about either public events or public figures. The early American women writers contributed to the development of the United States because they dared to step outside prescribed roles to make their voices heard.

Website

"New Jersey Historical Society." http://www.jerseyhistory.org

Poetry

Only for the Eye of a Friend: The Poems of Annis Boudinot Stockton. Charlottesville: University Press of Virginia, 1995.

References and Suggested Reading

Burt, Daniel. *The Chronology of American Literature.* Boston: Houghton Mifflin, 2004.

Claghorn, Charles E. *Women Patriots of the American Revolution: A Biographical Dictionary.* Metuchen, NJ: Scarecrow Press, 1991.

Clyne, Patricia Edwards. *Patriots in Petticoats.* New York: Dodd, Mead, 1976.

Davis, Gwenn, and Beverly Joyce, eds. *Poetry by Women (Bibliographies of Writings by American and British Women to 1900).* London: Cassell. 1997.

DePauw, Linda Grant. *Founding Mothers: Women of the Revolutionary Era.* Boston: Houghton Mifflin, 1975.

Ellet, Elizabeth F. *The Women of the American Revolution,* 2 vols. 1850 reprint. New York: Haskell House, 1969.

Green, Harry Clinton, and Mary Wolcott Green. *Wives of the Signers: The Women Behind the Declaration of Independence.* Aledo, TX: Wallbuilder Press, 1997. (Originally published in 1912 as volume 3 of *The Pioneer Mothers of America: A Record of the More Notable Women of the Early Days of the Country, and Particularly of the Colonial and Revolutionary Periods.* New York: G. P. Putnam's Sons).

Purcell, Edward L., and David F. Burg, eds. *The World Almanac of the American Revolution.* New York: Scripps Howard, 1992.

Silcox-Jarrett, Diane. *Heroines of the American Revolution: America's Founding Mothers.* Chapel Hill, NC: Green Angel Press, 1998.

Stedman, Edmund Clarence. *An American Anthology, 1787–1900; Selections Illustrating the Editor's Critical Review of American Poetry in the Nineteenth Century.* Brookfield, CT: Greenwood Press, 1968.

Zeinert, Karen. *Those Remarkable Women of the American Revolution.* Brookfield, CT: Millbrook Press, 1996.

Jean Toomer
(1894–1967)

Nathan Pinchback Toomer (subsequently known as Jean Toomer) was born in 1894 to Nathan Toomer and Nina Pinchback Toomer. The young Toomer's maternal grandfather was Pinckney Benton Stewart Pinchback, a free black who had been a Union officer in the Civil War and who became acting governor of Louisiana during Reconstruction and the first United States governor of African American descent. In 1895, financial problems and the separation of his parents forced the young Toomer and his mother to seek lodging with his maternal grandparents. Toomer's grandfather agreed to support his daughter and her son only if the boy's name was changed to eliminate reference to his daughter's husband; thus, the young Toomer underwent a name and identity change. At home, he was known as Eugene Pinchback; at school, he was known as Eugene Pinchback Toomer; when be began writing, the poet shortened his name to Jean Toomer.

Not unlike his parents, who were of mixed heritage, Toomer was often mistaken for white. Indeed, until age eighteen, he lived alternately as white and as African American. Just as often, however, he occupied both worlds simultaneously. In Washington, D.C., with his grandparents, Toomer lived in a white neighborhood but attended a segregated school for black students. However, in 1906, when Toomer was twelve years of age, his mother remarried and they moved to New Rochelle, New York. Here Toomer lived in a white neighborhood and attended a segregated school for white students. Upon his mother's death three years later, Toomer returned to Washington to live with his grandparents. After graduating from high school in Washington, D.C., Toomer decided to live as a member of no racial group; it was at this time that he declared himself an American, pure and simple.

The themes in Toomer's poetry reflect his effortless movement between the two racial identities as well as his struggle to reconcile the duality of self; his imaginative verse reflects a yearning for racelessness. Undoubtedly, his experiences as a young boy growing up in the house with a man of his grandfather's prominence shaped the young Toomer's perceptions and attitudes that we see reflected in his poetry. However, Toomer's efforts reflect as well his inventiveness and originality, for, along with other writers of his age, including Gertrude Stein, Ernest Hemingway, Ezra Pound, and T. S. Eliot, Toomer participated in the creation of a new, modern American literary tradition that eschewed conventional literary forms.

At age ten, the young Toomer was stricken with illnesses that would recur over most of his adult life; however, Toomer did not succumb to the adversity of ill health but retreated instead into his writing. After his graduation from high school, Toomer studied at five institutions of higher learning from 1914 until 1917. Possessed of an immense curiosity about most things in the world, he studied agriculture at the University of Wisconsin and at the Massachusetts College of Agriculture before leaving to take up a course of study in physical fitness at American College of Physical Training in Chicago. His curiosity not sated, Toomer enrolled in classes at the University of Chicago before relocating to New York, where he studied at the City College of New York and New York University. Unfortunately, Toomer did not earn a degree from any of the universities he attended. During this period of exploration and frequent movement and change, Toomer supported himself by selling newspapers and by working as a delivery boy, a soda clerk, a salesman, a shipyard worker, a librarian's assistant, a physical fitness director, a school teacher, and a grocery clerk. It was in Chicago that Toomer began to cultivate his interest in literature. It was also during this time that he discovered writers who gave him a contextual framework for his own love of language. He began reading work by William Shakespeare, George Santayana, Charles Baudelaire, William Blake, Sherwood Anderson, Leo Tolstoy, along with some major American poets and expressed a particular interest in the verse of the imagists. In fact, Toomer's romance with the use of imagery in his verse is clear: the poet constructs complex portraits of characters, places, and events in his work that are as finely drawn as a graphic artist's rendition.

In 1923, Toomer published *Cane*, a structurally fractured work of prose that contained poetry and a play. While Toomer had been an important contributor to the ideas and poetic models of the Harlem Renaissance, with the publication of *Cane* he became an equally important contributor to high modernism, which favored disjointed or fractured timelines over realistic representations. In 1926, Toomer traveled to France to attend the Institute for the Harmonious Development of Men, founded by G. I. Gurdjieff four years earlier. The institute, a spiritual school, encouraged fellows to work on self-improvement as a means of obtaining subjective consciousness, the third tier in the four stages of consciousness. Toomer maintained a relationship with Gurdjieff for approximately nine years, until 1935. However; the relationship turned sour for reasons neither Toomer nor Gurdjieff fully disclosed.

In 1940, Toomer became a member of the Religious Society of Friends (Quakers) and he began to give lectures around the country. Toomer enjoyed a fifteen-year relationship with the Quakers, and during his years of affiliation with the organization he was invited to lecture or to lead religious efforts in New Jersey, Philadelphia, Indiana, and Illinois. Toomer also worked with high-school students and wrote for the *Friends Intelligencer*, a pamphlet produced by the Quakers. In 1949, he was honored by the organization by being selected to present its prestigious William Penn Lecture. And in 1988, approximately twenty-one years after Toomer's death, his collected poems were published, containing work that had appeared in an earlier publication and including thirty-three unpublished poems obtained from the Jean Toomer Collection in the Beinecke Rare Book and Manuscript Library at Yale University. Toomer's daughter, Margery, edited the collection.

Website

"The Toomer Pages." http://www.math.buffalo.edu/~sww/toomer/jeantoomer.html

Poetry

The Collected Poems of Jean Toomer. Ed. Robert B. Jones and Margery Toomer Latimer. Chapel Hill: University of North Carolina Press, 1988.

Fiction

Cane. New York: Boni and Liveright, 1923.

Nonfiction

The Wayward and the Seeking: A Collection of Writings by Jean Toomer. Washington, DC: Howard University Press, 1980.

References and Suggested Reading

Feith, Michel, and Geneviève Fabre, eds. *Jean Toomer and the Harlem Renaissance.* New Brunswick, NJ: Rutgers University Press, 2001.
Ford, Karen Jackson. *Split-Gut Song: Jean Toomer and the Poetics of Modernity.* Tuscaloosa: University of Alabama Press, 2005.

Jean Toomer

Kerman, Cynthia Earl, and Richard Eldridge. *The Lives of Jean Toomer: A Hunger for Wholeness.* Baton Rogue: Louisiana State University Press, 1999.

Larson, Charles. *Invisible Darkness: Jean Toomer and Nella Larsen.* Iowa City: University of Iowa Press, 1993.

Rusch, Frederik. *A Jean Toomer Reader: Selected Unpublished Writings.* New York: Oxford University Press, 1993.

Scruggs, Charles, and Lee Vandemarr. *Jean Toomer and the Terrors of American History.* Philadelphia: University of Pennsylvania Press, 1998.

Taylor, Paul Beckman. *Shadows of Heaven: Gurdjieff and Toomer.* York Beach, ME: Samuel Weiser, 1998.

Wagner, Jean, and Kenneth Douglas. *Black Poets of the United States: From Paul Lawrence Dunbar to Langston Hughes.* Urbana: University of Illinois Press, 1973.

Woodson, Jon. *To Make a New Race: Gurdjieff, Toomer, and the Harlem Renaissance.* Jackson: University Press of Mississippi, 1999.

Robert Trammell
(1939–2006)

Robert Trammell. Courtesy of Jason Kyle, Shiny Red, Ltd., February 2005, WordSpace, Reading at Paperbacks Plus, Dallas, TX.

As much lyricist, cultural historian, filmmaker, and keeper of myths as poet, this American writer of imaginative verse published his first poem when he was thirty years of age. In fact, Trammell once quipped that he became a poet because he could not sing, and he credits musicians with being the real poets of any generation. Despite his reluctance to call himself a poet; Trammell has published imaginative verse in more than two hundred publications in the United States, in Mexico, and in Europe as well as on buses in two major American cities as part of the Poetry Society of America's public art series. In 1992, Trammell won a national contest that resulted in his poetry being reproduced on wind panels (the thin plastic sheets that protect commuters from the elements) at a bus terminal in Dallas, Texas, that serves as a major transportation hub.

A fifth-generation Texan, Trammell, who has recalled that his ancestors included circuit ministers, pioneers, and a horse thief, often intertwined his own history with that of Texas to create poetry that captures a historical moment in poignant, particular verse. In a prose piece titled "What does the River want to be?" (subtitled "Cold Water, Levees, Holy Men, Ancient

253

Hearths, Jack Ruby Stone Heads, and Salons on the Trinity"), Trammell combines poetry, history, and myth to reveal his admiration for his city, for its people, and for its history. Urging his audience to listen to the stories from the "wounded" Trinity River that courses through Dallas, dividing the town along racial and class lines, Trammell imagined a day when the neglected river might serve as a symbol of unity rather than of division. His words urged residents to reclaim the much maligned Trinity River, which he characterized as capable of harmonizing the "culture, spirit and thought" of the city he loved. Trammell has also published an essay that describes his own personal belief in angels. The prose piece appears in an anthology titled *The Angels.*

In addition to his diverse publishing interests, Trammell has given lectures at Notre Dame, the University of California at Santa Barbara, the University of Texas at Arlington, the University of Texas at Dallas, and the Dallas Institute of Humanities and Culture. He has published approximately twenty-five collections of poetry, including *Famous Men, Cicada, Jack Ruby and the Origins of the Avant-Garde in Dallas, Lovers/Killers, George Washington Trammel, Cam I Sole, Epics, No Evidence, Birds: An Almanac, A Book of Diseases*, and *Queen City of the Plains.* His poetry reflects his diverse interests and his obsessions with life, myth, and history. His poetry has also appeared in several magazines, including the *Southwest Review*, the *Exquisite Corpse, Another Chicago Magazine*, and *The Texas Observer.* And although his work requires a reader who is willing to be challenged, young readers will enjoy Trammell's use of imagery as well as his exacting, yet simple language in the often philosophical verse that succeeds in making relevant to present-day experience those forgotten events of historical and cultural significance.

In his youth, Trammell entered the political science program at prestigious Southern Methodist University, where he intended to pursue a degree in law. However, not unlike other celebrated American poets who either opted not to attend college or dropped out short of completing an academic program, Trammell left the academy before obtaining his degree, explaining his determination to prove that career options other than those of banker or developer were available to young people in his city.

Indeed, in his own work as a poet, Trammell modeled a successful life: he lived reasonably, collecting friendships rather than baubles, recording acts of renewal whether manifested in the birth of his son, or in the discovery of a fresh pollination in his garden. Trammell was instrumental in bringing young and not-so-young poets to public attention through his stints as a poet-in-residence in public schools in Dallas and through his work as a fellow at the Dallas Institute of Humanities and Culture. As the founder and executive director of *WordSpace: A North Texas Home for Imaginative Language*, he not only introduced new voices but took a special, almost fatherly interest in the poets, providing public venues for them to present their work and nurturing and encouraging them in their craft.

Described by friends as a gentle, giving man, Trammell was equally generous to mother earth. He felt a need to replenish and restore the world, and the backyard of his home attested to his attempts to do exactly that. Never taking more than was needed either from the earth or from his society, Trammell sought to repay even those things he took in need. Long before recycling and gardening became fashionable, Trammell cultivated vegetable and flower gardens as well as a mammoth compost heap of which he was particularly proud. Trammell loved the outdoors; he could often be found sitting quietly in his backyard, eyes closed, listening to the sounds of cicadas. In one of his poems, "Dreaming," Trammell asks, "What's he dreaming,/lying on grass,/eyes closed?". The answer is found several lines later as the poet responds: "he's remembering the good times." Trammell's gift, the simple act of remembering the good times, comes through in the body of his work that he left for young readers.

Prior to his death, Trammell had been collaborating with another writer and friend to produce a film documentary about the American Civil War. Robert Trammell died at his home in May 2006, more than two years after he had been diagnosed with a rare form of cancer and given six months to live. This beloved friend, poet, husband, father, and son was surrounded by friends and family who reluctantly bade him farewell. A collection of Trammell's books, many of which have become collector's items, are on permanent display at Paperbacks Plus Bookstore in Dallas, Texas.

Website

"WordSpace: A North Texas Home for Imaginative Language."
   http://wordspacetexas.org

Poetry

George Washington Trammell. Dallas: Salt Lick Press, 1978.
Lovers/Killers. Dallas: Salt Lick Press, 1980.
Jack Ruby and the Origins of the Avant-Garde in Dallas. Dallas: Barnburner Press, 1989.

Robert Trammell

References and Suggested Reading

Hill, Billy Bob. *Texas in Poetry: A 150 Year Anthology.* Denton: Center for Texas Studies, 1994.

Hill, Billy Bob. *Texas in Poetry 2.* Fort Worth: Texas Christian University Press, 2002.

Leonard, Frances. *Conversations with Texas Writers.* Austin: University of Texas Press, 2005.

Thomas, Gail. *The Angels.* Dallas: Continuum International Publishing Group (Dallas Institute of the Humanities), 1995.

Jane Colman Turell
(1708–1735)

Turell composed imaginative verse during the second period of literary production in American literary history. She was a poetic model for Martha Wadsworth Brewster (1725–1757), and like Brewster's, Turell's work provides an early example of the shift in themes in the poetry written by women of the colonial American period. In much of her work, Turell demonstrates a poetic consciousness of gender and of the importance of women's efforts to Western intellectual histories. However, Turell's poetry also reflects the contradiction both of her life and of the changing nature of literary traditions, for the recurring themes of religion and history that also appear in imaginative verse composed by this early American writer recall the first period of literary production; similar themes are found as well in work produced by such writers as Anne Bradstreet (1612–1672).

Still, despite the seemingly dual focus of Turell's work, there can be no doubt that her love of language was informed both by her early access to her father's library and by her early instruction in writing during a period in American history when few girls were taught to read or write. This daughter of a Harvard College president was lovingly encouraged in her precociousness; with such encouragement and support it is no wonder that Turell was a prolific writer who composed poetry on topics that went beyond those prescribed by Puritan culture.

So dedicated was Turell's father, Benjamin Colman, to his daughter's education that when the child's ill health prevented her interaction with peers and others outside the immediate family, he invented a game: the young Turell began to exchange letters as well as verses with her father. It was in this manner that the young girl, before reaching the age of ten, had composed her first hymn. Turell continued to write hymns and poetry throughout her young life; the majority of her work was written before she was married at eighteen years of age to Ebenezer Turell, one of her father's theology students.

Turell was not only a poet, she was also a correspondent and a diarist. However, her only extant works are those her husband included in a collection titled *Some Memoirs of the Life and Death of Mrs. Jane Turell*. The collection contains not only poetry but also essays that reveal Turell's use of wit and humor to examine the issues of her time. In her memoirs, as with her poetry, Turell provided a literary model for women writers of subsequent generations.

Website

"A Celebration of Women Writers." http://digital.library.upenn.edu/women/_generate/authors-T.html

Poetry

"1 Psalm CXXXVII Paraphras'd August 5, 1725"; "On reading the warning by Mrs. Singer"; "To My Muse." In *The Heath Anthology of American iterature,* 5th ed. Ed. Paul Lauter. Boston: Houghton Mifflin, 2005.

References and Suggested Reading

Cavalla, Guillermo, and Roger Chartier, eds. *A History of Reading in the West.* Amherst: University of Massachusetts Press, 1999.

Griffiths, Paul. *Religious Reading: The Place of Reading in the Practice of Religion.* New York: Oxford University Press, 199.

Hall, David D. "Learned Culture in the Eighteenth Century". In *A History of the Book in America,* Vol 1. Ed. Hugh Amory and David D. Hall. Cambridge: Cambridge University Press, 2000.

Kerber, Linda, and Jane Sherron De Hart. *Women's History: Refocusing the Past.* New York: Oxford University Press, 2004.

Kolodny, Annette. *The Land Before Her: Fantasy and Experience of the American Frontiers 1630–1860.* Chapel Hill: University of North Carolina Press, 1984.

Mercy Otis Warren
(1728–1814)

The first girl of her family, Mercy Otis Warren was born into a large family of boys, and she quickly learned the values of both family and independence, two themes that often appear in her poetry. As a young poet, Warren used imaginative verse to express her support of American independence from Britain. Warren was not published under her own name until later in life, and much of her work reveals her concern for the rights of women as necessary elements of the colonists' struggle for freedom from oversight by the British monarchy. Undoubtedly, her ideas and writings influenced many of her contemporaries to support the patriotic cause. Mercy Otis Warren was a member of a group of early women writers who used poetry and other imaginative verse to argue for specific reasons. For example, her poem "Massachusetts Song of Liberty" codifies and supports the colonists' arguments regarding their rights of self-governance. The poem was set to music, and it became a popular song of the colonists.

Warren's passionate love of independence may be reflected in the unusual facts of her life: she married late, by colonial American standards. In 1754, at the age of twenty-six, she became the wife of James Warren, a farmer and merchant whom she had met some eleven years earlier, in 1743, when she attended her brother's graduation from Harvard. Still, farm life may have been the perfect counterbalance to Mercy Otis Warren's activities as a counselor and advisor to her brother and his friends, Samuel Adams and John Hancock. Indeed, her counsel was sought by some of the more respected men in early American history. For in addition to her relationships with Adams and Hancock, Warren had opportunities to entertain George Washington, John Adams, and Alexander Hamilton in her home. However, the poet never ventured beyond eastern Massachusetts. Warren is one of several early American women writers, among them

Phillis Wheatley (1753(?)–1784) and Annis Boudinot Stockton (1736(?)–1801), who wrote poetry dedicated to George Washington, in his roles as general and as president.

Warren continued to write and publish until her death. In addition to a collection of poetry, *Poems: Dramatic and Miscellaneous,* published in 1790, Warren published her correspondences from and to John Adams as well as dramatic plays that criticized British taxation of American colonies. Warren was an early supporter of educational reform; her work reflects her attention to education as a means for women to achieve their rights in society.

Despite her prolific output, however, *Poems: Dramatic and Miscellaneous,* published when Otis Warren was sixty-two years old, was the first of her works that bore her name; the collection was also the only work she published during her lifetime. Other poetry was not published until almost two centuries after her death. Her letters to contemporaries, including Benjamin Franklin, Thomas Jefferson, Alexander Hamilton, and Abigail and John Adams, have also been published since her death. Critical reception to Warren's work has focused on the importance of her letters and other documents to history rather than on the importance of her poetry to the formation of early Western literary traditions.

Websites

"Mercy Otis Warren." http://library.thinkquest.org/10966/data/bwarren.shtml
"Mercy Warren." http://www.americanrevolution.org/women6.html
"PAL: Perspectives in American Literature—A Research and Reference Guide" (California State University, Department of English). http://www.csustan.edu/english/pal/chap2/warren.html

Poetry

Poems, Dramatic and Miscellaneous. Boston: I. Thomas and E. T. Andrews, 1790.

Nonfiction

Observations on the New Constitution, and on the Federal and State Conventions, 1788. Pamphlet against the Constitution, formerly attributed to Elbridge Gerry, now acknowledged as written by Mercy Otis Warren.
History of the Rise, Progress and Termination of the American Revolution, Vols. 1 and 2. Boston: Larkin, 1805; West Roxbury, MA: B & R Samizdat Express, 2004.

References and Suggested Reading

Anthony, Katherine. *First Lady of the Revolution: The Life of Mercy Otis Warren.* New York: Doubleday, 1958.

Brown, Alice. *Mercy Warren*. New York: Scribner's, 1986.

Davies, Kate. *Catherine Macaulay and Mercy Otis Warren: The Revolutionary Atlantic and the Politics of Gender*. New York: Oxford University Press, 2006.

Fritz, Jean. *Cast for a Revolution: Some American Friends and Enemies, 1728–1814*. Boston: Houghton Mifflin, 1972.

Garraty, John A., and Mark C. Carnes, eds. *American National Biography*. New York: Oxford University Press, 1999.

Gills, Jennifer B. *Mercy Otis Warren: Author and Historian*: Mankato, MN: Compass Point Books, 2005.

James, Edward T., Janet Wilson James, and Paul S. Boyer, eds. *Notable American Women, 1607–1950: A Biographical Dictionary*. Cambridge, MA: Belknap Press, 1971.

Zagarri, Rosemarie. *A Woman's Dilemma: Mercy Otis Warren and the American Revolution*. Wheeling, IL: Harlan Davidson, 1995.

Phillis Wheatley (Peters) (1753(?)–1784)

An original voice in American literature, this American poet was abducted from the Senegal–Gambia region of Africa and brought to the northern colonies on July 11, 1761, 142 years after the arrival of the first group of Africans abducted from their homeland. The young Senegalese girl was seven or eight years of age at the time of her arrival in Boston, according to the bill of sale, which made note of the youngster's missing front teeth at the time of her purchase by abolitionist John Wheatley as a companion to his wife, Susannah Wheatley.

As was the custom during the period of American chattel slavery, the young girl inherited the surname of her purchasers, who, in this instance, bestowed upon their acquisition a Christian name taken from the schooner, *The Phillis*, that delivered her to the Boston harbor and into slavery. Describing Wheatley's status upon arrival at the Boston harbor in market terms, her biographers indicate that auctioneers hired to sell the human cargo considered Wheatley refuse, and as a result of her declining monetary value, the Wheatleys were permitted to purchase her for a reduced price.

Phillis Wheatley's frailty most likely resulted from being one of approximately three hundred men, women, and children who were stolen from their homes or from play, forced to wear an eleven-pound metal ball attached to their necks or to their feet, interned for approximately three months at Ber (now known as Goree), a slave camp on an island off the coast of Senegal, loaded onto a ship, chained together in pairs, exposed to outbreaks of smallpox and measles that spread rapidly in the close quarters of the tightly packed slave vessels, and fed mash—a concoction of corn, yams, rice, and palm oil—during the months-long voyage from Africa to the American colonies. Even though the details of the young Senegalese girl's voyage to the colonies in the belly of a slave schooner are overwhelmingly horrifying, her arrival at the Boston harbor exemplifies a more sober statistic: between 1650 and 1900, she was one of approximately 479,900 Senegalese stolen from their families and conscripted for unpaid labor in the Americas.

However, it is probable that the young Senegalese, prior to her abduction by slave traders from the Americas, had been previously enslaved in her homeland by North Africans. Forms of slavery were practiced not only in Great Britain, Portugal, Brazil, Spain, and the American colonies; it was also accepted in Africa. However, unlike the systems of slavery enforced in other countries, slavery in Africa was employed as punishment for certain offenses. Africans enslaved by their neighbors were prisoners of war, or they were enslaved as punishment for engaging in criminal activity. In contrast to the systems of slavery in other countries, in Africa enslaved persons were not considered either subhuman or racially inferior; rather, they were viewed as unofficial members of the dominant group, and therefore, they could not earn that group's protection or regain their freedom unless they adopted the written language or religion of the dominant group or until they worked off their obligations. Yet another unmistakable distinction existed between slavery as practiced in Africa and as practiced elsewhere in the world. In Africa, enslaved women who had children by their masters became official members of the tribe that enslaved them, and thus not only were subject to the protection of the tribe but also were expected to share in its resources and in its decision making.

The young Phillis Wheatley, who spoke Arabic and who recalled her earliest memories as those of her mother prostrating herself before the morning sun, had no doubt experienced enslavement in which restoration of personal freedom was the norm upon conversion to her enslaver's religion, and her experience caused her to be acutely aware of the distinctions between enslavement in Africa and enslavement in America. Wheatley was baptized into the Christian religion at The Old South Meeting House on August 18, 1771, and she was well aware that although many enslaved Africans in America were also baptized, they remained enslaved, as had she. She knew that economic gain, rather than concern for the souls of Africans, was the reason slave traders abducted blacks from their homeland. In her poetry, often dismissed as marred because of its insubstantial or imitative nature, the young poet uses the language of eighteenth-century Enlightenment discourse to construct a new identity for enslaved Africans in America, to denounce Christian slave ownership, and to provide a model for subsequent British and American writers while appearing to celebrate her own enslavement.

Phillis Wheatley (Peters)

Almost immediately after being purchased by the Wheatleys and moving into their home at the corner of King Street and Mackerel Lane in Boston, the young Phillis Wheatley evinced an insatiable desire to read the many books owned by her new masters. Susannah Wheatley placed few, if any, restrictions on the young poet's aspiration; she recruited her own children to teach the young Wheatley, and within fifteen months of this American poet's arrival in the northern colonies, she was reading not only the Christian Bible, but also texts written in Latin as well as texts by two master poets, John Milton and Alexander Pope. The young poet studied the language and structure found in Milton's and Pope's poetry to recreate that language and structure in her own verse. Wheatley's poetry employs eighteenth-century neoclassical language and makes use of the iambic line to create a space from which the poet might articulate the African's natural right to freedom. Her first known writing, however, a letter dated February 11, 1774, to Samson Occom, the Mohegan Indian minister, was written when she was approximately twenty-one years old. This letter is generally recognized as her most direct antislavery statement.

In the years prior to the 1773 publication of her collection *Poems* in England, the poet created some of her most important literary work. A poem written in 1770, "On the Affray in King-Street, on the Evening of the 5th of March," commemorates the Boston Massacre, an event that the poet witnessed firsthand from inside the Wheatley home. Later that same year, the publication in England of "On the Death of the Rev. George Whitefield" established Wheatley as a poet of international distinction. Wheatley was manumitted in 1773, at the insistence of her supporters in Britain and shortly before the death of Susannah Wheatley. After manumission, Wheatley continued her correspondence with Arbour Tanner, a slave woman whom she had met on her voyage from Africa to Boston. It was through Tanner that Wheatley was introduced to John Peters, the man she married on April 1, 1778.

Wheatley died on December 5, 1784, at the age of thirty-one. At the time of her death, she and Peters had been married six years. During their marriage, the couple had three children, two of whom died during childbirth. A third child, a few months of age, was found dead in its mother's lifeless arms. At the time of her death, Wheatley was working on a second manuscript of poetry which was lost and has not been recovered. However, even in death, she remained a strong voice for the liberation of Africans enslaved in America. After her death, some of her previously published poems were republished on broadsides that protested the continued enslavement of Africans. Her 1773 collection, *Poems*, was eventually published in America. The manuscript was published in the United States, in

Pittsburgh, for the first time in 1786, two years after her death and thirteen years after the original publication in London.

More recently, in May 1998, the only known copy of a previously unpublished seventy-line poem by Wheatley, "Ocean," sold for $68,500 at an auction. Reuter's reports that the poem, sold to a book dealer, netted "significantly more than its estimate of eighteen to twenty-five thousand dollars." Wheatley wrote the poem, an ode to the sea, in Boston in 1773; however, it was not included in the 1773 collection. Phillis Wheatley Peters, an American poet, left behind a canon of work that stands among the first of that produced during the colonial period of American letters.

Websites

"PAL: Perspectives in American Literature—A Research and Reference Guide" (California State University, Department of English). http://www.csustan.edu/english/pal
"Archiving Early America." http://www.earlyamerica.com

Poetry

Poems on Various Subjects, Religious and Moral. Ed. John Shields. Schomburg Library of Nineteenth Century Black Women Writers. New York: Oxford University Press, 1988. (True copy of the original text published in 1773, including Wheatley's letters and poetry.)

References and Suggested Reading

Derounian, Kathryn Zabell, and William H. Robinson, eds. *Critical Essays on Phillis Wheatley.* Boston: G. K. Hall, 1982.
Mason, Julian. *Poems of Phillis Wheatley.* Chapel Hill: University of North Carolina Press, 1966.
Richmond, M. A. *Bid the Vassal Soar: Interpretive Essays on the Life and Poetry of Phillis Wheatley and George Moses Horton.* Washington, DC: Howard University Press, 1974.
Robinson, William H. *Phillis Wheatley: A Bio-Bibliography.* Boston: G. K. Hall, 1981.
Shockley, Ann Allen, ed. *Afro-American Women Writers 1746–1933.* Boston: G. K. Hall, 1988.

Janet S. Wong
(1962–)

Wong was born in Los Angeles to a Chinese father and a Korean mother. She received a bachelor of arts in history from the University of California at Los Angeles (UCLA), where she graduated summa cum laude. While enrolled at UCLA, Wong spent a year in France, where she studied art history. Upon her return to the university, she founded the UCLA Immigrant Children's Art Project to support her efforts to teach immigrant children to express themselves through art. It was also while she was enrolled at UCLA that Wong met the poet who would become her teacher and mentor, Myra Cohn Livingston. Although Wong's interest in poetry was piqued during this period of her life, after graduating from UCLA, she decided to continue her education at Yale University Law School, where she obtained a JD degree. After completing the course of study at Yale, Wong became director of the Yale Law and Technology Association, and she worked for the New Haven Legal Aid office. After practicing corporate and labor law for firms that included Universal Studios in Hollywood, she decided to devote her time to writing. Currently, Wong lives near Seattle. During her writing career, she has lived alternatively in Los Angeles, Bainbridge Island, and Medina, Washington, a suburb of Seattle.

Her poetry is often a simple yet candid reflection of her life as an Asian child. However, her representations of the hardships and concerns of childhood are those that are experienced by every child, regardless of race, economic class, gender, or sexual orientation. Wong's imaginative verse often focuses on issues of identity and customs relevant to young readers. Her work is lyrical, ironic, and humorous and it reveals her efforts to connect the many cultures of which she is part. Her first book of poetry, *Good Luck Gold*, contains sad, serious, and silly poems. A picture book, *The Trip Back Home,* teaches the value of the gift that is given from the heart.

Wong's poetry also captures the beauty of events familiar to young readers. For example, she has written poems that recall holiday dinners at her grandparents' house. In these poems, she recounts her grandfather's stories about his childhood in China and his later years in Northern California during the Depression. Wong memorializes those dinners as well as her grandfather's stories in poetry that delights readers. Wong's poetry recalls instances of families sharing love and encouragement, and it reminds readers of their own relationships with family and friends. In other poetry, she addresses the reader's sense of being alone, and describes the delight of recognizing another face that looks like his or her own in a room full of strangers. Although her poetry often rhymes, just as often Wong constructs in free verse.

Wong has received numerous awards and honors for her imaginative verse. The International Reading Association presented her with its Celebrate Literacy award for her service in the promotion of literacy. Wong also received the Stone Center Recognition of Merit, a prestigious award granted by the Claremont Graduate School. In addition, she has been appointed to two terms on the Commission on Literature of the National Council of Teachers of English, and she has received a Notable Children's Trade Book Award from the Children's Book Council for her book, *A Suitcase of Seaweed and Other Poems.*

As a youngster, Wong never had an opportunity to meet a poet. Perhaps that is one reason she visits schools across the United States each year to promote her love of books. In addition, her poems are used by teachers, librarians, and parents to develop programs in a growing number of classrooms, and her books are available in many libraries. In fact, Wong visits about forty schools each year to share her poetry and stories with young people in kindergarten through high school. She conducts teacher workshops at universities, and she speaks at various conferences such as the International Reading Association (IRA), the American Library Association (ALA), and the National Council of Teachers of English (NCTE). Wong tries to make poetry fun so that children will be encouraged to read and to realize their own creative genius.

Websites

"Strangers to Us All: Lawyers Who Were Poets." http://www.wvu.edu/~lawfac/ jelkins/lp-2001/intro/contemp_pt2.html

Poet's web page: http://www.janetwong.com

Poetry

The Rainbow Hand: Poems about Mothers and Children. New York: Simon & Schuster, 1999.
This Next New Year. Illustrated by Yangsook Choi. New York: Farrar, Straus & Giroux, 2000.
Behind the Wheel: Poems about Driving. New York: Simon & Schuster, 2001.
grump. Illustrated by John Wallace. New York: Simon & Schuster, 2001.
BUZZ. New York: Harcourt, 2002.
Apple Pie Fourth of July, New York: Harcourt, 2002.
Night Garden: Poems from the World of Dreams. New York: McElderry Books, 2002. *Knock on Wood: Poems about Superstition.* New York: McElderry Books, 2003.

Nonfiction

You Have to Write. Illustrated by Teresa Flavin. New York: McElderry Books, 2002.
Alex and the Wednesday Chess Club. New York: Simon & Schuster, 2004.

References and Suggested Reading

Austin, Patricia. "Janet Wong—The Making of a Poet." *TALL: Teaching and Learning Literature with Children and Young Adults* 6.4 (March/April 1997): pp. 62–70.
Avery, Gillian. *Everyman Anthology of Poetry for Children.* Portland, OR: Powell's Books, 1994.
Baek, Eunice H. "Through the Eyes of Children: Postwar Modern Korean Literature." *Korean Culture* 11.4 (Winter 1990): pp. 24–29. Huck, Charlotte. *Children's Literature in the Elementary School.* New York: McGraw-Hill, 2003.
Prelutsky, Jack, and Meilo So. *The 20th Century Children's Poetry Treasure.* New York: Alfred A. Knopf, 1999.
Sullivan, Joanna. *The Children's Literature Lover's Book of Lists.* San Francisco: John Wiley & Sons, 2004.

Ray Anthony Young Bear
(Ka ka to) (1950–)

This American poet is an enrolled member of The Mesquakie People, pioneers in U.S. history who, unlike other Native Americans who were forced onto reservations, purchased the land near Tama, in central Iowa, where they have lived for generations. Their name translates as "The Red Earth People," and it is rendered properly in the English alphabet according to their own practice—syllabically rather than morphologically—as Me skwa ki; historically they have been known as the Fox Indians, a misinterpretation of their name. The Me skwa ki respect all earthly kinds of life, whether it is a tree, a stone, or a river; they believe that even these items breathe, feel, and share in a human existence.

Young Bear's almost one-hundred-year-old connection to the customs, traditions, and belief systems of the Me skwa ki can be traced to 1856, when his great-great-grandfather purchased the land on which his family now lives. Young Bear owns journals that once belonged to his great-great-grandfather. He has described his own processes of writing as "word-collecting," and he characterizes his writing as a personal, intimate link to his ancestors. In his poetry, Young Bear records the voices and stories of a people who have lived separate from but very much a part of U.S. history and culture.

Although the Me skwa ki adopted the English alphabet in the 1600s, Young Bear describes being uncomfortable with English until he was approximately seventeen years old. Until that time, he wrote most of his poetry in Me skwa ki and later translated it into English. He credits his grandmother with being the greatest influence on his growth as a writer. From her he learned the mythology, language, and customs of his ancestry. Early in his career, Young Bear was befriended by the poet Robert Bly. Other early influences included the Upward Bound program, a well-respected, national summer program for youth. Upward Bound is sponsored by colleges for working class and other disadvantaged students who perform well academically but whose family resources are not sufficient to allow them the experiences afforded by the program.

In his poetry, Young Bear attempts to maintain equilibrium with his tribal history and with the larger world. He is a conservative poet who writes out of a tradition that is at once Native American and Midwestern, and while Young Bear's imaginative verse primarily records what it means to be Me skwa ki, his poetry also marks a place of common ground across the two cultures. His poetry is deceptively simple in its use of structure and language. In a poem titled "for the rain in march," Young Bear, who has identified himself as "incomplete," writes "I may never know who I actually am" and attributes such unknowing to the human condition. The narrator in the poem observes that "many/different minds drift across each other" suggesting that cultures overlap, each influencing and being influenced by the other. In "Quall and his Role in Agriculture," Young Bear's narrator recalls "a hot September day" when he finds himself in a line with local farmers as they all await their turn at an ice cream stand.

Still, Young Bear's poetry often takes writers to task for their stereotypical portrayals of Native Americans. In a poem titled "in disgust and in response" Young Bear critiques the portrayal of Me skwa ki identity by a writer who used pejorative language and imagery to describe a sacred Native American ritual, the Pow Wow. In this work, Young Bear characterizes the ritual as a homecoming, a celebration of the season, family, and life. He alludes to the massacre and eradication of Native Americans by whites to suggest that group's lack of both authority and wisdom. Young Bear often writes about identity and about the particular circumstances of his identity as a Me skwa ki. In a poem titled "one chip of human bone," Young Bear appears to acquiesce to the common stereotypes of Native Americans, but he does so to make an observation. He understands the despair of "being an Indian with nothing to lose"; his poetry records the moments of such loss in haunting, persistent language.

Young Bear attended Claremont College in California, as well as the University of Iowa, Iowa State University and Northern Iowa University. He has been a visiting faculty member at Eastern Washington University and the University of Iowa. Young Bear and his wife cofounded the Woodland Song and Dance Troupe of Arts Midwest in 1983, and his troupe has performed traditional Me skwa ki music in this country and in the Netherlands.

Website

"Modern American Poetry." http://www.english.uiuc.edu
Ellefson, Elias. "A 1994 Interview with Ray Young Bear." http://www.english.uiuc.edu/
    maps/poets/s_z/youngbear/1994.htm

Poetry

Winter of the Salamander: The Keeper of Importance. San Francisco. Harper & Row, 1980.
The Invisible Musician. Duluth, MN: Holy Cow! Press, 1990.
Black Eagle Child: The Facepaint Narratives. Iowa City: University of Iowa Press, 1992.
Remnants of the First Earth. New York: Grove/Atlantic, 1997.
The Rock Island Hiking Club. Iowa City: University of Iowa Press, 2001.

References and Suggested Reading

Bataille, Gretchen. "Ray Young Bear: Tribal History and Personal Vision" (review of
    Winter of the Salamander). In *Studies in American Indian Literature 6.3* (os, 1982):
    pp. 1–6; reprinted in *Studies in American Indian Literature 5.2* (ns, 1993): pp. 17–20.
Bruchac, Joseph. "Connected to the Past: An Interview with Ray Young Bear." In
    Survival This Way: Interviews with American Indian Poets. Tucson: University of
    Arizona Press, 1987, pp. 337–48.
Callender, Charles. "Fox." In *Handbook of North American Indians, Vol. 15: Northeast.*
    Ed. Bruce G. Trigger. Washington, DC: Smithsonian, 1978.
Castro, Michael. *Interpreting the Indian: Twentieth-Century Poets and the Native American.*
    Albuquerque: University of New Mexico Press, 1983.
Ellefson, Elias. "An Interview with Ray A. Young Bear." In *Speaking of the Short Story*:
    Interviews with Contemporary Writers. Ed. Farhat Iftekharuddin, Mary Rohrberger,
    and Maurice Lee. Jackson: University Press of Mississippi, 1997.
Gearing, Frederick O. *The Face of the Fox.* Chicago: Aldine, 1970.
Gildner, Gary, and Judith Gildner. *Out of This World: Poems from the Hawkeye State.*
    Ames: Iowa State University Press, 1975.
Gish, Robert E. *Beyond Bounds*: *Cross Cultural Essays on Anglo, American Indian, and Chicano*
    Literature. Albuquerque: University of New Mexico Press, 1996.
McTaggart, Fred. *Wolf That I Am: In Search of the Red Earth People.* 1976. Norman: University
    of Oklahoma Press, 1984.
Niatum, Duane, ed. *Carriers of the Dream Wheel*: *Contemporary Native American Poetry.*
    New York: Harper & Row, 1975.
Swann, Brian. *Coming to Light*: *Contemporary Translations of the Native Literatures of North*
    America. New York: Vintage Books, 1996.
Wiget, Andrew. *Native American Literature.* Boston: Twayne, 1985.
Woodland Singers. *Traditional Mesquakie Songs.* Canyon Records, CR-6194, 1987.

Selected Bibliography

Baker, Houston A., Jr. *Afro-American Poetics: Revisions of Harlem and the Black Aesthetic*. Madison: U of Wisconsin P, 1996.

Baker, Houston A. Jr., and Patricia Redmond. *Afro American Literary Study in the 1990s*. IL: U of Chicago Press, 1992.

Baym, Nina, editor. *The Norton Anthology of American Literature*. Fifth edition. NY: W. W. Norton and Company, 1998.

Bruchac, Joseph, ed. *Breaking Silence: An Anthology of Contemporary Asian American Poets*. NY: Greenfield Review Press, 1983.

Castro, Michael. *Interpreting the Indian: Twentieth Century Poets and the Native American*. Norman: University of Oklahoma Press (reprint edition), 1991.

Davidson, Cathy N. and Linda Wagner Martin, editors. *The Oxford Companion to Women's Writing in the United States*. NY: Oxford UP., 1995.

Elliott, Emory. *The Cambridge Introduction to Early American Literature*. Cambridge UP, 2002.

Gray, Jeffrey, James McCorkle and Mary McAleer Balkun, editors. *The Greenwood Encyclopedia of American Poets and Poetry* [Five Volumes]. Westport, CT: Greenwood Press, 2005.

Howe, Florence, editor. *No More Masks! An Anthology of Twentieth-Century American Women Poets*. NY: HarperCollins Publishers, 1993.

James, Edward T. Janet Wilson James and Paul Boyer, editors. *Notable American Women 1607-1950: A Biographical Dictionary*. Rhode Island: Belknap Press, 1974.

O'Neill, Michael, editor. *Literature of the Romantic Period: A Bibliographical Guide*. Oxford: Clarendon Press, 1998.

Roth, John K., editor. *American Diversity, American Identity, the Lives and Works of 145 Writers Who Define the American Experience*. NY: Henry Holt and Company, 1995.

Susag, Dorothea. *Roots and Branches: A Resource of Native American Literature—Themes, Lessons, and Bibliographies*. Urbana, Illinois: National Council of Teachers of English, 1998.

Ware, Susan and Stacy Braukman, editors. *Notable American Women: A Biographical Dictionary Completing the Twentieth Century*. Rhode Island: Belknap Press, 2005.

Index

Bold page numbers indicate main entries.

Index

276

About the Authors

MARY LOVING BLANCHARD is an Assistant Professor of English at New Jersey City University. In summer 2004, her poem, "Here" was inscribed on a memorial built to commemorate former enslaved African Americans of Dallas County, Texas. In 1995, her poem, "Quilting," was commissioned by the Children's Choir of Greater Dallas to commemorate its twenty-fifth year. Blanchard has published scholarly articles, fiction, and poetry.

CARA FALCETTI received her B.A. from Fordham University and is pursuing graduate work at Queen's College in New York City. She has held several positions in middle school education and library science.